International Relations & Diplomacy

Theory and Practice

International Relations & Diplomacy

Theory and Practice

Edited by

Dr. Aparna
Dr. Ranvijay

MANAK
PUBLICATIONS PVT. LTD

Published by

MANAK

PUBLICATIONS PVT. LTD

B-7, Saraswati Complex, Subhash Chowk,
Laxmi Nagar, New Delhi 110092
Phone: 011-22453894, 22042529
E-mail : manak.publications@gmail.com
Website: manakpublication.com

Subsidiary Office in USA
MANAK PUBLICATION, INC.
8145 Kolb Ave, Allen Park, M.I. 48101 USA
E-mail: manakpublication.USA@gmail.com

First Edition 2019

ISBN 978-81-943035-4-1

Laser Typeset by: Tabrez Ali, Aadil Printographics, Delhi
Printed in India by: Nice Printing Press, New Delhi (India)

Dedicated to

My Mother

Contents

Foreword

International Relations theory is now a subject of growing interest in universities across India, beyond the metropolitan cities. Not long ago, IR was embedded as an integral part of courses in political science. However, before long and in tune with the global trend particularly in the west, IR emerged out of the shadows of political science ad Indian institutions began to pay close attention to IR as a separate and distinct discipline and study. The increasing complexities of the world scene stemming from rapid globalization, emergence of new blocs and fresh equations among the nations, growing interdependence for resources—all these combined to generate a substantive content and practical need for IR studies, in addition to plain academic and intellectual pursuits. What happens in OPEC deliberations or a crisis I want Asia may impact oil imports, balance of trade, rupee-dollar exchange rate, retail price of oil and gas. Similarly, decisions of WTO could affect farm products pricing policies. Thus two crucial non-traditional security concerns—energy and food—closely interplay with developments in the world scene. Similarly, shared interest in global commons like environment, oceans, space etc., further underscore the importance of International Relations studies.

Indian foreign policy establishment is run by the Indian Foreign Service (IFS). The entry into the IFS is through a Combined Civil Services examinations held annually and open to all University graduates of certain age. Thus at entry level, it is a generalist service. Over time as their careers progress, the officers acquire some expertise in certain areas, through self-initiative, meeting at the same time the need to hold different position caused by rotation of posts. Universities with IR departments can play a significant role in providing expertise and experts to foreign policy establishment through their specialists and analytical studies of global development.

It is gratifying to note that the Department of Politics and International Relations of the Central University of Jharkhand, Ranchi, though still in formative years has organized an international seminar on the important subject of IR Theory and Foreign Policy.

I congratulate the Department, particularly its faculty member Dr. Aparna, for the commendable initiative, which no doubt will help in laying an enduring foundation for International Relations Studies in Ranchi, Jharkhand.

Ambassador Dayakara Ratakonda
Former Ambassador to Jordan, Sweden and Iraq

Acknowledgements

The present edited volume is a seminar proceeding book. Is isan outcome of the International Seminar on "International Relations in India: Evidences from History, Scholastic Writings and Diplomatic Practices", organised in collaboration with the ICSSR, New Delhi and the Department of Politics and International Relations, Central University of Jharkhand, Ranchi, during April 25-27, 2018. Firstly, I would like to thank ICSSR, New Delhi and CUJ administration and finance for granting us funds for this gentle academic exercise.

Many faculties and research scholars from India and abroad have rigorously discussed on the theme and sub-theme of the seminar for three days. The seminar was blessed with the presence of Honourable Vice Chancellor of the University, Prof. Nand Kumar Yadav 'Indu', Ambassador Lok Raj Baral (Nepal), Ambassador Dayakara Ratakonda, Prof. Ashwani Mahapatra, Prof. Satish Kumar, Prof. Sanjay Srivastava, Prof. Sanjay Kumar Jha, Prof. Ripu Sudan Singh, Prof. Ulzit Luvsanjav (Magnolia), Dr. Saurabh, Dr. Praveen Kumar, Dr. Tapan Bihari and number of efficient research scholars. They have presented their papers in different technical sessions and subsequently many of them have contributed their articles for this volume. I sincerely express my heartfelt thanks to all the contributors for writing scholarly articles.

I would take the opportunity to thank upon Dr. Ranvijay for all of his support and valuable suggestions. Acknowledging the hidden and continuous efforts of Dr. Pradeep Kumar Singh is noteworthy here. I sincerely extend my thanks to him.

The value of the book immensely increased with a Foreword by Ambassador Dayakara Ratakonda, a 1976 batch IFS officer and former Ambassador to Jordan (2005-2008), Iraq (1978-82), and Sweden. He was the first Secretary in Embassy of India, Doha, Qatar (1982-85). Thanks would be a smaller word for appreciating Dayakara sir efforts in my editing work. Without his motivation, conscientious, untiring and unconditional efforts this book couldn't have come in the present form.

I also express my sincere thanks to Mr. M.P. Yadava, Director, Manak Publications Pvt. Ltd., New Delhi for readily accepting the proposal to come up with a volume on the subject. Our effort will achieve its goals if this volume is useful to the academia, research scholars, civil society, policy makers and students.

List of Contributors

1. Dr. Aparna, Assistant Professor, Department of Politics and International Relations, Central University of Jharkhand, Brambe, Ranchi.
2. Siv Charan Singh, Senior Journalist, Freelancer.
3. Dr. Rajani Bala, Assistant Professor, Department of Political Science, SPM College, University of Delhi, New Delhi.
4. Zheer Ahmed, Ph.D. Scholar at Centre for West Asian Studies, School of International Studies, Jawaharlal Nehru University, New Delhi.
5. Sudhir Parida, Ph.D. Scholar, Centre for Russian and Central Asian Studies, School of International Studies, Jawaharlal Nehru University, New Delhi.
6. Dr. Saumya Maniny Sinha, Assistant Professor, Department of Political Science, St. Xaviers College, Ranchi, Jharkhand.
7. Dr. Subhash Kumar Baitha, Assistant Professor, Department of Politics and International Relations, Central University of Jharkhand, Brambe, Ranchi.
8. Kumar Adarsh, Graduate Student, Department of Politics and International Relations, Central University of Jharkhand, Brambe, Ranchi.

9. Dr. Alok Kumar Gupta, Associate Professor, Central University of South Bihar, Gaya, Bihar.
10. Vandana Mishra, Research Scholar, Central University of South Bihar, Gaya, Bihar.
11. Gitesh Kumar, Research Scholar, Department of Politics and International Relations, Central University of Jharkhand, Brambe, Ranchi.
12. Jyoti Gupta, Ph.D. Research Scholar at Centre for South Asian Studies, School of International Studies, Jawaharlal Nehru University, New Delhi.
13. Niraj Kumar, Research Scholar, Central University of South Bihar, Gaya, Bihar.
14. Mohammad Janesar, JRF Scholar, Department of Politics and International Studies, Pondicherry University, Puducherry.
15. Salma Zafar, Research Scholar, Central University of South Bihar, Gaya, Bihar.
16. Sanchana Srivastava, M.A., Department of Politics and International Relations, Central University of Jharkhand, Brambe, Ranchi.
17. Shaily, Research Scholar, Centre for Political Studies, Central University of South Bihar, Gaya, Bihar.
18. Abhishek Mohanty, Junior Research Associate, German Southeast Asian Centre of Excellence for Public Policy and Good Governance, Bangkok.
19. Ritesh Kumar Rai, Ph.D. Scholar at Centre for Inner Asian Studies, School of International Studies, Jawaharlal Nehru University, New Delhi.

Introduction

Acharya and Buzan's book tried to prompt non-western experiences to bring their historical and cultural voices into the theoretical debates about International Relations. However after passing approximately one decade, there has not much work produced since the publication of that provocative book. Book contains wide range of work produced by the non-western scholars particularly from Asia and Africa. Both also clarifies that starting a debate for non-western theory on IR does not mean that it wanted to replace western International Relations. Theory but to point out the narrowness of thee western perspective which failed to address the wider project to understand the social world in which we act and live.

Prof. Navnita Behera in her informative essay in the same book lamented about the poor state of IR in Indian academics. She pointed out lack of conceptual clarity and teaching of IR as an additional elective subject with political science, not as a separate discipline engendering the scientific knowledge production of IR in India. However she elucidated many critical writing on IR by Indian leaders and scholars who had presented quite contrary view on essential concepts of IR such as conception of self-rule, internationalism nationalism or nation. For instance, Gandhi, Tagore, Savarkar, Bose presented very critical view on nationalism from west, nevertheless, Indian writing fails to or still lacking to herald its presence in the global scientific knowledge production on IR.

Off course, there are rich source of writing on IR by many Indian scholars with alternative perspectives on the understanding on IR. At the same time there are also various attemptsfor theorisation of IRT, for instance, Gujral doctrine, minimalist approach to nuclear power, NAM, as well as from ancient era such as, state craft from Kautilya, just war (dharmuddhya) in Mahabharta, rules of war in religious text so on and so forth. Similarly, 20th century also witnessed in the production of many seminal works which implicitly or explicitly destroyed the many assumption of so called scientific knowledge by pointing out the rigid binary in western parlances.

Keeping above ideas in mind this book intends to collect scholarly writings on the theoretical and practical aspect of International relations in general and diplomacy and Indian foreign policy in particular.

The first chapter titled "Geo-politics and Methods of Guerrilla Warfare of Chatrapati Shivaji Maharaj, Aparna tried to examine the context of politics, warfare, and impact of geography on strategy of war during the reign of Chatrapati Shivaji Maharaj. The reign and time of Shivaji was significant in many ways; the imperial overreach of European nation and use of modern weapons in warfare, the expansion of Mughal Empire towards Deccan plateau. As Maratha state was located at Deccan Plateau, the geographical terrain was not favourable for foreign army. Shivaji had a great knowledge of the terrain and that gave him opportunity to grow its army for guerrilla warfare. Shivaji developed his army not only innovative in their warfare methods but unique in defending their territory. Maratha's main rival Mughal' could not match themselves in guerrilla warfare with Shivaji army. Guerrilla warfare is irregular warfare where a small group of troop, armed civilians use military tactics to fight a larger enemy. This paper aims to evaluate the geo-political strategy of Chatrapati Shivaji Maharaj and his Guerrilla warfare.

Shiv Charan Singh's second chapter titled, "Intellectual Voyage of the Indophilians to the Haloed Sub-Continent: An Incessant Passage to Self-inquiry and Elevation" enlightened that the haloed land of India has ever been reverberating with the silent chants of *Vasudhaiva Kutumbakam* perceptible from the hospitable faces of its proud residents, about whom Apollonius of Tyana had long back in the very first century (Common Era) said *In India I found a race of mortals living upon the Earth, but not adhering to it. Inhabiting cities, but not being fixed to them, possessing everything but possessed by nothing*. This has actually been a one-way traffic of spiritually, emotionally and intellectually thirsty people from across the globe embarking on a perpetual flight to the oriental firmament in their bid to seek answers to the mysteries of the world and the self. They have been the 'Indophilians' opposed to the 'Indophobians' including a large segment of self-loathing Indians, who, for a variety of reasons, spew venom against India with their choicest vituperatives such as 'un-progressive', 'barbarians' and 'superstitious heathens'. But then, the proud Indians remain silent and unshaken by the Indophobians' slugfest. However, their reticence finds loud echoes in the Indophilians such as 2nd century Roman philosopher Arrian, who celebrated India to be '*the nation of free people*', reiterating that he had found '*no slaves in India at all*'. And what's more, Arrian almost decreed '*No Indian ever went outside his own country on a warlike expedition, so righteous were they*'.

Undeterred by Indophobians' malice, the proud Indians welcome complimentary and grateful utterances from other lands in their patient stride. For, they know only the enlightened ones with perfect pair of eyes could see radiant glow of knowledge emanating from the oriental sky and sift through innumerable scriptures to seek answers to the gnawing mysteries. And that's why, when French philosopher Voltaire sang paeans in the words – *"I am convinced that everything has come down to us from the banks of the Ganges, – astronomy, astrology, metempsychosis, etc... It is very important to note that some 2,500 years ago at the least Pythagoras went from Samos to the Ganges to learn geometry...But he would certainly not have undertaken such a strange journey had the reputation of the Brahmins' science not been long established in Europe"*[3] the proud Indians only smile in silence. Among the names galore in this one-way traffic, some came here (India) to seek knowledge and entered into the club of Indophilians. Rest of them, though were not so fortunate but were equally proud to have realized the worth and supremacy of the land and its immeasurable treasure of knowledge.

In the third chapter, Rajani Bala and Zheer Ahmed make an analysis on "India in South Asia: Debating Regional Strategies". Together they examined that in South Asia, India is the most important country in context of living democratic values. India is a pioneer member of the SAARC organization which is a great platform for discussing the multilateral issues with each other. India is also trying to engage with the SAARC members so that they can tackle issues like terrorism, health, education, poverty, under-development and so on. On the other hand, India's engagement with its neighbours has received a policy reinvigoration after the National Democratic Alliance (NDA) government assumed power and announced its 'Neighbourhood first policy'. The 'Neighbourhood first policy' seems to be conscious response to the String of Pearls policy of China.

Sudhir Parida in the following chapter, "*Vasudhaiva Kutumbakam*—A Right Cord between Internationalism and Anti-nationalism" focused upon the Indian philosophy especially, *Vasudhaiva Kutumbakam* which is the milestone of Indian culture and philosophy, support the whole world as the one home and favor brotherhood at the mainstream platform. He gives arguments that the current wave of anti-nationalism has been spear headed through the idea of liberal internationalism as well as proletariat internationalism. In the contemporary debate towards internationalism has failed to secure the nations and the world from turbulence and sprouted anti-national movements in nations. Powerful nations are using globalisation as a subversion tool, spreading anti-national movements among other countries which is the negative view of developing world. Thus, he pointed out that the goal of *Vasudhaiva Kutumbakam* is non-hegemonic, multi-polar, multi-cultural, free, open, diverse, inclusive, and cooperative engagement with each other. The engagement among nations should focus with mutual respect and stable bedrock of peace.

Saumya Maniny Sinha in the fifth chapter, "Area Studies towards the Construction of a New South Asia" has produced an argument that the construction of New South Asia needs for Indian Scholarship to strike a consensus among her neighbours on a range of issues. It also aims at providing ambitious suggestions for the construction of new theories for a New South Asia. There is an ardent need for theory construction and building a structural interpretation of the rise and nature of social movements in South Asia, the challenges of terrorism, global warming, role of religion, and ethnicity in South Asia and exploring new areas of economic co-operation. Focusing Area Studies scholarship in these spheres will not just help this region, but also strengthen SAARC as a regional forum. The approach of the area studies was primarily multi-disciplinary, each isolated and secluded from the other. Thus, this chapter argued that it is obvious the groundwork done by the west on South Asia as a region had a definitive impact in building its own academic edifice in the literature. Hence, the west started playing an important role in theorizing the international relations in South Asia.

In chapter six, Subhash Kumar Baitha & Kumar Adarsh through light upon the topic "Assessment of India's Foreign Policy in the Modi Regime". The paper discussed that there is visible influence of history, culture, Buddhism etc. on Indian foreign policy. At different international platforms randomly, Prime Minister Narendra Modi has also emphasised upon the ideals of international peace, co-operation and theory of *Panchsheela*. Therefore, he gave priority on having strong partnership with Japan, Australia, and United States of America and so on. Furthermore, South-East Asia, managing the China challenge through a mix of competition and cooperation, the sustained and expanding engagement with Africa and the reaching out to the large and influential Indian diaspora are all elements of continuity but there are a new vigour and energy with which these are being pursued. In this paper they have also discussed some of the major policy initiatives taken by the Modi government to prove that India is going to be more assertive i.e., Look East to Act East, Para-diplomacy, and Indian Ocean Outreach.

In the very next chapter, Alok Kumar Gupta and Vandana Mishra has opined on, "Indo-Thailand Relations: Cultural Connectivity and Role of Buddhism". This paper describes the soft power in the context of Buddhist philosophy towards the bilateral relations between Indo-Thailand and has also ensured the role of Act East Policy for promoting India's bilateral engagements with other East

Asian countries. Buddhist pilgrimages are paving the way for the same. From this perspective, cultural connectivity is also an instrument to frame a soft power. On the other hand, religious factor will also lead to consequent benefits in the area of science and technology, research and development, trade and commerce etc. Thus, both countries could also be transformed into India's 'Gateway to ASEAN' and would help to promote India's Act East Policy in the coming years. This paper has examined three factors, namely, history, geography, and capability.

In the eighth chapter, "Eurasian Region and India in 21st Century: Diplomatic Victory" by Gitesh Kumar argues that in the 21st century, changing environment and engagements of India with the Eurasian region is emerging a mid and long term strategy for effective arrangement. Since 2017, there is recognition of India's membership in SCO. This is a result of India's continuous and dynamic cooperation with the region and it would be able to make potential platform in order to engage SCO economically and geo-strategically. At the same time, there can be opportunities to continue interactions with Pakistan during the SCO summits. There will be opportunities to discuss the energy issues, drug trafficking and also terrorist activities in the region. Thus, this paper has aimed to find out India's diplomatic strategies in the area of security, trade and cooperation in the 21st century.

Jyoti Gupta, in her chapter,"Afghanistan and China: Political and Strategic Relations in Post 9/11 Period" analyses that there has been expansion in the bilateral engagement between Afghanistan and China on regional politics. It has a greater focus on peace, development, security and cooperative approach between both countries. From this perspective, Afghanistan-China relations in the field of security cooperation have been steadily growing since 2012.

The agreement on Strategic and Cooperative Partnership of 2012, provided to maintain a hope of greater support of China in the wake of improving the international support. Afghanistan not only enhanced its interactions bilaterally but also in tri-lateral, quadrilateral and multilateral framework with China on the regional as well as international platform. China did not effectively put pressure to on the Taliban to accept the peace process in the region. Thus, Afghanistan got Chinese various assistance and supports like financial, technology and so on, but it did not result in any solution to the conflict. Despite the failure of peace talks, Afghanistan is still looking towards China's supportive role in the future.

In the tenth chapter, "Locating Nehru's Approach towards Regionalism: A Challenge to Western Hegemony" Kumar Niraj opines that the Nehruvian approach of regionalism is still relevant after the fifty four years of his death. Because, the dramatic changes at the global level initiated a process of reorientation of the power distribution in international politics. After the decline of cold war, disintegration of USSR and the unification of Europe for the construction of single European identity have changed the world order. On the other hand, the security scenario of world politics has been changed due to power transition like, the decline of communism, the sudden rise of Asian countries mainly, India, China and ASEAN, emergence of resurgent Russia and the establishment of new economic bloc such as BRICS and G-20. From this perspective, India should raise the voice of developing countries through highlighting the different rules in different spheres, such as missing the rules of global macroeconomic management, international financial structure, cross-border movement of people and international public good.

Mohammad Janesar's chapter titled, "Analyzing India

and Central Asia Relations: Challenges and Opportunities" argues that the Central Asian region emerged as a separate geographical entity after the collapse of erstwhile Soviet Union in 1991 and emerged as five Central Asian Republics. All Central Asian countries namely Kazakhstan, Uzbekistan, Turkmenistan, Tajikistan and Kyrgyzstan get excluded from the part of Soviet Union without any struggle for independence. Hence, their independence was as a God gift. Due to its' geographical location, geostrategic and geopolitical significance this region has become as a battle ground for big power and some adjoining states what is called as New Grate Game. India is not considered as a player of this battle ground but playing as a role of balancer in the high politics of Central Asia. He argued that India has the largest software industry in the world and also she has an established growing economy. Hence India should utilize this strength in information technology, banking and small and medium-scale enterprises sectors.

In the twelfth chapter titled, "Democratic Assistance: Emerging Dimension of India's Foreign Policy in South Asia" Salma Zafar puts an argument that, India has adopted a great technique for delivering democratic assistance that goes beyond far-fetched interpretations such as those associated with India, i.e. democratic values support with Afghanistan and respect human right. While India is making the effort to support and strengthen the democracy around its region when they are called by neighbors to assist them. Though sometimes, India's democratic assistance has been criticized as based on realist ground as where its national interest collide, it tries to exclude itself from supporting democracy. Thus, this engaged that India continues to provide its democratic assistance and democracy promotion as an important principle in its foreign policy agenda.

The thirteenth chapter, "Construct of Peace and Security

System in Indian Perspective" Sanchana Srivastava pointed out that in the era of transformation, the collective security has come to mean something more than simply the defense of the community against an internal or external aggression regarding human rights. A democratic India with valuable experiences in building a federal multi-ethnic union and the accompanying security challenges has to work with other like-minded states to build an equitable, prosperous and secure future through the deepening of multilateral structures even as it takes independent steps to safeguard its security. She argued that there is a growing debate on the need to expand the traditional notions of security to address the non- traditional threats and so to develop a more comprehensive approach to security.

Shaily makes an argument in the paper, "New India and Legacies of Indira Gandhi: A Critical Analysis of her contributions" that India is going to make a transformation society with the highest population as a young country in the world. This is possible through social media and information communication and technology, giving a platform for exchanging ideas with each other at a very low cost. The people have been also using the constitutional right that is freedom of speech in a New India led by Prime Minister Narendra Modi, which focuses digital India. On the other hand, PM Modi is pointing his double-barreled gun towards the Congress, one barrel of which is towards Nehru and the second one on the present National Congress Party dispensation. He is attacking both the past and the present with and avowed aim of destroying the Congress for all time to come; whereas the fact remains he is carrying the legacy of Indira Gandhi, the strongest personality of the Congress party that emerged so far.

Abhishek Mohanty in the fifteenth chapter titled, "India-ASEAN Evolving Security Cooperation In 21st

Century: Challenges and Prospects" through light upon a crisp summary of cordial relations among India and ASEAN, examines the spheres of engagement in the area of security cooperation, also throws light on the challenges being faced and then concludes with possible prospects of security cooperation in the near future with the intention of making way for the Asian century. Since the last few years, ASEAN has discussed with India to play a larger role in the maritime security of the Indo-Pacific region, due to the worldwide respect of India's defence capabilities and a well-balanced foreign policy approach. For India, the shifting geopolitical scenario in the Indo-Pacific and the hostile activities of Chinese government in the South China Sea has thrown an opportunity to India to play a dominant role and ascertain itself as a regional power. Thus, he argued that India and ASEAN share mutual security dilemmas in both traditional non-traditional spheres. Therefore, prospering of India-ASEAN Security Cooperation is not only an obligation but also a mutual objective.

In the last chapter titled, "The Dynamics of Growth Amid India-Mongolia Relations" Ritesh Kumar Rai attempted to analyze the geo-political as well as geo-economic developments of the Mongolian region. It assesses emerging trends in India-Mongolia relations in changing political environment at the world stage. He argues that it may reduce the overarching influence of Russia and China in Mongolia to some extent because of concerning the impact of Mongolia's third neighbour approach on India-Mongolia bilateral relations. It is evident of the emergence of a new dimension in the region. From this perspective of bilateral ties seem to have been transformed into a comprehensive partnership suggesting ways in which both sides have redefined their geostrategic interests. Thus, he agreed that both countries have benefitted from improving the bilateral ties and needs each other's help.

1

Geo-Politics and Methods of Guerilla Warfare of Chatrapati Shivaji Maharaj

Aparna

It was a sultry April evening of 1663. Thanks to the draconian rules prohibiting Marathas' entry into Pune, the city streets wore a deserted look. Nevertheless, a wedding party consisting of a little over 400 men conscientiously slithered into the city precisely on the 5th of that month. Having duly obtained special permission from the authorities for holding this marital procession, the wedding party was a traditional treat to the people who slipped into a blissful reverie caused by the rhythmic beat of the band party.

But there wasn't a real marriage nor was it a marital procession. The phony marriage party comprised men on mission in disguise – majority as bridegroom's relatives, others as band party members, and a chosen few as the 'soldiers' from the Mughal authorities – but they all waited for the precise moment around midnight when the palace compound of a viceroy from Mughal emperor Aurangzeb, Nawab Shaista Khanturned into the nocturnal battlefield thanks to the disguised men, the Marathas led by their valiant leader Shivaji, the Great.

In their undeterred bid to assassinate the Mughal viceroy, the Marathas had broken into the courtyard of the palace and slaughtered the palace guards. Evidently caught unaware and unprepared, though the target Shaista Khan could not be finished in the midnight skirmish, his son was killed by the Marathas while the former lost three fingers. Forty attendants were also killed. The heavy camping of Mughal forces notwithstanding, the Marathas escaped the palace and Pune in the ensuing confusion and vanished into the darkness.

Shocked by the sudden and bold attack in Pune, Aurangzeb angrily transferred Shaista Khan to Bengal, even refusing to give him an interview at the time of transfer as was the custom. For, Shivaji's attack on Khan was anexpress slap on Aurangzeb's face – an act unthinkable for most Indian kings at that time. And obviously it was a great victory for Shivaji, who avowed to rid the country of foreign rulers.

Attack on Aurangzeb's viceroy was one of the many military guerilla feats successfully accomplished by Shivaji, who had become a legendary character of many a folktale during his own lifetime. Thus Sir J.N. Sarkar, a prominent Indian historian's remarks – "States fall, empires breakup, dynasties become extinct, but the memory of a true 'hero as King' like Shivaji, remains animperishable historical legacy for the entire human race." – continue to echo in our hearts painting an inspiring image of the towering personality this great Indian hero had.

In a concerted bid to understand the magnitude of this Indian hero's personality and time, this paper humbly tries to examine albeit on a minuscule scale the vast extent of the context of politics, warfare, and impact of geography on strategy of war during the reign of Chatrapati Shivaji Maharaj.

Shivaji's time and reign was significant in many ways, characterize by the imperial overreach of European nation and use of modern weapons in warfare and the expansion of Mughal Empire towards Deccan plateau. The expanse of the Maratha state, located in the difficult and draining geographical terrain of the Deccan plateau was not favorable for the foreign army. Shivaji, however, knew the tortuous Deccan terrain as a camel knows the fear-invoking interminable desert and now-here-but-ever-vanishing sand paths. Naturally, Shivaji's knowledge enabled him to raise his army for the famous and singular in many ways guerilla warfare. Shivaji developed his army not only in an innovative way in his warfare methods but also in a unique manner in defending his territory.

Maratha's main rival Mughals could not match themselves in Guerilla warfare with Shivaji's army. Guerrilla warfare, where in small troops or armed civilians use military tactics to fight a larger and superior enemy, was used by Chatrapati Shivaji Maharaj in a most befitting way against his rivals. Shivaji's armed victories over the major empires of his time were of course the triumph of his heroism; but more than that they brought about a definite change in the perception of the time that the major empires could not be paid back in their own coin and also showed the capacity ofthe 'oppressed' people to rise in revolt against the 'oppressors' and their zeal to free themselves by means of guerrilla warfare under the innovative leadership of their new hero. This paper aims at evaluating the geo-political strategy of Chatrapati Shivaji Maharaj and his Guerilla warfare.

Geo-political Understanding: Key of his strength and success

Shivaji, founder of the Maratha kingdom of India, had

reigned between years1674–80. Words can describe the acts and historical facts, but they seem feeble and small in describing the towering personality of Shivaji the Great. But then the following words from J.N. Sarkar describe Shivaji and his time in a most appropriate and convincing way.

"Shivaji has shown that the tree of Hinduism is not really dead, that it can rise from beneath the seeming crushing load of centuries of political bondage, exclusion from administration and legal repression, it can put forth new leaves and branches, it can again lift up its head to the skies." Sarkar continues: "I regard him as the last great constructive genius and nation-builder that the Hindu race has produced."

Shivaji had a great understanding of geo-politics that is why, before waging wars he traveled a lot and collected information about the forests and hills of the Sahyadri range and used it on time. Geographically analyzing Deccan region would clearly indicate that why and how Shivaji has successfully opted and conducted the strategy of guerrilla warfare. Since his childhood Shivaji has witnessed the ruthless ruling of Mughals and Muslim Sultans. At that time contemporaneous India was under Muslim rule and the ancestral estate of Shivaji was situated in the Deccan. Three Islamic sultanates were sharing power and ruling over Deccan region, Bijapur, Ahmednagar and Golconda. On the one hand Deccan plateauis a catchment area for rivers like Godavari, Kaveri, Krishna and their tributaries and the other hand, its impenetrable forests, uneven landscape and mountains turn this region unassailable for aliens. For western travellers, Golconda was a "source of wealth, advantages or happiness."

India Office was the headquarters of East India Company in London that chiefly worked for keeping eyes on the trade of the East India Company in India. Its records namely, 'Factory Records' give vital information about the activities of the Marathas during the period from 1600 to 1707, according to which "Shivaji made Anthony Smith write a note to the company (page 76 line 4) that he had not come to do any harm to the English or other merchants but only to revenge himself on Aurangzeb who had invaded his country..."

1655 was the year when Shivaji defeated the weaker Bijapur. In continuation, he destroyed some of the influential regimes, who had generous relations with the sultans. He got admiration and support from all over because of his military skills and strictness towards the Mughals. Furiously in 1659 Afzal Khan, with a huge army about 20, 000 was sent to defeat Shivaji by the Bijapur sultan. But unexpectedly he could not meet the success and got killed by Shivaji. Bal Krishna has beautified the fear of Afzal Khan before meeting Shivaji in the following words,

"Afzal Khan alone came forward to bring Shiva alive or dead to Bijapur. But he was really doubtful of his success. According to Abbe Carre, he shut himself up in his mansion for several days to enjoy the last pleasures of this world. The climax of this round of enjoyments was an incredible tragedy. He was afraid that after his death, his wives might be taken up by others. Therefore, he killed 120 ladies of his harem. The Muslim world of those days was not stunned with the demoniac murder of so many innocent ladies. This tragedy is a strange commentary on the unlimited power enjoyed by the nobles of those times. Instead of being hanged for such a brutal inhumanity, he was honored by his ruler and given command of the forces sent against Shivaji. It is evident that Afzal Khan came with a determination to conquer or die."

Now, an established Chieftain Shivaji attacked the wealthy coastal areas of Surat. But later on he got defeated and house-arrested by the Maharaja Raja Jai Singh, a prominent general of Aurangzeb.

The Shivaji kingdom's security was based on religious toleration and on the functional integration of the Brahmans, Marathas, and Prabhus. Chhatrapati Shivaji Maharaj (1630-80) was, and is, the great Hindu hero of India. He fought with the Mughals and the Muslim rulers of the Deccan, and overawed the British, the Dutch and other European trading companies of the time. In the process, he created an empire of his own that stretched from the Central Indian plains to the western coastline.

Hindavi Swaraj: A Futuristic Vision

Bal Krishna in his book *'Shivaji the Great'* emphasized on the thirstof Shivaji for Swaraj, "Shivaji for the first time used the magnetic words "Hindavi Swaraj" which has become popular since then. It should be noted that it was not merely Swaraj for Maharashtra, not even Swaraj for the Hindus, but an All-Indian Swaraj. He was against foreign rule and religious persecutions. He even tried to win the Indian Muslims to his cause and made an alliance against the foreign Pathans, Moguls and Persians."

Lala Lajpat Rai (*Writings and Speeches, Vol. I*) brilliantly complimented Shivajis's version of Swaraj. He seriously objected to the popular conception that Nationalism is a modern idea taught by the Europeans to the rest of the world. By putting his argument he claims, "The ideas of "nationality" and "patriotism" are as old as the different countries into which the earth is divided, as ancient as the distinctions of race and religion that have been existing in this world from times immemorial and pre-historic."

Continuing with this argument in the next place he hastily condemned and says, "We the English educated Hindus of the present day, who claim to have imbibed the new spirit of nationality and patriotism from the West would really do well to study a few chapters of the Vedic literature with care and thought, and I am confident that this study will open a panorama of new ideas to our view."

Shivaji was a true worshipper of Swaraj/ Hindavi Swaraj. Till his last breath he had fought for the same. Bal Krishna says, the last will and testament of Shivaji is significant in showing his ideals and ambitious programs, "It was my intense desire to conquer the whole of India, but I have not fulfilled it on account of my premature death. You should all attempt to realize this high ideal. The kingdom founded by me should be consolidated and extended with more heroism than I have ever exhibited." Intellectually and rationally, we should not overlook or undermine the greatness of Shivaji Maharaj's idea of Hindavi Swaraj.

Naval Enterprises: A Progressive Statesman

Shivaji Maharaj was the first Indian ruler who understood the importance of naval forces not for trade but for defense as well. He had learned this strategy from the English and the Portuguese traders. Shivaji's policies were far ahead of the time. For strengthening his naval forces he had taken help from all the people who were well familiar with the coastal areas like Malabar pirates, Muslim mercenaries and a number of Portuguese sailors etc. *Encyclopedia Britannica* says that horrified by Shivaji's escalating figure, Aurangzeb imposed a poll tax (tax of a uniform amount levied on each individual or head) on them.

During medieval period, Shivaji understood the changed nature and strategy of warfare. After that he made a survey before developing new naval bases in coastal areas and building his own ships. Outlining the deep understanding of Shivaji Maharaj on the importance of navy,

Jagdeep Singh says, "Shivaji was one of the few Indian rulers who tried to develop a navy. His conquest of the ports of Kalyan, Bhivandi and Panvel in North Konkan brought him adjacent to the Portuguese possessions at Goa. He realized quickly that without a navy he would not be able to control the creeks on which places of trade and commerce were located. Nor would he be able to defend the coast and areas from the depredations of the Sidis of Janjira, an African group of people who dominated the island of Janjira and its adjacent areas. There were a few reasons because of which Shivaji had developed navy of his own:

1. The peninsular India was full of wealthy resources.
2. For establishing a mighty empire Shivaji was in need of increasing state income. Because of the established administration system of Mughals and Muslim rulers he was getting skimpy revenue.
3. All Indians were compelled to buy passports from the Goa government for their movement in the Indian Ocean. To free the coastal areas from the subjugation of Portuguese government, Shivaji has developed parallel naval bases in different coastal areas, i.e. Vijaydurg (Gheria), Suvarn-Durg (Songarh), Ratnagiri, Sindhudurg, Jaygarh etc.

Marathi chronicles say at its height, his fleet counted some 400 military ships, though British chronicles counter that the number never exceeded 160 ships. Because of the above mentioned qualities, H. S. Sardesai called Shivaji a 'born statesman'.

Guerrilla Warfare: A Liberator

Guerrilla warfare is a bunch of irregular fighting tactics by the comparatively weak side against the superior military forces. Popularly it can be used to overthrow the existing political establishment or it may be used as the alternative to the conventional warfare. Usually the Guerrilla combatants use the hit-and-run formula. Samuel Huntington defines Guerrilla warfare, "As a form of warfare by which the strategically weaker side assumes the tactical offensive in selected forms, times, and places. Guerrilla warfare is the weapon of the weak. It is never chosen in preference to regular warfare; it is employed only when and where the possibilities of regular warfare have been foreclosed."

During the medieval period, Shivaji Maharaj was one of the first practitioners of Guerrilla warfare as the means of his strategy. From Russian Guerrilla warfare (against Napoleon army) to the Chinese Red Army (against Japanese imperialism) and the popular Vietcong (against the mighty USA forces) we have ample examples in different time and space wherein Guerrilla warfare has been tactically, strategically and successfully accomplished. S. Kalyanaraman in his article *'Conceptualizing Guerrilla Warfare'* produces arguments from T. E. Lawrence's writing and says that guerrilla warfare could be proved as an exact science. The factors which prove it science as are: an unassailable guerrilla base, a regular opposing army of limited strength with the task of controlling a wide area and a sympathetic population. Far ahead of this discussion, Shivaji hadtactically combined all of them together. Before adopting Guerrilla warfare defence strategy Shivaji had developed hundreds of forts as the back-bone, i.e. from Sahyadri mountain range to so many sea forts (Suvarnadurg, Vijaydurg, Sindhudurg, Kolabaetc). Other than this, Shivaji has maintained a very high standard of morality and discipline in the army and he got unequivocal support of the people from every corner of Maharashtra. Ashish Kumar says, "King Shivaji gave world new optimum war technique known as Guerrilla warfare."

Chatrapati Shivaji Maharaj: A Rebel?

This part of my paper critically analyzesif Chatrapati Shivaji Maharaj was just a'Rebel'? Dealing with this question, Bal Krishna maintained that he was a rebel with a noble purpose. In his words: "It is true that he was a rebel against the Muslim monarchies of Delhi and the Deccan. He aimed at their overthrow, and worked for the restoration of the freedom and independence of his own country. He stands in the foremost rank of such liberators as Washington, Garibaldi, De Valera and Lenin. Each one of these rebels fought against the foreign or despotic government then prevalent in his country. Shivaji rebelled against political oppression, religious intolerance, social injustice, and cultural suppression, rampant under the Muslim monarchies."He was a revolutionary, a reformer who transformed "the whole people from down-trodden, persecuted, passive, patient, submissive and suppressed sheep into fearless, revengeful and conquering lions that was the immortal work of the great king." In his short life time Shivaji substantiated his self as a great administrator and strategist.

The lost treatise of Rayatwari system and Asth Pradhan system got due place in the civilian administration of Shivaji Maharaj ruling. His ranking of his officers both in the infantry and the cavalry, payment of wages of soldiers on the fixed day, personal supervision of their recruitment, training and promotion, etc. were all successful measures.

Conclusion

Dr. R.C. Majumdar writes of him, "He was not merely a daring soldier and successful military conqueror but also an enlightened ruler of his people."

दावा द्रुम दंड पर, चित्ता मृगझुंड पर, भूषण बितंड पर, जैसे मृगराज हैं।
तेजतम अंश पर, काह्न जिम कंस पर, त्यों मिलेच्छ वंस पर शेर शिवराज हैं।।

(As forest-fire is to the forest trees, a leopard to the deer-herds and a lion to the stately elephants, as the sun is to the darkness of the night, as Krishna was to Kansa, so was king Shivaji, a lion, towards the hordes of Mlechchas.)

— *Swami Vivekananda*

Notes

1. Bal Krishna, *Shivaji the Great,* Retrieved from https://archive.org/stream/shivajithegreat035466mbp#page/n43/mode/2up
2. J.N. Sarkar, (1973), *Shivaji and his Time,* Orient Longman Ltd, New Delhi.
3. G.S. Sardesai, "3 Most Powerful Rulers of the Maratha Empire", *Indian History,* Retrieved from http://www.historydiscussion.net/history-of-india/maratha-empire/3-most-powerful-rulers-of-the-maratha-empire-indian-history/6554
4. V. Madhukar Jadhav, *Geo-Political and Warfare Characteristics of Medieval Deccan.*(Doctoral dissertation). Retrieved fromhttp://shodhganga.inflibnet.ac.in/bitstream/10603/138292/7/07_chapter%201.pdf
5. Madhukar Joshi, *Relevance of Shivaji at the Dawn of 21st Century,* Retrieved from https://www.maayboli.com/arch/1/shivaji/shivaji1.shtml
6. Independent. (2010) *Shivaji: At Home With A Hindu Hero.* Retrieved from https://www.independent.co.uk/travel/asia/shivaji-at-home-with-a-hindu-hero-2160480.html
7. K.N. Vaswani, *Shivaji in Stories, Vivekananda Kendra Patrika,* Retrieved Fromhttp://prakashan.vivekanandakendra.org/sites/default/files/Final%20Sivaji.pdf
8. Shiva Chanitra Karyalay, *English Records on Shiveji 1659-1682.* Retrieved from https://archive.org/stream/EnglishFactoryRecordsOnShivaji1659To1682/EnglsihRecords OnShivaji_djvu.txt
9. H.S. Sardesai, *Shivaji, The Great Maratha.* Retrieved from https://books.google.co.in/books?id=W6d-Hd5UceUC&pg=PA633&lpg=PA633&dq=english+factory+ report+1664&source=bl&ots=QdnN3rDbKO&sig=duBxzgbPHc2OFVuU3RKSFlRBdRI&hl=en&sa=X&ved=0ahUKEwipx7fA39jbAhUIfn0KHcgLCn EQ6AEITTAI#v=onepage&q&f=false

10. Ranjit, Ramchandra Desai, *Shivaji.* Retrieved from https://www.britannica.com/biography/Shivaji
11. Chellappan Kumar, (2018, 17 June). *A glimpse of Shivaji.* Retrieved from http://www.dailypioneer.com/sunday-edition/agenda/books/a-glimpse-of-shivaji.html
12. *India Today*, (2017). *5 Facts about Chhatrapati Shivaji Maharaj that every Indian should know.* Retrieved from https://www.indiatoday.in/education-today/gk-current-affairs/story/shivaji-jayanti-interesting-facts-961344-2017-02-19
13. Mohnish Nelarwar, (2018, 19 February). *Fight for pride like Shivaji Maharaj did, says Patra.* Retrieved from https://timesofindia.indiatimes.com/city/nagpur/fight-for-pride-like-shivaji-maharaj-did-says-patra/articleshow/62974479.cms
14. Ukessays, (2016, 5 December).*Shivaji: The Great Guerrilla History Essay.* Retrieved from https://www.ukessays.com/essays/history/chapter-iv-shivaji-the-great-guerrilla-history-essay.php
15. M.C. Rao Nanjunda. *Swami Vivekananda's talk on Shivaji.* Retrieved from http://www.hinduhumanrights.info/swami-vivekanandas-talkon-shivaji/
16. Jagdeep Singh, (2016). *The Rise and the warfare methods of Marathas.* Retrieved from http://www.allresearchjournal.com/archives/2016/vol2issue7/PartG/2-7-88-438.pdf
17. LalaLajpat Rai, *Writings and Speeches*, Vol. I, Retrieved from https://archive.org/stream/in.ernet.dli.2015.237291/2015.237291.Lala-Lajpat_djvu.txt
18. Ashish Kumar Lammata, *Protection of Unlawful Combatants with Specific Study on Guerrilla Warfare.* Retrieved from http://sajms.com/wp-content/uploads/2016/11/Ashish_Kumar_Paper.pdf
19. Shodhganga. *Italian and Indian Nationalism—Unity of Thought and Action.* Retrieved from http://shodhganga. inflibnet.ac.in/bitstream/10603/74210/14/14_chapter%205.pdf
20. Dipesh Karmarkar, (2013). *Understanding the Geographical Vision of Chatrapati Shivaji Maharaj.* Retrieved from https://www.researchgate.net/publication/303594245
21. S. Kalyanaraman, (2003). *Conceptualisations of Guerrilla Warfare.* Retrieved from https://idsa.in/system/files/strategicanalysis_skalyanaraman_0603.pdf
22. Samuel P. Huntington, "Introduction", in Franklin M. Osanka, Ed. *Modern Guerrilla Warfare: Fighting Communist Guerrilla Movements, 1941-1961. 1962.* The Free Press; New York. p. xvi.

2

Intellectual Voyage of the Indophilians to the Haloed Sub-Continent

An Incessant Passage to Self-inquiry and Elevation

Shiv Charan Singh

The Voracious Seeker from Hungarian Soil

Everything was normal in the Transylvanian part of Hungary: the snowy clouds in the sky unrewardingly trying to skirt the penetrating rays of the rising sun and the sluggishly waking people. But a non-descript house in Nagyenyed witnessed an unusual scene.

With a stick in his hand and a knap-sack on his back, a thirty-five year-old man was getting ready for a longest journey eastward. The man was Alexander Csoma de Koros, a Hungarian Indologist, who undertook his journey India in the Autumn of 1819 with just 200 florins in his pockets. The journey on foot in pursuit of the knowledge heritage scattered across the Indian subcontinentwas not an easy task.

Csoma had to manage many an authority of the countries and frontiers he passed through. Anyway, he traveled from Rumanian frontier to Greece; got on a small merchant ship to Egypt; headed for Aleppo, in North Syria; undertook his wanderings into Asia; joined a caravan to reach Mosul in present day Iraq; and was on a raft down the Tigris riverto reach Baghdad. At Baghdad he dressed himself as an Armenian and arrived at Tehran, where he came across an English ambassador. The latter was impressed by Csoma's pursuit of oriental knowledge and thus gave him a grant of Rs 300, a sizeable sum at that time, which in turn enabled Csoma to move further north-eastward in his bid to reach Central Asia in hope of meeting the descendants of their ancestors, who, according to an old Hungarian tradition, were believed to have been living in the central Asian region. But the central Asian region in Csoma's mind was a definite territory. It consisted of Tibet and other Himalayan regions.

Owing to prevailing circumstances, Csoma could not make any advance in north eastward direction and made a detour towards Afghanistan in his attempt to reach his final destination the inner Asia in the lap of Himalayan heights on completion of a journey in April 1822 that had begun in autumn of 1819.

His biographer Dr. Ernest Hetenyi paints a dramatic picture of Csoma's arrival on the Indian frontiers. "On the Indian border he met with two French officers in the service of Ranjit Singh, the Rajah of Punjab. As former generals of Napoleon the two French officers were able to reform and modernize the army of the Rajah who was making a determined stand against the expanding British power in India. The Frenchmen stood in surpriseas they gazed at the strange wanderer in whom, in spite of the queer Asiatic attire, they recognized the Scientifically educated European. Csoma was offered a job but he did not accept it. After a short timeset out alone again, walking as usual. His plan was to go through Kashmir to the Karakorum pass. But he was only able to reach Leh, capital of Ladakh, adjoining the Highlands of Western Tibet. By nowhis meagre funds had run out and he learned that the journey into Central Asia was very expensive—and very dangerous. He had toreturn again, hoping to find another route to reach his destination." (Alexander Csoma de Koros: The Hungarian Bodhisattva—Dr. Ernest Hetenyi)

On his next Himalayan sojourn, Csoma met explorer and British Government agent Moorcroft, who was convinced that Csoma had extraordinary mental powers and dauntless will power. Csoma's meeting with the British agent paved way for British assistance for his study of Tibetan language. Anyway, back in Csomaengaged a learned Lama as his tutor. What followed next was going to be Csoma's mission of devoting his whole life to the study of oriental languages and culture and bringing forth things which even the natives were just unaware of.

He studied Tibetan language, published first book of Tibetan grammar and dictionary, studied Sanskrit texts and stunned Indian scholars by his revealing commentaries.

Csoma was of course not the first European traveler to Indian soil in search of knowledge and contentment of soul, but one of the most devoted ones, who left material comfort behind and came to the Indian soil never to return. Whether in coldest region of Himalayan region or in sweltering Calcutta, Csoma lived a life of monk subsisting on meager diet in order to satiate his hunger for knowledge till he breathed his last in 1841 in Darjeeling.

Flow of Indophilians Continues

Be it Csoma de Koros of Hungary or other Indophilians from across the globe, the haloed land of India has ever been reverberating with the silent chants of *Vasudhaiva Kutumbakam* perceptible from the hospitable faces of its proud residents, about whom Apollonius of Tyana had long back in the very first century (Common Era) said *'In India I found a race of mortals living upon the Earth, but not adhering to it. Inhabiting cities, but not being fixed to them, possessing everything but possessed by nothing.'* ("Brand New World: How Paupers, Pirates, and Oligarchs are Reshaping Business", . 74, by Max Lenderman from original source Philostratus's book Life of Apollonius of Tyana)

This has actually been a one-way traffic of spiritually, emotionally and intellectually thirsty people from across the globe embarking on a perpetual flight to the oriental firmament in their bid to seek answers to the mysteries of the world and the self.

They have been the 'Indophilians' opposed to the 'Indophobians' including a large segment of self-loathing Indians, who, for a variety of reasons, spew venom against India with their choicest vituperatives such as 'un-progressive', 'barbarians' and 'superstitious heathens'. But then, the proud Indians remain silent and unshaken by the Indophobians' slugfest. However, their reticence finds loud echoes in the Indophilians such as 2nd century Roman philosopher Arrian, who celebrated India to be 'the nation of free people', reiterating that he had found 'no slaves in India at all'. And what's more, Arrian almost decreed 'No Indian ever went outside his own country on a warlike expedition, so righteous were they'. ("Slavery", by Richard Oluseyi Asaolu / "The Origins of the Europeans: Classical Observations in Culture and Personality", William S. Shelley)

Undeterred by Indophobians' malice, the proud Indians welcome complimentary and grateful utterances from other lands in their patient stride. For, they know only the enlightened ones with perfect pair of eyes could see radiant glow of knowledge emanating from the oriental sky and sift through innumerable scriptures to seek answers to the gnawing mysteries. And that's why, when French philosopher Voltaire sang paeans in the words – "I am convinced that everything has come down to us from the banks of the Ganges, – astronomy, astrology, metempsychosis, etc... It is very important to note that some 2, 500 years ago at the least Pythagoras went from Samos to the Ganges to learn geometry...But he would certainly not have undertaken such a strange journey had the reputation of the Brahmins' science not been long established in Europe" ("Letters surl'orgine des sciences et sure celle des peoples del'Asie"–Voltaire–dated December 15, 1775–first published in Paris in 1777) the proud Indians only smile in silence.

Amongthe names galore in this one-way traffic, some came here (India) to seek knowledge and entered into the club of Indophilians. Rest of them though were not so fortunate but were equally proud to have realized the worth and supremacy of the land and its immeasurable treasure of knowledge.

From the Canadian foothills..,

About most of the Indophilians, who amazed me by their love for our country, I have read extensively. However, I had chance of interacting with some of them. Ishwar Sharan, who was born in a God-fearing Protestant Christian family and was brought up in the foothills of western Canada, is one of them. He does not speak about his Christian name. For, he was "a never believing Christian." I had a very brief encounter with IshwarSharan, who came to India in 1967, became a Sanyasi (Swami Devanand) and has been living here thence. He kept this name (Ishwar Sharan) for writing purpose.

He describes himself as a devotee of the Mother Goddess from an early age. He attributes this devotion to his samskara, 'a very deeply embedded memory'. Delving deeper into the books on oriental sacred texts, he realized that Hinduism was the only religion that remembered the Goddess today.

Speaking about 'the turning point in his life' Sharan said: "The turning point in my life came when my righteous father beat me for going to see a circus that had come to town. He beat me so badly the school authorities wanted to take legal action against him. I stopped them from doing that as it would have been a scandal in the closed Christian community we lived in. But I also lost respect for him and he became a complete stranger to me. He was a good man but he was obsessed with the stories of the Old Testament prophets and tried to emulate them. I left school and the family house soon after this event, at the age of sixteen. I wanted to see the world which I had been taught was a very wicked place and destined for destruction. By leaving the family, I became a free man. Or so I believed at the time. I would learn soon enough that there are very few free men in this world. Most men and women are bound by their desires or their minds are imprisoned in the same fundamentalist ideologies my father's mind was imprisoned in." (E-mail interview given to Pradeep Krishnan in August 2013 and published by him on the *Haindava Keralam* website on September 19, 2013.")

In the same interview, he spoke about the reasons for his decision to settle in India and seek a spiritual path. "I arrived in India in 1967 with the specific desire to find a spiritual teacher. I had learned from my travels and reading that a guru was needed to guide a seeker in the spiritual life. I deeply desired a spiritual life and I was sure India had an answer for me. India was quite a different place in 1967, than it is today. It was poorer but it was much gentler and closer to its cultural and spiritual traditions."

Ever since he came to the Indian soil, he has not only

been championing the cause of Indian values, but also writing about the nexus of people who are bent on making dents in the cultural fibre of this country. He is particularly critical of Christianity and the missionary machinery.

The fervent hunter of Sanskrit texts..,

On a cold January evening of 2012, I had a call from an acquaintance, who told me that his German relative, a lover of Sanskrit and oriental languages, was staying with them and if I could have a meeting and write something about in the newspaper (I was then reporting-writing for the *Hindustan Times*, Jharkhand edition). My meeting with Prof. Stefan Baums was very heartwarming. Baumsloves to describes himself as a secular Buddhist. He was teaching Sanskrit at the University of California (Berkeley). I had a very lovely conversation with him. Like hundreds of Germans, who were known for their love for India, Baums had a natural inclination towards anything and everything that concerned with the knowledge heritage vouchsafed by the rishis and munies of India.

With this burning passion in heart, Baums looked and hunted for droplets of oriental wisdom which also included a love for the haloed scripts and manuscripts. He discovered his love for Sanskrit during his pursuit of European classical languages including Latin and Greek.

He began as a student of western classical languages. However, a chance exposure to Sanskrit left an everlasting impact on the young German, who discovered that his destiny lay eastward in the oriental studies with Sanskrit as its main vehicle.

He traced his passionate journey in Sanskrit to the enchanting love story of Nal-Damyanti in the Mahabharata. "I was pursuing Greek at the University of Gottingen in 1994. During a session on the comparative literature, a teacher dwelt on the story of Nal-Damyanti segment and I fell in love with the language called Sanskrit, " he told me during our conversation in 2012 and the same was published in the *Hindustan Times* dated January 7, 2012.

The teacher at the University of Gottingen had set the ball rolling for Baums, who scanned Sanskrit texts and hunted similar beautiful tales. The fire was ignited and thus soon after leaving the University of Gottingen, Baums went in for Sanskrit and oriental languages studies and till then had studied over 50 Sanskrit texts in their original Devnagari script.

However, at the mention of Devnagari script, Baums chuckled and told me his unique love story that culminated into his marriage with Rita Banerji of Ranchi. Baums met Rita at a book fair in Washington in 2005. At one of the stalls, there was a book titled "Why People Should Write in Devnagari!" It so happened that both Baums and Rita made their moves for the same book at the same time. However, the latter picked up the book and browsed through the pages while Baums impatiently waited for her to put down the book on the stall. Rita realized Baums' fascination for the book and what followed was an academic love story culminating in their marriage. However, the marriage only accelerated Baums' pursuit of Sanskrit and oriental studies.

A unique Thai connection..,

In July 2010, I had a long interview with the first Jnanpeeth Awardee (in Sanskrit), Professor SatyaVrat Shastri, who had come down to Ranchi in connection with a seminar. Prof. Shastri shared with me several anecdotes about his pursuit of divine language and the people. However, the one that he fervently recalled fascinated me much. It was his teaching assignment abroad for single student in Thailand.

Inspired by the depth and charms of the divine language, Thai princess Maha Chakri Sirindhorn desperately longed to learn Sanskrit under the tutelage of a learned scholar preferably from India. Resultantly, the Thai authorities got in touch with their Indian counterpart and a hunt for the learned scholar from India began. The Indian authorities got Shastri engaged for the assignment for two years (1977-79). He helped Princess Sirindhorn learn many a Sanskrit text.

Helena: the Russian Indologist..,

Born in Southern Russia in 1831, Helena Petrovna Blavatsky was an exceptional child reportedly in possession of certain psychic powers, which astonished her family and friends. When she was 20, Helena met the person, about whom she claimed to have known in her psycho-spiritual visions from childhood. He was an Eastern Initiate of Rajput birth, the Mahatma Morya or simply M. She accepted him as her guide and on his instructions she set her future goals.

She came to India twice. On her second visit, Helena stayed in the country for about six years between 1879 and 1885, during which she got in touch with several learned Indian minds, who gave definite shapes to what she claimed to have already foreseen in her psychic visions and the result was "the accumulated Wisdom of the ages, tested and verified by generations of Seers..., " under the umbrella of Theosophical Society. (Boris de Zirkoff and published in *Theosophia* (Los Angeles, California), Summer 1968, pp. 3-8.)

"... Madame Blavatsky... stands out as the fountain head of modern occult thought, and was either the originator and/or popularizer of many of the ideas and terms which have a century later been assembled within the New Age Movement. The Theosophical Society, which she cofounded, has been the major advocate of occult philosophy in the West and the single most important avenue of Eastern teaching to the West." (J. Gordon Melton, Jerome Clark and Aidan A.

Kelly, editors, New Age Almanac, Detroit, Michigan, Gale Research Inc., 1991, p. 16.)

Pseudo indologists..,

Those who pursued their interest in the oriental studies also included certain big names such as Max Muller, H H Wilson, Monier Williams among others. But then they were pseudo indologists interested in India with an ulterior motive.

Max Muller, for instance, was a devout student of Vedanticscriptures. But he did it with purpose. He was assigned the task of undertaking this study by the British to further the latter's colonial interest and proselytization project of the Christian missionary.

Muller expresses his intention in his writing: "The translation of the *Veda* will hereafter tell to a great extent on the fate of India, and on the growth of millions of souls in that country. It is the root of their religion, and to show them what the root is, is, I feel sure, is the only way of uprooting all that has sprung from it during the last 3,000 years." (Edwin Bryant (2001). Eliot Weinberger (2000).

His intentions were more manifest in his letter (1868) to George Campbell, the newly appointed Secretary of State for India: "India has been conquered once, but India must be conquered again, and that second conquest should be a conquest by education. Much has been done for education of late, but if the funds were tripled and quadrupled, that would hardly be enough (...) By encouraging a study of their own ancient literature, as part of their education, a national feeling of pride and self-respect will be reawakened among those who influence the large masses of the people. A new national literature may spring up, impregnated with Western ideas, yet retaining its native spirit and character (...) A new national literature will bring with it a new national life, and new moral vigour. As to religion, that will take care of itself.

The missionaries have done far more than they themselves seem to be aware of, nay, much of the work which is theirs they would probably disclaim. The Christianity of our nineteenth century will hardly be the Christianity of India. But the ancient religion of India is doomed—and if Christianity does not step in, whose fault will it be?" (Müller, Georgina (1902) *The Life and Letters of Right Honorable Friedrich Max Müller*, Vol. 1, London: Longman, pp. 357–358)

In fact Max Muller appears to be a confused and at loggerheads with himself or else how can we reconcile with shower of praise in his lecture at the Cambridge in 1883, when he had said: "If I were to look over the whole world to find out the country most richly endowed with all the wealth, power, and beauty that nature can bestow—in some parts a very paradise on earth—I should point to India. If I were asked under what sky the human mind has most full developed some of its choicest gifts, has most deeply pondered on the greatest problems of life, and has found solutions of some of them which well deserve the attention even of those who have studied Plato and Kant—I should point to India. And if I were to ask myself from what literature we, here in Europe, we who have been nurtured almost exclusively on the thoughts of Greeks and Romans, and of one Semitic race, the Jewish, may draw that corrective which is most wanted in order to make our inner life more perfect, more comprehensive, more universal, in fact more truly human, a life, not for this life only, but a transfigured and eternal life—again I should point to India." (Max Müller, India – Lecture I What Can India Teach Us? A Course of *Lectures Delivered before the University of Cambridge, Project Gutenberg*)

Wrapping up..,

Indophobians' intention notwithstanding, the flow of indophilians or India lovers and their deep interest in the liberating philosophy have continued for ages and will ever continue to inspire the travelers on the one-way traffic to destination India.

References

Hetenyi, Dr. Ernest, *Alexander Csoma de Koros: The Hungarian Bodhisattva.*

Lenderman, Max, "Brand New World: How Paupers, Pirates, and Oligarchs are Reshaping Business", 74, by from original source Philostratus's book *Life of Apollonius of Tyana.*

Shelley, William S. "Slavery", by *Richard Oluseyi Asaolu* / "The Origins of the Europeans: Classical Observations in Culture and Personality".

Letters surl'orgine des sciences et sure celle des peoplesdel'Asie" - *Voltaire* - dated December 15, 1775 - first published in Paris in 1777) the proud Indians only smile in silence. E-mail interview given to *Pradeep Krishnan* in August 2013 and published by him on the HaindavaKeralam website on September 19, 2013.

Singh, Shiv Charan, "German prof. devotes himself to study of Sanskrit", *Hindustan Times*, Jharkhand edition, January 7, 2012.

Singh, Shiv Charan, "Ranchi Reminds Me of My honeymoon", *Hindustan Times*, Jharkhand edition, July 19, 2010.

Theosophia, Boris de Zirkoff (Los Angeles, California), Summer 1968, pp. 3-8

Melton, J. Gordon, Jerome Clark and Aidan A. Kelly, editors, *New Age Almanac*, Detroit, Michigan, Gale Research Inc., 1991, p. 16.)

Bryant, Edwin, (2001). *The Quest for the Origins of Vedic Culture: The Indo-Aryan Migration Debate*. Oxford University Press, p. 289.

Weinberger, Eliot, (2000). *Karmic Traces, 1993–1999*. New Directions Publishing.p. 174.

Müller, Georgina (1902). *The Life and Letters of Right Honorable Friedrich Max Müller*. Vol. 1. London: Longman, pp. 357–358)

Müller, Max, *India – Lecture I What Can India Teach Us?* A Course of Lectures Delivered before the University of Cambridge, Project Gutenberg.

3

India in South Asia
Debating Regional Strategies

Rajani Bala and Zheer Ahmed

Introduction

India got its independence with the speech called 'tryst with destiny'. The speech set up India's political goals that were to be achieved in future. India's independence came with some serious challenges, such as partition and rehabilitation of people, free and fair elections, existing caste hierarchy, issue of reservations and land reforms. These challenges posed serious threat to the newly formed Indian state. At SAARC forums, the government of India has been insisting that the economies of South Asia are complementary and that on the basis of this complementarity there should be a harmonization of economic plans in this region. By harmonization, India refers to the point that it should be the industrial power in the region, manufacturing enough to meet the needs of the entire region, while the other countries of South Asia should concentrate on production of agricultural or other primary products. Pakistan has opposed this notion of complementarity, pointing out that its exports are largely competitive with those of India.[1]

India then is trying to turn South Asia into its own market. It is important to note that this regional market is not being captured in defiance of the Trinmool National Congress out in subsidiary collaboration with them. Regional hegemony goes along with a regional market. The two help each other. But in analyzing the factors in India's regional hegemony, one must not make a simple transition from economics to politics. Rather, it is necessary to look at the overall strategic situation and analyze the relation between the superpowers' competing global hegemonies and India's regional hegemony.[2]

Former Prime Minister Atal Bihari Vajpayee buried the idea of undoing partition during his visit to Lahore in February 1999 by visiting Minar-e-Pakistan, which symbolizes the creation of Pakistan. He also propounded the forward-looking approach of developing trust, confidence and creating "a solid structure of cooperation". Manmohan Singh carried this thinking forward in presenting a vision of South Asia where, with the cooperation of all its neighbors, India moves from poverty to prosperity, ignorance to knowledge and insecurity to lasting peace. Instead of pursuing the unrealistic goal of undoing partition, this approach sought to leverage the large Indian economy in building mutually beneficial trade, economic and other linkages within South Asia[3].

Ever since the 1990's economic reforms, India's foreign policy has gone through many transitions. This was also the period where many changes were taking place at the global level. It was the phase of the post-cold war period. Along with the conventional challenges, there were new challenges thrown for facing by policy makers. Non-governmental sector, foreign investment and other pro development measures became significant issues to be addressed thereafter.[4]

As a result the making of the foreign policy became complex. There were many factors which drove the Indian foreign policy in the post cold war era. Such as, India's aspiration to attain the great power status had a major impact on its foreign policy. There were many reasons for this; however India's location in South Asia provided it with the many advantages. Among the major steps taken during this time were the Civil Nuclear Cooperation with the US and India-ASEAN Free Trade Agreement. India's Foreign Policy in early 2000s and later as well was a radical transformation to approach its neighbors in South Asia. Some scholars are of the view that the foreign policies of the present government are in fact the continuation of the Manmohan regime. Such arguments are based on the fact that the concrete decisions to link India's economic transformation and growth of India with its foreign policy approach and objectives.[5]

The broad territorial division of ethnic groups within India and the strength of regional ethnic identities ensure that Indian policy towards the countries in question is always attentive to the preferences of domestic actors in these regions. In South Asia there are many ethnic groups that share their identity with several groups in India. The Tamil ethnic group is one of them. As a result of this India has often been dragged into the conflict between the LTTE and the Sri Lankan state. The Indian state closely watches the developments and reconstruction activities to ensure that the Tamil ethnic groups are not oppressed. New Delhi often comes under pressure from the domestic groups to intervene with the Sri Lankan government to provide calming assurances.[6] The same remains true of the Madhesis in Nepal.

In 2008, New Delhi bent to political pressure from Tamil

Nadu to intervene with the Sri Lankan government, at a time when it was in the military ascendance against the LTTE, to provide calming assurances. Similarly, the International Crisis Group reports in regard to the Madhesi movement for autonomy in the Tarai region of Nepal, that there is "widespread sympathy" in Indian border regions and "most politicians and bureaucrats do not hesitate to express moral support" for the cause.

Due to its diverse nature, India often becomes vulnerable to secessionist and separatist conflicts. The reasons could be far and wide. Unequal distribution of the resources, uneven democracy, apathy of the Indian state towards few regions such as Kashmir and Nagaland, and other factors often lead to the regions calling for a separate state. To this day India struggles with the secessionist movements. The consequences of the armed movements are the use of the territories of adjacent countries to stage their attacks on the Indian state, the cross-border activities of secessionists creating obstacles to neutralize these movements and secessionist movements allowing neighboring countries with an interest in destabilising India to interfere in its internal affairs in an adverse manner.

The political observers are of the view that the global political architecture is in the process of transformation. This transformation focuses on power shifting from the west to the east. South Asia forms an important part of this transformation.[7] In particular India has a bigger role to play. However such shifts are also brought about by another important actor in the East that is China. China being one of the emerging global powers itself, wants to increase its influence in the region. In recent times they have established economic relations with Pakistan in the form of the massive China Pakistan economic corridor as part of One Belt One Road. The same thing can be seen when it played a pivotal role in managing and building of the Hambantota Port in Sri Lanka. This is coupled with their territorial claims over many of the India's territories such as Arunachal Pradesh.

Along with this, there are many other factors that are relevant. For instance, they do not support India's membership to the UN Security Council. As a result, China is an important factor that is shaping India's foreign policy today. The recent Indo-US bilateral meetings and other agreements such as Comicosa and 2+2 dialogue initiatives should be seen to tackle China's growing might as a global power. India's look east policy should also be seen as its reaction against the China Pakistan economic corridor. Despite this, Harsh Pant opines that India's ability to think strategically on issues of national security is questionable. George Tan Ham takes the same narrative when he says that the Indian elites have shown little evidence of having thought coherently and systematically about the national strategy.

There are many reasons that support their claims. National Security Council established in the 1990s to evaluate the military, economic and other strategic challenges facing the nation. It advices the government to tackle these challenges effectively. Though meant to be guiding the Government and in policy formulation but it lacked the institutionalization. As a result it faces many drawbacks. There are no institutional arrangements at place to meet its advices. Hence it faces difficulties in bringing about any structural changes. There are times the decisions are often taken in ad hoc manner without consulting the cabinet committee and other strategic policy groups. India's stand on Maldivian political crisis is an example of national strategy weaknesses. Maldives is a small country located strategically in the Indian Ocean. It is connected with the major sea lanes of communication. It acts as a major trading route to the Indian Ocean countries. As the country is located so closely to India, India watches the developments happening in Maldives closely. The Government in Maldives led by president Abdulla Yameen said to be dictatorial in exercising power. His rule has often come under attack by the democratic forces for curbing the freedom of expression and rights. There are many business enterprises of Indian origin that are working in the Maldives today. GMR remains one of them. Besides Maldives is a member of the SAARC. Recently, Maldives was in news for political uncertainty facing it. India showed no intervention except the statement calling upon the Maldives to restore all the articles of constitution and allow other institutions to operate freely.

This was not good news for India as the Maldives has come under the forces that are not friendly as the regime before.[8] Traditionally Maldives has sought India's help time and again. Ambassador A.K. Banerjee opines that India should bat for a friend. It should work for a unitary government and persuade all to agree to early elections. Besides it should recommend that the Maldivians agree to a long term strengthening of democratic institutions and resolve their differences peacefully. Considering the case of India's approach to South Asia, even the recent initiative by the current regime of "Neighborhood First" approach also seems a failed attempt by the government of India to establish its friendly relations in South Asian region.

Changing Dimension of India's Foreign Policy in the South Asia

India's neighborhood, namely, Afghanistan, Bangladesh, Bhutan, Nepal, Maldives, Pakistan and Sri Lanka, has a fairly complex geographical entity. These regions represent a world of historical links, shared legacies, commonalities as well as diversities which are so elaborately reflected in their ethnic, linguistic, religious and political fabric. The principal thrust of India's engagement with the countries of South Asia bilaterally as well as with the region as whole is to develop and grow its society. India advocates the policy of constructive engagement, despite such serious provocations as have been in the past (Attacks on Parliament, Mumbai etc). It believes that violent retaliation and confrontation can only complicate the matters. This applies in particular to Pakistan—the origin of state-sponsored terrorism targeted at India. A rising India has interest in the success of its neighbors since the stability in the region contributes in establishing an environment to grow and develop. India's engagement in South Asian region is both bilateral and multipronged. Multipronged under the ambit of SAARC and through sub regional or even trans regional mechanisms such as Bay of Bengal Initiative (BIMSTEC) which includes some SAARC members and some ASEAN ones and Indian Ocean Rim Association for Regional Cooperation. India had already intensified its cooperation at the regional and sub-regional levels and the NDA government is proactive in taking these engagements forward. Regional as well as sub-regional cooperation became major vehicles of India's neighbourhood policy. The importance of the region for India is not because of the fact that it is a geographical *fait accompli* but its significance as a contiguous cultural space based on a shared heritage that needs to be nurtured and sustained.

India and Afghanistan

India and Afghanistan share 2000 years old cultural heritage via music, arts, architecture, language and cuisine. Afghanistan has been a significant trading centre, connects India with Central Asia and Persia. This people-to-people relationship has further been strengthened by both the nations in recent past. The strategic partnership agreement between the two nations is a chalk-up example of strength in partnership. The agreement signed in 2011, provides assistance to rebuild Afghanistan's infrastructure and institutions[9]. The second partnership agreement was signed in 2017, which is considered as development partnership in building dam, provide drinking water and water for irrigation[10]. Along with, India also takes up high impact community development projects aim to invest in areas of education, health, agriculture, renewable energy, micro-hydropower and administrative infrastructure.

Diplomatic and political relations have always been estimable between India and Afghanistan. However, Taliban is an exception in this history of relations. Indian support to anti-Taliban resistance turned Taliban more hostile. Overthrow of Taliban regime in 2001, full diplomatic relations were restored between India and Afghanistan. India is providing financial aid for Afghanistan's reconstruction and development. With the worth of $1.2 billion financial aid to Afghanistan, India becomes largest donor to Afghanistan in South Asian region. The relations grow up bilaterally as well. India is the largest market for Afghan products in the region. Bilateral trade between India and Afghanistan was $800 million in 2016-17. High level visits from both the sides signify the importance of bilateral trade. The dam earlier known as Salma dam has renamed as Afghan-India friendship dam, after Prime Minister Modi visited Afghanistan in 2016. Along with, India also completed construction of the Zaranj-Delaram highway in southwest Afghanistan near the Iranian border, built new parliament and trained Afghan police officers, diplomats and civil servants.

Afghanistan holds strategic importance for India. It is a gateway for India to Central Asia. Afghanistan being neighbor of India and Pakistan, Pakistan influences interests of India in Afghanistan. However, Afghanistan states, that it follows the policy of neutralism. Pakistan views India's growing influence in Afghanistan as a threat to its interests in the region. However, New Delhi blames Pakistan and its support to Taliban for attacks Indian personnel and assets in Afghanistan. Afghanistan and Indian tie have grown up significantly. Pakistan as a fear factor always influences India-Afghanistan bilateral relations.

India-Bangladesh

India and Bangladesh share a common border of 4096 Km running through five Indian states, West Bengal, Assam, Meghalaya, Tripura and Mizoram. Traditionally, India shares cultural, economic and social relations with Bangladesh. Along with, India not just shares its typical history of battle for flexibility and freedom, but friendly and familiarly ties. Linguistic and cultural ties bring the countries close. While India played a crucial role in 1971 in the birth of Bangladesh, the bilateral relations have been witnessed of ups and downs thereafter.

India's role in Bangladesh's war of liberation is that, for few years India enjoyed a privileged relationship with the new state[11]. India immediately acknowledged the sovereignty of new state and became first state to give recognition to Bangladesh. In 1972, the two nations strengthened the relationship by signing a 'treaty of friendship and peace' for a term of 25 years. The treaty declares that both sides would respect their mutual independence, sovereignty and territorial integrity. Also, the treaty refrain both the nations from interfering in each other's internal affairs. Muzibur-ur-Rehman's assassination in 1975 pulled India-Bangladesh ties downward. New regime under General Zia-ur-Rehman was based on more of Islamic ideology than linguistic nationalism. Consequently, India's relations with Bangladesh backfired and the relationship was characterized as belligerence and insensitivity on the Indian part and oversensitivity and suspicion on the Bangladeshi side[12]. However, both the nations realized the need of cooperation to address mutual problems. This had been seen in 1977 agreement on sharing the waters of the River Ganges during the dry season and India lease over Tin Bigha corridor to Bangladesh in 1992.

The coming to power of Bhartiya Janta Party (BJP) government in India in 1998 was not welcomed by Bangladesh. Dhaka viewed the regime in India with suspicion because of BJP's desire to re-establish India that expands from Kyber Pass in the northwest to Chittagong in the east. In 2004, the scenario was changed and Bangladesh welcomed new 'United Progressive Alliance' regime led the Congress party. However, bilateral relations tumbled after New Delhi refused to participate in the SAARC summit at Dhaka in February 2005, citing law and order problems in Bangladesh. In recent trends, there are ample issues that shape India-Bangladesh relations. Water issue, illegal migration, maritime boundary demarcation and Islamic fundamentalism weaken ties between India and Bangladesh.

Bangladesh is heavily dependent on India for its water flow. The construction of Farakka Barrage is a major bone of contention between the two countries[13]. The water dispute was resolved in 1996 with signing the 30 years water sharing agreement for the Ganges. Treaty also has not been a permanent solution of the problem. Therefore, water concerns significantly derive the bilateral relations time to time. Another issue of contention is illegal Bangladeshi migration streams to India. The migration has altered the demography of Indian border areas resulting in ethnic imbalance, electoral irregularities and loss of employment opportunities for Indian nationals[14]. Recently, there were violent clashes in Assam, while implementing National Register of Citizens of India. This act has already hampered India's relations with Bangladesh. However, many North Eastern States are also opposing the Citizenship Amendment Bill 2016. Islamic Fundamentalism has been seen as a threat by the Indian side, which has been growing in Bangladesh. Since 2009, under the Sheik Hasina regime, the relationship has been tremendously improved with 'India-Positive' by the Bangladesh. Land Limit Understanding is a new beginning in relationship between India and Bangladesh under the leadership of Prime Minister Narendra Modi. These issues of bilateral importance had been slowed down since 2009.

India-Bhutan

Bhutan was a British India's protectorate that allowed Britain to guide its foreign and defense affairs through the 'Treaty of Punakha' signed in 1910. Till 1948, India handled Bhutan's political and foreign affairs through a political officer based in Sikkim. In 1948, the treaty was revisited and both the countries signed a new 'treaty of friendship and cooperation' in 1949, which declares that "Bhutan's internal affairs shall function without any interference from India while the foreign relations will take place its guidance"[15]. However, in 2007 article 2 of the treaty was revised and termed India's relations with Bhutan as bilateral. Formal diplomatic relations was established in 1968 after a special office of India was opened in Thimpu.

India shares a special relationship with Bhutan. Both the countries share deep religious-cultural relationship. Buddhism cemented traditional ties between the people of the two countries. India shares a 605 km border with Bhutan. In terms of trade, India is the largest trading partner with Bhutan, accounting for 98 percent of its exports and 90 percent of its imports. India's financial aid to Bhutan was raised from US$ 600 million in 2012-2013 to US$ 985 million in 2015-2016, which made Bhutan a largest beneficiary of India foreign aid.

Since late 1950s, Bhutan is incessantly asserting its independent identity and making its efforts to reduce its dependency on India. After getting full membership of the United Nations in 1971, Bhutan opened full ambassadorial diplomatic relation with India and with other countries as well. Recently, in 2017, Bhutan withdrew from Bhutan-Bangladesh-India-Nepal Motor Vehicle Corridor for the reason that it would adversely affect its environment and sovereignty. However, economic ties were governed by the India-Bhutan Trade and Transit Agreement of 1972, and the bilateral trade stood at Rs. 8723 crore in 2016 making India, Bhutan's largest trading partner.

Apart from some obstacle-cum-issues, such as India's paternalistic attitude towards Bhutan, Bhutans geographical location, China's role in India-Bhutan relations, both the countries benefit from each other. Under Prime Minister Modi's policy of 'Neighborhood first' and 'Act East', India gives special emphasis on India-Bhutan relations. Prime Minister Modi's 'Bharat to Bhutan' vision which says, that Bharat should stand for Bhutan and Bhutan for Bharat is also significant in this aspect. The relationship is largely sustained by the regular high level visits and dialogue. Both the countries share mutual cooperation in the areas of Security, border management, trade, hydro-power and many more. Hydro-cooperation is the single most important area of mutual beneficial cooperation in India and Bhutan ties. Under the 2006 Agreement on cooperation in hydro-power, India has pledged to assist Bhutan in developing at least 10,000 MW of hydro-power and import the surplus of electricity to India by 2020.

India-Maldives

Maldives located is located south of India in the Indian Ocean. India established ties with Maldives immediately after Maldives got independence from British rule in 1965. India established its mission at Male in 1972 and contributed to the maintenance of security of the island nation[16]. India and Maldives officially decided their maritime boundary in 1976. However, in 1982 Maldives claimed Minicoy Island, which officially has been the part of India. Apart from small regional strains, both the countries share ethnic, linguistic, cultural, religious and commercial link steeped in antiquity and enjoy cordial and multi-dimensional relations.[17]

In 1988 India launched 'Operation Cactus' to counter an attempt of military coup by the People's Organization of Tamil Eelam in Maldives. The then president of Maldives Maumoom Abdul Gayoom requested India for military support. The Indian Prime Minister at that time Rajiv Gandhi dispatch of 1600 Indian troops and squashed the military coup attempt. This operation had solidified relations between the two nations. Analysts of the Operation argue that in the absence of Indian military help, external powers would have been tempted to intervene or even establish bases in Maldives, which being in India's backyard, India could not allow.[18] India's action in Maldives was endorsed by great powers such as USA and Great Britain and regional neighbors such as Nepal and Bangladesh.[19]

Ever since the success of 'Operation Cactus', commercial relations between the two have enlarged significantly.[20] In 2013-2014 bilateral trade had reached to Rs. 677. 15 crore. India has provided extensive economic aid and participated in bilateral programs for the development of health, aviation, infrastructure, telecommunications and labor resources. The relations hit an all-time low after Maldives canceled the GMR airport contract. However, in

2014, during the drinking water crisis, India came to rescue Maldives by sending bottled water to the Island. Military relations have also expanded significantly. In 2006, Indian Navy gifted a Trinkat Class Fast attack Craft to Maldive's National Defense Force. Since 2009, both the countries share strong military ties. Maldives in a way is dependent on the security provided by India. India signed many military agreements with the island nation, which cover a range of military pacts.

Apart from military and commercial aid to Maldives, both the countries have rich political relations. There is a regular exchange of high level ministerial visits at regular intervals. India has always supported Maldives in internationals forums such as United Nations and SAARC. There is rich tradition of people-to-people contacts between India and Maldives. They have rich heritage of cultural relations. India opened a India Cultural Centre at Male in 2011. The Centre conducts regular courses of Yoga, Classical music and Dance[21]. Recent political upheavals in Maldives have affected India-Maldives relations. However, regime under Ibu Solih has a positive attitude towards India, which has been seen in recent visit by the president.

India and Nepal

India and Nepal share a unique relationship of friendship and cooperation. The relationship is characterized by open borders and deep rooted people to people contacts of kinship and culture[22]. India shares its border with Nepal of over 1850 Km in the East, South and West with the five Indian States, namely; Sikkim, West Bengal, Bihar, Uttar Pradesh and Uttarakhand. The 1950 India-Nepal treaty of Peace and Friendship forms the bedrock of special relations that exist between India and Nepal. Under the provisions of this treaty, Nepalese citizens enjoy unparallel advantages in India. They avail facilities and opportunities at par with Indian citizens. Currently, around 600, 000 Indian are inhabitants in Nepal. Both the nations share significant cultural relations. In 1990, Indians living in Nepal set up Indian Citizens Association of Nepal, providing a platform for discussion on matter pertaining to the legitimate interests of resident Indians in Nepal[23]. To promote its cultural heritage, India established India Cultural Centre in Nepal in 2007.

The proposal for the creation of 'Zone of Peace' in 1975 tarnished India-Nepal relations. On the one hand India taught it as a violation of friendship treaty of 1950, while other regional actors, such as China and Pakistan welcomed the move towards an independent Nepal's foreign policy. In 1989, it was Rajiv Gandhi's Government in India which blew-down the relationship. After the expiration of Trade and Transit treaty of 1987, India put economic blockade against Nepal[24]. 240-years old monarchy in Nepal was abolished in 2006 with the help of India. India welcomed newly formed government through Comprehensive Peace Agreement in 2006. This was a first step towards political stabilization in Nepal. India consistently supported the peace process towards the multi-party democratization and institutionalization[25]. India extended its support to constituent assembly to frame a new constitution. At the same time, during the promulgation of constitution, violence erupted by the Madhes-based parties and other groups. India expressed its grave concern over the situation in Nepal.

Economic relations between India and Nepal have blown up since 1990s. Since 1996, India-Nepal bilateral trade has grown more than eleven times till 2013-2014. India's export to Nepal was increased from US$ 605 million to US$ 4.81 billion in 2014. India is one of the highest contributors to Nepal's foreign direct investment[26]. Nepal gets substantial financial and technical assistance from India. The aid focuses in the areas of infrastructure, health, water resources, education and rural and community development[27]. In the area of education, India's contribution to the development of human resources has been one of major aspects of bilateral cooperation. The relations are not always abundant and gets setback time to time. Factors but influence India-Nepal relations broadly are distribution of water and China's infiltration in Nepal's domestic affairs. However, a three-tier mechanism has established in 2008 to discuss all bilateral issues relating to cooperation in water resources and hydropower which has been working fine. India shares 'Roti-Beti' relations with Nepal, which China lacks and put India-Nepal in an unique relationship.

India and Sri Lanka

Sri Lanka is separated from Indian subcontinent by a stretch of water known as Palk Strait. India shares its maritime boundary with Sri Lanka. India's policy towards Sri Lanka is an extension of its domestic policy dealing with the Tamil issue. Sri Lankan Tamils have been numerical minority as against the Sinhalese majority, but they are regionally in majority in dominating the northeastern Sri Lanka[28]. Ever since its independence in 1948, Sri Lanka initiated controversial and discriminating policies of education, employment and citizenship towards minority Tamils[29]. The discriminatory policies of Sri Lankan government resulted into Tamil secessionist and separatist movements in the country. The secessionist movement in Sri Lanka, by and large, affected the bilateral relations between the two countries. Ethnic violence was a common phenomenon in Sri Lanka in 1950s[30]. Most prominent ethnic violence and riots occurred in 1956, 1958, 1977 and 1983. However, the bilateral relationship started blossoming in mid-1960s.

The ethnic conflict between Tamil ethnic group and Sri Lankan Sinhalese in 1983 caused influx of 1, 25, 000 Sri Lankan Tamils to Tamil Nadu in 1983[31]. It was the worst ethnic crisis ever had been seen in the history of Sri Lanka. Sri Lankan Tamils were demanding for separate Tamil Ealam, which was not accepted by the Sri Lankan government. Consequently, both the nations were affected from the ethnic conflict. On the Indian side, India never supported independent Tamil Eelam disturbing Sri Lankan unity and territorial integrity[32]. However, Indian assistance to Tamil guerillas had worsened Indo-Sri Lankan relations. It was blamed on India that LTTE was established and nurtured in India. This paved the way for outside powers to enter the region as Sri Lanka moved to Western powers and looked at China as an alternative to counter India. In this background, China and Pakistan established their feet in Sri Lankan soil.

The ethnic crisis continued till 1987. All the negotiations and efforts to establish peace were failed. Indian efforts were severely criticized on the ground of breach of Sri Lankan sovereignty; however, USA supported India's action in Sri Lanka on humanitarian grounds. Both the countries had come to common understanding for establishing peace in the region. Eventually, Prime Minister Rajiv Gandhi and President L. Jayawardene signed an accord known as Indo-Sri Lanka Accord on 29th July 1987 to establish peace and normalcy in Sri Lanka. According to the Accord, the Indian peacekeeping force was introduced in Jaffna. To counter the violence erupted by LTTE, IPKF sought to disarm the Tamil militant group through the 'Operation Pawan'. After the failure of IPKF and subsequent assassination of Rajiv Gandhi by the LTTE, India has formulated hands off policy towards Sri Lanka[33]. In 2002, India strongly supported the cease-fire agreement between LTTE and Sri Lanka.

Thus, India's involvement in Sri Lanka was unavoidable not only because of Tamil ethnic problem, but for its own national security concerns, given Sri Lanka's geopolitical location.[34] On the commercial and military side, both the nations share good relations, apart from some dispute such as fishing and China's military base in Sri Lanka's Hambantota Port.

India and Myanmar

India shares 1600 km of land boundary with Myanmar as well a maritime boundary in Bay of Bengal. Four states in India's northeast namely; Arunachal Pradesh, Nagaland, Manipur and Mizoram share their boundary with Myanmar. Both the countries share a heritage of ethnic, religious and linguistic ties[35]. India established its diplomatic relations with Myanmar in 1948 immediately after Myanmar got independence. India-Myanmar bilateral relations have been flourishing until 1988, when military Junta took over power. India and an arch, supporter of democracy criticized the act and extend its support towards pro democracy movement. However, Indian foreign policy under the leadership of PV Narasimha Rao and Atal Vihari Vajpayee changed its course and established wider relations with Myanmar. India's 'Act East Policy[36]' is one effort in this regard.

Since 1990s, Government-to-Government relations have been improved between India and Myanmar. Defense and security cooperation has been strengthening over the period of time. Both the nations have signed a memorandum of understanding on Border Cooperation, army training and naval staff talks[37]. Commercial cooperation is guided by the bilateral agreement signed in 1970. Trade relations grew steadily, but remain below potential dominated by agricultural sector. Total trade in 2016-17 was US$ 2178.44 million. With this number of trade, India stands tenth largest investor with an approved investment of US$ 740.64 million[38]. Energy is another important sector of cooperation between India and Myanmar. Along with financial aid, India also assists Myanmar in humanitarian relief operations. India extends its developmental assistance to Myanmar worth of US$ 1726 million. On the humanitarian grounds, India assisted Myanmar during Cyclone Nargis in 2008 and earthquake in Shan state in 2010.

Myanmar is the only country among the ASEAN that shares its border with India. Myanmar being a member of ASEAN becomes gateway for India to connect it with South East Asia. Myanmar, given its geo-strategic location, plays crucial role in India's 'Look East' now become 'Act East' policy. Apart from member of ASEAN, Myanmar also holds membership of other regional organizations, such as BIMSTEC and Mekong Ganga Cooperation, which boost up the bilateral relationship.

India and Pakistan

India shares land as well as maritime boundary with Pakistan. The relations have been complex and largely hostile. Kashmir issue and military conflict fought between the two aid hostility between the two nations. A long standing confrontation has witnessed four major armed conflicts in 1948, 1965, 1971 and 1999 respectively. Confrontation throughout the history has limited bilateral ties. Therefore, India's relationship with Pakistan is the most intractable and intense of those with neighbors.[39]

For past sixty five years, India-Pakistan relations have been burdened. The core of conflict is Kashmir, whereas many other factors bedeviled resentment and anxiety between the hostile neighbors. This is one of the most enduring rivalries of the post World War II era[40]. Numerous agreements have signed in late 1980s, including the protection of nuclear facilities, bus service between the India and Pakistan, human trafficking, illegal immigration and the establishment of trading roots.[41] Even on the issue of Kashmir, there was a two track discussion from both the sides[42]. But little has come out of exertions made by both the parties, because of lack of trust between the two governments and political risk aversion in tackling their fundamental differences.[43]

The 1999 Kargil war and spectacular incident of terrorism against India backed by Pakistan such as hijacking of Indian Airlines flight in 1999 and attack on Indian Parliament in 2001[44] and deadly terrorist attack in Mumbai in 2008 have worsened the relationship. Beyond the individual terms, the greater challenge is that Pakistan defines itself in anti Indian terms.[45] The government in Pakistan civilian or military plays 'India card' to consolidate their regime. The sole purpose of Pakistan's military build-up is to counter India. According to Pakistani scholar Ahmed Rashid "The Pakistani army seeks to ensure that a balance of terror and power is maintained with respect to India and the Jihadis are seen as part of this strategy.[46]

Kashmir remains at the crux of the tortured relationship between India and Pakistan.[47] Tussel elements in Pakistan see Kashmir issue as quixotically as a key to unraveling the cohesion of India.[48] Mistrust between the two results regular violence along the Line of Control. The Line of Control becomes central issue of tussle and violation of armistice agreements occurs every then and now. Pakistan levels the Kashmir issue as a territorial, ideological and moral dispute[49] and had fought three consecutive wars over the issue. However, it is power asymmetry causing India-Pakistan rivalry that has prevailed between antagonists for over half a century argued by T.V. Paul[50]. Stephen Cohen argues that if terrorism is the core issue for India, Kashmir is for Pakistan[51].

Bilateral trade could be a weapon to overcome the military differences. Optimists from both the sides hope for peace through the economic cooperation. However, the value of trade is minimal. India's imports and exports are little in terms of trade value[52] India's main interests in economic cooperation lie in hydropower, water management, gas transportation and tourism. Road connectivity to Iran and Afghanistan and proposed US$ 7.6 billion 'Iran-Pakistan-India' gas pipeline is a major roadmap for economic cooperation. At the level of people-to-people, people are well treated during their visits in each country.

China's infiltration in bilateral relations between India and Pakistan however, is not welcome by the Indian side. Pakistan's inclusion in China's Belt and Road initiative and its active participation in China Pakistan Economic Corridor has been worrying India for its territorial violation in Pakistan Occupied Kashmir. Therefore, Pakistan has been known as China's bulwark for keeping India – its main rival tied down to South Asia.[53]

India and China

China's entry into the South Asian region has opened up new avenues for smaller neighbours which can be leveraged in their dealings with India. As a result, the very idea of what South Asian geography means is undergoing a change. This is true in the sense that SAARC could not play its role effectively in India's engagement with South Asia. In that sense, it is about reimagining India's strategic geography altogether. From Sri Lanka to Bangladesh, Pakistan and Myanmar, a string of South Asian states seem politically and economically beholden to Beijing, many falling victim to debt traps created by the Chinese Belt and Road Initiative and string of pearls strategy.

In Sri Lanka, domestic political developments are

affecting India-Sri Lanka's relationship with China having strengthened in recent years. It extended billions of dollars of loans to Sri Lankan government for infrastructure project. Moreover the Sri Lankan government has handed over strategic port of Hambantota. While in the Maldives, India has found its clout diminishing.

In the Seychelles, India is struggling to operationalize a pact to build a military facility. China's clout, meanwhile, is growing markedly around India's periphery, further constraining New Delhi's ability to push its regional agenda. What has rankled even more is China's propping up of regimes unfriendly to India, following which many smaller island states are choosing to overlook New Delhi's interests.

Therefore, the questions that arise are: Is India now prepared for a regional leadership role given the government's emphasis on economic connectivity and neighborhood-first policy? And to what extent would sub-regional cooperation among the Bangladesh, Bhutan, and India and Nepal (BBIN) framework impact on the success of SAARC as a regional cooperation organization is to be assessed.

India needs to address the three important issues. Maldives represents a tipping point, which did not mean that India's decline influence is irreversible. Second, the changing geopolitics of the region demands India to construct favorable alliances to achieve balance of power. India had an imperative to forge closer ties with its Quadrilateral partners. India needed a counter-containment strategy to arrest China's growing military rise in South Asia. The way to do this is not so much to play a defensive game in the Indian Ocean but to expand Indian naval presence to the Western Pacific.

India and BIMSTEC

The South Asia-Southeast Asia grouping is known by

its rather unwieldy name of the Bay of Bengal Initiative for Multi-Sectoral Technical and Economic Cooperation or by the acronym BIMSTEC. It comprises Bangladesh, Bhutan, India, Myanmar, Nepal, Sri Lanka and Thailand, and brings together 1.5 billion people or 21 per cent of the world population and a combined gross domestic product (GDP) of over $2.5 trillion. In terms of connectivity, BIMSTEC has major projects that, when finished, could transform the movement of goods and vehicles through the countries in the grouping.

One is the Kaladan Multimodal project that seeks to link India and Myanmar. The project envisages connecting Kolkata to Sittwe port in Myanmar, and then Mizoram by river and road. India and Myanmar had signed a framework agreement in 2008 for the implementation of this project. Another is the Asian Trilateral Highway connecting India and Thailand through Myanmar. The highway will run from Moreh in Manipur to Mae Sot in Thailand via Myanmar and represents a significant step in establishing connectivity between India and Southeast Asian countries. The project is expected to be completed soon.

Bangladesh, Bhutan, India and Nepal (BBIN)

Bangladesh, Bhutan, India and Nepal (BBIN) have signed a pact for the movement of goods and vehicles among them. Trial runs of trucks between Bangladesh and India have begun. As India shifted from bilateralism to pursue sub-regional and regional approaches towards the neighbourhood, its geographical location provided it with a distinct advantage. It has now emerged as a gateway to Nepal, Bhutan and Bangladesh for their trade with each other and beyond. Some analysts term this 'new regionalism' 'whereby the interrelation between the market and (global) political order is restructured'.

Conclusion

Through SAARC India is engaged with the countries on core areas of development, especially health, education, energy, agriculture, infrastructure and fight against terrorism. There has been serious debate with regard to China's string of Pearls policy in encircling India. But India has not responded with an official policy to counter String of Pearls policy. The recent announcements, however, do suggest that India seems to have taken note of designs of China. India's engagement with its neighbors received a policy reinvigoration after the National Democratic Alliance (NDA) government assumed power and announced its 'neighborhood first' policy. The 'Neighborhood policy' seems to be conscious response to the String of Pearls policy of China. The first sign of this policy was visible when Prime Minister Narendra Modi invited all the heads of state of the neighboring countries for his oath-taking ceremony, on May 26, 2014. India's interest and engagement with the South Asian Association for Regional Cooperation (SAARC) has also intensified in the past few years – from being a reluctant player to driving the regional economic agenda. Unlike in the past, Prime Minister Modi undertook his first foreign visit to Bhutan, followed by visits to Nepal, Sri Lanka, Mauritius, Seychelles and Bangladesh, to synergize bilateral relations. The fact that the neighborhood was given such a prominent position generated hopes among neighboring countries about India's intensive engagement with the region.

The main emphasis of neighborhood policy of India is on trade, connectivity and people to people contact which is evident in the initiatives taken by India in 18th SAARC summit where PM Modi announced slew of initiatives such as immediate medical visa for the patient and attendant, business visa for 3-5 years, support for monitoring and surveillance of polio-free countries, develop and launch of

SAARC satellite, promote use of solar energy. India has contributed US $1.05 million for up-gradation of the SAARC Tuberculosis & HIV/AIDS Centre laboratory in Kathmandu to a super national laboratory. India has set up Special purpose facility to finance infrastructure project in region. Under SAFTA India unilaterally offered duty free access on all items to SAARC LDCs.

It has contributed $200 million for SAARC Development Fund, in the establishment of South Asian University in New Delhi, which is open to the students from eight SAARC members and in the establishment of an Endowment for climate change with a corpus of Rs 25 crores to finance environment related projects.

Notes

1. D.N. (1988). "India in South Asia", *Economic and Political Weekly*, 23(25): 1262-1263.
2. Ibid.
3. *Indian Foreign Policy for a cohesive South Asia.* Online: web] Accessed 18 Decembar, 2018 URL:, https://www.orfonline.org/research/indias-foreign-policy-past-present-and-the-future/.
4. Chris Ogden has discussed it in Indian foreign policy ambition and transition, Online: web] Accessed 18 December, 2018.URL https://www.orfonline.org/research/indias-foreign-policy-past-present-and-the-future/
5. Shashi Tharoor, *Accessed 18 December*, 2018.URL https://www.orfonline.org/research/indias-foreign-policy-past-present-and-the-future/.
6. James F. Hoge, Jr (2004). "A global power shift in the making", *Foreign Affairs*, 83(4): 3.
7. Dahiya Rumel (2018). *Maldives needs help now and india alone can provide it. Institute for Defence Studies and Analyses*, New Delhi., Accessed 18 December, 2018.URL https://idsa.in/idsacomments/maldives-needs-help-now-and-india-alone-can-provide-it_rdahiya_090218.

8. Government of India, (2017). Ministry if External Affairs "India-Afghanistan Relations", Online: web] Accessed 1 January 2019 URL: https://www.mea.gov.in/Portal/ForeignRelation/1Afghanistan_October_2017.pdf.
9. Ibid.
10. Sumit Ganguly, (1994). *The Origins of war in South Asia: Indi-Pakistani Conflict Since 1947*, Boulder, Colo: Westview Press: 82.
11. Jacques Kathryn, (2000). *Bangladesh, India and Pakistan: International Relations and Regional Tension in South Asia*, New York: St. Martin Press. 4-6.
12. Shaukat Hussan, (1991). "Environmental issues and Security in South Asia", *Adelhphi paper no 262: 69* International Institute for Strategic Studies: London, England.
13. R. Sengupta, (2005). "Why India is Concerned about Bangladesh", *India Abroad*, December 22, 2005.
14. *India-Bhutan Treaty of Friendship and Cooperation* (1949). Article 2. [Online: web] Accessed 1 January 2019 URL: https://www.refworld.org/docid/3ae6b4d620.html.
15. T. Devin Hagerty, (2005). *South Asia in World Politics*, Maryland: Rowman and Littlefield. 2.
16. *Op.cit.*
17. Laskar Rejaul (2014). "Rajiv Gandhi's Diplomac: Historic Significance and Contemporary Relevance", *Extraordinary and plenipotentiary Diplomatist*, 2(9): 47.
18. T. Devin Hagerty (2005). *South Asia in World Politics*, Maryland: Rowman and Littlefield. 2
19. Ibid.
20. Government of India, (2014). *op. cit.*
21. Government of India (2015). *op. cit.*
22. *Op. cit.*
23. Sneha Patel (2017). "A New Journey in the New Context: Nepal-India Relations", *Journal of Humanities and Social Sciences*, 22(9): 75.
24. Government of India (2015). *op. cit.*
25. Ibid.
26. Ibid.
27. Khorbragade F. Vinod (2008). "Indian Approach towards Sri Lankan Conflicts", *The Indian Journal of Political Science*, 69(4): 911.
28. Ibid.
29. Ibid.
30. Bernadeen Silva and Balasurya, Fr. Tissa (1988). "Sri Lanka-India Relations", *Economic and Political Weekly*, 23(21): 1038.

31. Khorbragade F. Vinod (2008). *op. cit.*
32. *Op. cit.*
33. J.N. Dixit, (2002). *Assignment Colombo,* Konark Publisher. 327.
34. Government of India (2017). *op.cit.*
35. Formerly known as Look East Policy.
36. Government of India (2017). *op. cit.*
37. *Op. cit.*
38. David Malone, (2012). *Does the Elephant Dance,* London: Oxford University Press. 105.
39. T.V. Paul (2006). "Why has India-Pakistan Rivalry been so Enduring? Power Asymmetry and an Intractable Conflict", *Security Studies,* 15(4): 603.
40. Steve Coll, (2009). "The Black Channel", *The New Yorker,* New York, 2 March 2009.
41. David Malone, (2012). *op. cit.,* 108.
42. Jaswant Singh, (2006). *A Call to Honour: In Service of Emergent India,* New Delhi: Rupa and Co., 240.
43. Stephen Cohen, (2009). speech delivered at the International Development Research Centre, Ontario on "Rising India has a Pakistan Problem", on 9 April 2009.
44. Ibid.
45. David Malone, (2012). *op. cit.,* 109.
46. Ibid.
47. Rashid Ahmed, (2009). "Pakistan on the Brink", *New York Review of Books,* 56(10): 14-15.
48. T.V. Paul, (2006). *op. cit.* 15(4): 601.
49. *Op. cit.*
50. Nisha Taneja, (2007). "Trade Possibilities and Non-Tariff Barriers to Indi-Pak Trade", *ICRIER Working Paper, 200,* New Delhi: Indian Council for Research on International Economic Relations. Full paper is available at http://www.icier.org/publication/working_paper_200.html.
51. Swaran Singh, (2016). "China's Global Activism: Implications for US Security Interests", paper presented at National Defense University's Annual Pacific Symposium, *China-South Asia: Changing Contours,* on 20 June 2016. Full Paper is available at Https://Www.Researchgate.Net/Publication/242312337Jawaharlalnehruuniversity.

4

Vasudhaiva Kutumbakam

A Right Cord between Internationalism and Anti-nationalism

Sudhir Parida

The changing dynamics of world has witnessed the transposition of the forms of governments; and hence the nature of the state. The concept of nation, which has emerged from the rudiments of the series of religious wars between Catholic and Protestant nations in Europe, had actually a negative connotation for being ethnic exclusiveness. Conceptually and theoretically, the notion of nation had promoted ethnic superiority, language chauvinism, racism, parochialism etc.; and had gained ground in the world history only after Treaty of Westphalia in 1648 (Cavendish, 1998). The definition and usage of the term have changed over time. In contemporary world politics, the meaning of nation has juxtaposed; and the predominant state concept is the nation-state. Although literally, nation-state explicates an ethnic state with own land and government; this explanation became redundant now a days; and it is being expressed as the land with distinct ethnic groups mutually co-habitating and forming a state (UNESCO, n.d.). Shri Pranab Kumar Mukherjee (2018), former President of Bharat (India) emphasizing the contemporary understanding, reiterated that nation is "a large group of people sharing the same culture, language or history and inhabiting a particular state or area". The concept of state and the concept of nation, though not same, are being used interchangeably with the concept of nation state. The Nation still connotes the sense of commonness among diverse people.

Diverse ideas have flourished throughout history. In Bharatiya intellectual tradition, there are abundant examples of pluralistic discourse as seen in Shastrarth Parampara; from Vedic, Upanishadic, Budhist, Jain and many other traditions (Matilal, 1998). Dialectic Method (debate among people of opposite views) had been used by Zeno of Elea; and successively had been used by Socrates and Plato and Aristotle, and by Kant to theorise idealism (Cooper & Hutchinson, 1997; Barnes, 1984; Kant, 1781). Though Karl Barth (1959) described Hegel as the Protestant Aquinas, still Hegel made some distinct articulation of the progress of history using dialectic materialism (Abstract-Negative-Concrete which is also termed by Fichte, as thesis-antithesis-synthesis) (Barth, 1959; Hegel, 1821). The argument here is history follows progression through a constant dialectical method of ideas. No one can arrest the progress of history and the differences of ideas. But when difference in idea converts to discontent, dissatisfaction, dissociation, antagonism, hatred and aversion, it transforms into mercilessness, ruthlessness, savagery and violence.

People live with multiple identities based on different ideas. Political, economic, social and cultural difference sometimes results in discontent among diverse ethnic group inside as well as outside of nation-state. Religious and ideological differences exacerbate the discontent to more chronic level. Diversity of identities like gender, religion, and ethnicity are being exploited as fault lines by powerful nations, and being weaponised to spread internal disturbance.

Fukuyama (2002) employing Hegelian argument, in The End of History and the Last Man, emphasized that we are not only witnessing the end of the Cold War, or the passing of a particular period of post-war history, but "the end of history". He contended that "the end point of mankind's ideological evolution and the universalization of Western liberal democracy is the final form of human government". He was quite optimistic about future world order as peaceful and conflict free; he was confident about the minimisation of fault lines through the universalisation of liberal democratic values. Again while making an effort to lay out elements of a post-cold war paradigm, Huntington (2003) elucidated that "...the fundamental source of conflict in this new world will not be primarily ideological or primarily economic. "The great divisions among humankind and the dominating source of conflict will be cultural" (p. 22). To him, "Nation states will remain the most powerful actors in world affairs, but the principal conflicts of global politics will occur between nations and groups of different civilizations. The clash of civilizations will dominate global politics. (p. 22)". Unlike Fukuyama, Huntington contended that "The fault lines between civilizations will be the battle lines of the future" (p. 22).

Viewing the contemporary conflicts throughout the world, we can say, the precarious fractures of world politics were there, are there, and will be there; only the refurbishment of rift will be there. Because, the course of war is nothing but the human ambition of creating history. To register the name of person or of the state in history, wars may continue. The epidemic of conflict may spread to every nation and to every person; beyond space and time. The fault lines are being designed to warfare and to destabilise world order. Many nations are in turbulence due to internal class of civilisation and external clash of civilisation. Economic interests, power politics, the ambition of hegemonic powers and neo-imperial forces made the condition worst (Cox, 1996; Beyer, 2009; Waltz, 1979; Wendt, 1992). Though the epicentre of turbulence lies within the boundaries of a nation the nation became the battle ground of powerful nations. The resultant conflict around these fault line has cascading effect. Spanish Civil War, Libya, Egypt, Iraq, Syria and many more had already been the testing grounds of new mothers and fathers of bombs, new missile technology, new laser weaponry, new fighter planes, new submarines (Sanchez, 1987; Beevor, 2006; Fuller, 2015). Apart from these tools of hard powers, demonstration, march, protest for false propaganda of oppression, inequality, human rights, MNCs, NGOs and many other sophisticated liberal weapon

are also being used for destabilizing less powerful nations (Cartalucci & Bowie, 2012; De Mars & Dijkzeul, 2015). History is replete with such mass butchering of people, which started as protest and ended with the destabilising the nation-state (Coverdale, 1975). Bharat is also not immune to this chaos. Recently, it has been noticed the wave of anti-nationalism in Bharat, when some university students shouted anti-Bharat slogans inside their university campuses. Simply, the end is to destroy the people where the means are also people. Both end and means are decided by neo-imperial forces and strike hard at the fault-lines of each nation. Since there exist fault lines in each societies and in every nation, the basic question "how to minimise the amplification of clashes?", still persists. To understand this we need a comprehensive understanding and inevitability of the state or the modern nation.

Why the state?

Naturally, man tends to survive with others. This, in other words called civility. This is actually a stark contrast to the principle of survival of the fittest. Along with survival, man tends to prosper with others. This tendency must have followed from the beginning of evolution (Collins, 2014). With course of time, humans have developed an exceptional cognitive ability and reasoning capacity. As Great Power comes with great responsibility; so it is expected from human, who has a comparatively developed cerebrum, to prosper with others without shading harm to others. But time and space have procreated the human, as the species full of greedy, selfish, voracious, avaricious, acquisitive, ravenous, materialistic, possessive, imperialist, merciless, brutish, nasty, violent behaviour (Hobbes, 1651; Rousseau, 1762). Majority of humans, whose history has less ink and less pen, are relatively cooperative and peaceful in nature and with the nature. We can find these people who are not directly involved in power politics. But the history is replete of violent and brutish people who have devastated the nature for their lust of power, in the name of change (Carr, 1961; McCullagh, 1998).

The devastation made by a few people, had generated an anarchic society. The condition of this kind of anarchic society, is expounded in ancient Hindu intellectual tradition as Matsya Nyaya (Law of fishes), where large fishes eat small fishes; a metaphor meaning the powerful devours powerless in the absence of law (Sarkar, 1921; Kautilyan.d.). The human had changed himself from peaceful coexistence to the might is right principle; and so the new tendency became Matsya Nyaya. After millenniums, this condition is also theorised as state of nature in western intellectual tradition. It is believed that this anarchic condition of Matsya Nyaya had forced mankind to form states and governments (Hobbes,

1651). The ultimate aim of mankind behind the formation of state was the

hope: to return to their glorious past; to be a civil animal like they were before; to think together about the future of the societies and to reflect together; not merely through natural laws but through laws of human. The whole argument is to shed light on the importance of maintaining law and order; the inevitability of a formal institution which can discharge this function; the most prominent and inevitable modern institution; the state. The sovereign state or the nation is the modern paramount institution for protection of natural laws of its inhabitants.

Nation and Nationalism

In international relations, the word "nation" and "state" are used interchangeably. Amitav Acharya (1995), in "The Periphery as the Core: The Third World and Security Studies", narrated nation and national security keeping in mind, nation as nation state. Morgenthau (1948) exemplified nation as a unit and an independent political actor in international politics. Kenneth Waltz (1959) in "Man, the State and War" interchangeably uses state and nation at equal meaning. Bull (1977), Wendt (1992) Oye (1995), Mearsheimer (2001) and many other eminent theorists consider nation as an independent sovereign political unit and actor in international arena. Marxist writers still are in the old view where nation has its literal meaning. They consider nation (nation state) is multinational nation or nation of nations.

In medieval period Machiavelli, Locke, Hobbes, and Rousseau conceptualised state as independent unit. In modern times Carlton J. H. Hayes, Henry Maine, Ferdinand Tonnies, Rabindranath Tagore, Emile Durkheim, Max Weber, Arnold Joseph Toynbee and Talcott Parsons and many other theorists theorised nation as sovereign political unit. Almost all modern thinkers conceptualised nation as an integrated single and sovereign unit in international politics. As Heywood (2004) asserts, "It has almost been taken for granted that the nation is the only legitimate political community, and therefore that the nation-state is the highest form of political organization" (p. 89). So the contemporary idea of nation should not be confused with conventional idea of nation; it should understood as the nation-state.

Connotation of the concept of nationalism evolved with the evolution of concept of nation. What meaning it had carried during medieval period is not compatible and can't be an appropriate understanding today. While defining nationalism, we will proceed with the positive and contemporary meaning of nation (nation-state). Nationalism is the powerful emotion among diverse population irrespective of contrast ethnic groups. Nationalism is a strong sense of commonbelongingness with unity and diversity as guiding principle. This connotation completes with having common boundary for a nation. This common belongingness is derived from a sense of common history, common territory and common political aspiration (Griffiths et al., 2008; Heywood, 2004).

Internationalism

There are two major currents of internationalism: Liberal Internationalism and proletarian (social) internationalism. Liberal internationalism as political thought is being epitomized by Richard Cobden and John Bright, John Struat Mill and Herbert Spencer (Bell, n.d.). As argued by Adam Smith and subsequently emphasized by Cobden, free trade would pacify the world by interdependence. Liberal Internationalism flourished under the patronage of British Foreign Secretary and Prime Minister Lord Palmerston in nineteenth century, and also by Woodrow Wilson the USA president. The goal of liberal internationalism was to create a liberal world order through international organisations which in turn will ease the worst exercise of power politics among nations. It advocated global free trade, liberal economics and liberal political systems. It argued that liberal democratic states have relations which are characterized by non-violence and peace will prevail everywhere with liberal democratic world order (Ikenberry et al., 2018).

In direct ideological opposition to liberal internationalism, Communist League had been formed in the summer of 1847 in London by Engels and Marx (Marx & Engels, 1847). Afterwards, socialists and radicals of that time formed the International Workingmen's Association, in 1864 known as the First International; Second International or the Socialist International was constituted in 1889; the Communist International known as the Comintern or the Third International, was formed in 1919; the fourth and last Socialist International was founded in 1938. The Communist Internationalism is famously known as proletarian internationalism or international socialism (Marxists Internet Archive, n. d). Marx & Engels (1848) in Communist Manifesto pronounced that workingmen have no country and on this philosophy proletarian socialism had opposed the concept of nationalism. Proletarian socialism identified capitalism as an international system; a system exploitative in nature and exploits the surplus labour of proletariat class. It stressed that working-class people of all countries must unite across national boundaries in order to overthrow capitalism, and replace it with communism as an international system. Then only proletariat class can have the ownership and control of means of production, and hence the redistribution of property is possible. This will in turn create a classless international communist society ((Marx & Engels, 1848; Avineri, 1991). Though many other had proposed some methods of internationalism, either they are being subdued under any two of above ideologies or not had any impact on international society. Both liberals as well as communists tried to flex their ideological muscles by intervening in the internal matters of different nations (Jacobsen, 2017; Byrnes, 2017; Allison, 2013). After the dissolution of USSR, the world is being dominated by liberal order. But the internal conflicts of nations are still instigated either by liberals or by communists. Thus, the major anti-national activities are being controlled by external forces, under the veil of either liberal dogma or by communist dogma.

There also existed supra-national institutions which are backed by international treaty. To Heywood (2011) "Supra-nationalism is the existence of an authority that is higher than that of the nation-state and capable of imposing its will on it" (p. 458). This institutionalisation is somehow based on the principle of liberal internationalism. Supra-national institutions like BeNeLux, European Union (EU), African Union (AU), ASEAN, EAEU, SAARC, BRICS, WTO and many others give the hope that internationalism is possible with some caution. But the Brexit dynamism diminished the hope for further supranational institutions. In this frequently changing world, almost all the systems have fault lines. So, on these fault lines Britain left from EU. After the Brexit, supra-nationalism is crumbling to find the conceptual ground (Blackwell, 2018).

Anti-nationalism

Anti-nationalism is an antithetic concept to nationalism. Nationalism is the sentiment of commonness among diverse people with definite boundary; hence, its antithesis i.e. anti-nationalism is the opposite sentiment of commonness, and of diversity within definite boundaries of states. Anti-national movements are rarely a self-instigated phenomenon. It always has been propelled by external forces to change regimes and destabilise nations.

Liberal internationalism was a foreign policy doctrine that advocated the radical way to propagate the doctrine; either by preaching or by punitive method. Liberals argued that liberal states should intervene in other sovereign states in order to pursue liberal objectives by military invasion or by humanitarian aid or by both (Ikenberry et al., 2018). This is a major challenge to the sovereignty of a nation. History has several instances of liberal interventions by powerful liberal nations by the means of liberal violence. As globalisation prevailed over everywhere, liberal nations use their NGO to wage proxy wars against not so powerful nations and to destabilise their internal systems (Hoffmann, 1995). The intention behind is to plunder the natural resources by destabilising; mounting pressure on national government, and by breaking a nation into many nations and installing their puppet regimes or even occupation. So, anti-nationalism is not only an individual activity, but also a state activity. It started from individual issue and ends with the destruction of nation.

Communist thinkers such as Karl Marx, Friedrich Engels, and Vladimir Lenin had argued that state is an instrument of class oppression; nation is in the ruling class interest and to promote nationalism in order to hide the inherent class conflicts at play within a given society. Further communist thinkers contended that economic class, rather than nationality, race, or culture, is the main force which divides people in society, and that nationalist ideology is a propaganda tool of a society's dominant economic class (Marx & Engels, 1948; Lenin, 1916). Thus, Proletarian internationalism is antithetical to the concept of nationalism. It undermines the very notion of sovereignty i.e. the sovereignty on which the modern nation state is stood.

The third facet is the anarchist facet, which in the disguise of freedom of speech, are spewing venom against their own nation. The anarchists are hammering regularly to the idea of state with their ivory-tower approach. For them a society without state or government is both possible and desirable" and state is parasite upon nation (Bakunin, 1873). This approach is not only an existential threat to themselves, but also a threat to human civilisation as whole and consequently to the whole world.

Failures of Models of Internationalism

We are witnessing the continual wars among nations. The root cause of global chaos and wars is the failure of existing models of internationalism. Both liberal internationalism and proletarian internationalism had failed miserably and felicitated either war, anti-national activities within Nation or both. The liberal internationalism was designed to exploit the wealth. It was the link between global economic competition and imperialism. The proletariat internationalism was in opposition of liberalism and against the people who owned wealth at that time. This was a chaos designed to counter liberal chaos. Marxist interpretation of internationalism which never materialise, is the fundamental and ideological force behind the urban naxlites who are leading their anarchical arguments with classical Urbano-guerrilla warfare style hugger-mugger theatrics in Bharat. Anti-national movement in Bharat came into light, when some students shouted to break Bharat into many pieces of land. The movement challenged the very notion of sovereignty and integrity of Bharatiya state. The said motive behind these activities is to be greater autonomy or self-determination for a geographic region but the real motive is to exploit the fault lines already presented in nation for self-interest (Malhotra & Neelakandan, 2011). These campaigns are often fuelled by ethnic or linguistic splits, or economic grievances. So, are there any solutions to this violence, violent protests and lies of internationalism?

Yes there is Bharat from its civilisational ethos adopted the principle of "*Vasudhaiva Kutumbakam*" – the philosophy of the world being one family. If Bharatiya discourse of internationalism is to carve out a niche for itself in the International Relations arena, the scholars of Bharat, according to Kalyankumar (2015), "have to necessarily immerse themselves in studying India's own experience of war, diplomacy and statecraft as practiced by the great Indian empires and various kingdoms and dynasties over the last 2500 years" (p.3). Though many IR theorists from Bharat put this concept even before the *Bharatiya foreign policy* envisioned and in academic discipline, the concept became a buzzword worldwide after 23 January 2018, when Prof. Klaus Schwab, the president of the World Economic Forum, emphasized the idea, while welcoming Prime Minister NarendraModi todeliver the keynote address at the plenary session of the World Economic Forum in Davos (WEF, 2018).

Vasudhaiva Kutumbakam (VK): The World Future

Vasudhaiva Kutumbakam is a holistic theory which embodies environmental, cultural, political, economic and social aspects of life. The mention of this *VK* is found in an ancient Hindu epic Maha-Upanishad (*Maha Upanishad*, 6:71). This concept has elaborated the enlightenment and liberation from earthly bondage through spiritual means. Later the concept was found in Hitopadesha and extensively influenced the social and political orders in Bharatiya subcontinent; and till now influencing the Bharatiya foreign policy as well as common life (Narayana, n.d.). The literal meaning of *VK* is "the world is a family" and so it is the spirit of true internationalism.

The concept of family is central to *VK*. The philosophy should be theorised more as a modern concept of internationalism for peace and prosperity. *VK* is an integrated, multidimensional concept for internationalism rather than a unidirectional vector. During Maha-Upanishad, there was no Westphalian treaty, no nation state defined. But it conceived the whole world as a family based on mutual trust and peace and cooperation. The political aspects of VK and the concept of state can be derived from Atharva Veda. The Bhumi Shukta, mentioned in Atharva Veda, states that "matabhumiputroahmpruthibyam" which literally translates as 'the whole earth is my mother and I am her offspring' (Atharva Veda, 12:1-18). It preaches unimpeded freedom through mountains, slopes and plains. This delineates the relation of individual and state; and the state being the whole earth. It does not differentiate nations as enemies of each other.

VK is transcendence of nationality not an antagonistic to nation. It is a confluence of political economy with environmental protection as core theme. This is value ridden rather than territorial and economic ambition. This concept provided Bharat, a unique political philosophy of universalism which guided it's relation with other nations. Bharat had no history of attacking other nations and exploiting others property. It always stood firmly for high value and humanity, without any territorial ambition. Bharat is the only land where Jews, Parsis, Tebatians and many other non-Bharatiya lived. Without any territorial ambition, Bharatiyas took part in WW I and WW II. After independence, Bharat is largest contributor to UN peacekeeping force. In modern times, without any expectation Bharat had evacuated hundreds of foreign nationals from war torn Yemen. These all exemplified the concept of *VK* as political internationalism.

Cultural aspect of *VK* is co-existence and cooperation. Most of sects and religions in the world had been affected by reaction of a particular existing dominant ideology and religion. Like anti-nationalism has evolved against the backdrops of nationalism. So the emerging ideology saw the existing ideology as an enemy and as the evil of all instances. But in contrast, we will find many ideas in Bharat which are independent, dynamic and optimistic such as Vedic, Charvak, Buddhist, Jaina, and residing here for centuries. Some ideas also evolve due to crisis of identity of its propounder and its followers. In this fractured world, everyone wanted to be famous overnight without efficiency and hard work. The social dimension of *VK* gives primacy to family rather than individual. One can have multiple identities within a family like male, female, boy, girl, son, daughter, uncle, aunt, grandfather, grandmother and so on. These identities are not created by man. These are naturally existed. Only nomenclature has been done. If a single identity will dictate, there will be fracture in the family, so is in international politics. Because if there is only one hegemonic power, there will be unilateral exercise of power (Ikenberry et al., 2009). *VK* focuses on cooperation rather than struggle. It is a principle of construction rather than destruction.

The destruction of a gigantic structure requires only a fraction of second but to construct it, it takes years. In this fractured world, the concept of *VK* is more relevant and important today than ever before; because of its constructive internationalism. The economic interpretation of *VK* gives responsibility to powerful and developed nations to provide the basic needs to the needy nation like a family member instead of benefit seeking, greedy, hegemonic nation. Means of the achievement of *VK* can be derived from Isha Upanishad "Tenatyaktenabhunjita" (enjoy whatever in this world with renunciation) (Isha Upanishad 1). There will be no shortage of resources for all, if consumption is limited only to the necessity. It is less of capitalism as it forbids accumulating wealth. It is the only sustainable development model without which the world will reel under scarcity. We need market economy with social welfare instead of a socialist economy because though theoretically, it stands for equal distribution of property but it has been seen on many instances that nations adopted socialism and instead of distributing means of production equally, they distributed poverty equally. It is, because you can't dictate to others what to do and how to do. If so, then there will be erosion of creativity and that will lead to non-up gradation of economy and subsequently economic stagnation will prevail. Simply, the need is of a market economy accompanied by a strong welfare state. The finest example of development of *Vasudhaiva Kutumbakam* and internationalism is seen in the document of economic development pattern prepared by American government about world GDP of 2000 years. It shows that for approximately 1600 years Bharat and China contributed more than 50 per cent of world economy and there are rare instances of conflict or altercation (Madison, 2001, 2006; Chakravarti, 2010).

Bharat is committed to the principles of justice, equality, liberty, rule of law etc. for peaceful international order. Bharat derives these ethos from the principle of *VK*. We should create a shared future in a fractured world. Glimpses of changing world should be free, open, inclusive which embraces us all in a common pursuit of progress and prosperity. It is rightly pointed out by Prof Klaus Schwab, "Globally we are moving towards a multipolar and a multi-conceptual world. This echo the resemblance of old Bharatiya tradition of *Vasudaiva Kutumbakam*." He also emphasized that Bharat, in seemingly fractured world, presents "a bright image of dynamism, optimism" (WEF, 2018).

Conclusion

If widespread mistrust and resentment continue to spread, it would pulverise and decimate the vulnerable. It would be the poorest and weakest who would be the first victims. So, the world has to choose a right concept of internationalism. As discussed above *VK*, through all its elements can be the right option between the contemporary forms of internationalism and anti-nationalism. We need to maintain a balance between individual liberty, community liberty and liberty of nations. The end or the goal of VK is non-hegemonic, multi-polar, multi-cultural, free, open, diverse, inclusive, and cooperative. The engagement among nations should focus with mutual respect on stable bedrock of peace. With the Rig Vedic hymn "*ekamsatyaviprabahu-davadanti*", which enjoins the philosophy of co-existence with pluralism, we should thrive on the lines of *Vasudhaiva Kutumbakam* as an inevitable internationalism option for world which ultimately brings down anti-nationalism and will prevail peace and prosperity among nations and among people.

References

Acharya, A. (1995). *The Periphery as the Core: The Third World and Security Studies*. Retrieved from https://yorkspace.library.yorku.ca/xmlui/bitstream/handle/10315/1412/YCI0071.pdf?sequence=1&isAllowed=y

Allison, R. (2013). *The Soviet Union and Cold War Interventions*. DOI:10.1093/acprof:oso/9780199590636.003.0002 Atharva Veda, 12, 1-18. Bhumi Shukta. Retrived from https://vedpuran.files.wordpress.com/2013/12/atharva-ved.pdf

Avineri, S. (1991). "Marx and Nationalism". *Journal of Contemporary History*, 26 (3), 637-657.

Bakunin, M. (1873). *Statism and Anarchy*. Retrieved from https://www.marxists.org/reference/archive/bakunin/works/1873/statism-anarchy.htm

Barnes, J. (1984). *Aristotle: The Revised Oxford Translation*. New Jersey: Princeton University Press.

Barth, K. (1959). *Protestant Thought: From Rousseau to Ritshl*. New York: Harper and Brothers.

Beevor, A. (2005). *The Battle for Spain: The Spanish Civil War, 1936-1939*. Great Britain: The Orion Publishing Group.

Bell, D. (n.d.). *Liberal Internationalism*. Retrieved from https://www.britannica.com/topic/liberal-internationalism

Beyer, C. (2009). "Hegemony, equilibrium and counterpower: A Synthetic Approach". *International Relations*, 23(2), 411–427.

Blackwell, N. (2018). *The real divide over the UK's post-EU future is hope and despair*. Retrievedfrom https://www.ft.com/content/d55387d8-4d58-11e8-97e4-13afc22d86d4

Bull, H. (1977). *The Anarchical Society: A Study of Order in World Politics*. New York: Columbia University Press.

Byrnes, S. (2017). *The pernicious influence of liberal interventionism*. Retrieved fromhttps://www.thenational.ae/opinion/the-pernicious-influence-of-liberal-interventionism 1.65713

Carr, E. H. (1961). *What is History*?. London: Penguin Publishers.

Cartalucci, T. & Bowie, N. (2012). *Subverting Syria: How CIA Contra Gangs and NGO's Manufacture*, Mislabel and Market Mass Murder. California: (Smashwords) ProgressivePress.

Cavendish, R. (1998). *The Treaty of Westphalia*. Retrieved fromhttps://www.historytoday.com/richard-cavendish/treaty-westphalia

Chakravarti, M. (2010). *World history by per Capita GDP*. Retrieved from https://www.livemint.com/Opinion/Nb7KkZ3yOVSNW3vHf9K1oM/World-history-by-per-capita-GDP.html

Collins, M. (2014). *The Unselfish Spirit: Human Evolution in a Time of Global Crisis*. United Kingdom: Permanent Publications.

Cooper, J.M. & Hutchinson, D. S. (1997). *Plato: Complete Works*. USA: Hackett Publishing

Coverdale, J.F. (1975). *Italian Intervention in the Spanish Civil War*. Princeton: Princeton University Press.

Cox, R. (1996). Gramsci, hegemony, and international relations: An essay in method. In R. Cox & T. Sinclair (Eds.), *Approaches to World Order* (pp. 49–66). Cambridge: Cambridge University Press.

DeMars, W.E. & Dijkzeul, D. (2015). *The NGO Challenge for International Relations Theory*. New York: Routledge.

Fukuyama, F. (2002). *The End of History and the Last Man*, New York: The Free Press.

Fuller, R. (2015). *Beasts and Gods: How Democracy Changed Its Meaning and Lost Its Purpose*, London: Zed Books Ltd.

Griffiths, M., O'Callaghan, T & Roach, S. C. (2008). *International Relations: The Key Concepts*. London: Routledge.

Hegel, G. W. F. (1821). *Elements of Philosophy of Right* (Edited by Allen W. Wood). United Kingdom: The Press Syndicate of University of Cambridge.

Heywood, A. (2004). *Political Theory: An Introduction*. London: Palgrave Macmillan.

Heywood, A. (2011). *Global Politics*. London: Palgrave Macmillan.

Hobbes, T. (1651). *Leviathan or The Matter*, Forme and Power of a Common-Wealth Ecclesiasticalland Civil. (Trans. by W.G. Pogson Smith in 1909). Great Britain: Clarendon Press. Hoffmann, S. (1995). *The Crisis of Liberal Internationalism*. DOI: 10.2307/1148964

Huntington, S.P. (1993). "The Clash of Civilizations?". *Foreign Affairs*, 72(3), 22.

Ikenberry, G. J., Mastanduno, M. & Wohlforth, W.C. (2009). *World Politics*, 61 (1), 1-27

Ikenberry, G. J., Parmar, I. & Stokes, D. (2018). "Introduction: Ordering the world? Liberalinternationalism in theory and practice", *International Affairs*, 94 (1), 1-5.

Isha Upanishad 1. Retrieved from http://www.sriaurobindo-ashram.org/ashram/sriauro/downloadpdf.php?id=32

Jacobsen, K.L. (2017). *Liberal Interventionism: The Crisis Within*. Retrieved fromhttp://www.cips-cepi.ca/2017/07/09/liberal-interventionism-the-crisis-within/

Kalyanaraman, S. (2015). "Arthashastra, Diplomatic History and the Study of International Relations in India". In P.K. Gautam, S. Mishra & A. Gupta (Eds.), *Indegeneous Historical Knowledge: Kautilya and His Vocabulary*, 1-4. New Delhi: Pentagon Press.

Kant, E. (1781). *Critique of Pure Reason*. (Trans. By Meiklej J.M.D.). London: J. Billing Printerand Stereotyper, Woking, Surrey.

Kautilya. (n.d.). *The Arthashastra*. (Trans. by L. N. Rangrajan in 1987). New Delhi: Penguin Books India (P) Ltd.

Lenin, V. I. (1916). *The Socialist Revolution and the Right of Nations to Self-Determination*. Retrieved from https://www. marxists.org/archive/lenin/works/1916/jan/x01.htm

Maddison, A. (2006). *The World Economy: A Millenium Perspective.* Paris: OECD Publishing

Maddison, A. (2006). *The World Economy*. Paris: OECD Publishing.

Maha Upanishad. 6:71. Retrieved from https://sanskrit documents.org/doc_upanishhat/maha.pdf

Malhotra, R. & Neelakandan, A. (2011). *Breaking India*. Princeton: Infinity Foundation.

Marx, K. & Engels, F. (1848). *The Manifesto of Communist Party.* Retrieved fromhttps://www.marxists.org/archive/marx/works/download/pdf/Manifesto.pdf

Marx, K., & Engels, F. (1847). "Draft Rules of the Communist League". In *Marx & Engels Collected Work,* Vol. 6. London: Lawrence &Wishart.

Marxists Internet Archive. (n.d.). Retrieved from https://marxists.catbull.com/archive/index.htm

Matilal, B. K. (1998). *The Character of Logic in India*. New York: State University of New York Press.

McCullag, C. B. (1998). *The Truth of History*. London: Routledge.

Mearshiemer, J. J. (2001). *The Tragedy of Great Power Politics*. London: W. W. Norton & Company.

Morgenthau, H. J. (1948). *Politics Among Nations: The Struggle for Power and Peace*. New York: Alfred A. Knopf INC.

Mukherjee, P.K. (2018). *Nation, Nationalism and Patriotism*. Retrieved fromhttp://pranabmukherjee.nic.in/sp070618.html

Narayan. (n.d.). *Hitopadesha*. In Narayan Ram Acharya (Ed.), Pt. Rameshwar Bhatta (Trans.), Varanasi: Chaukhamba Sanskrit Pratishthan.

Oye, K.A. (1995). "Explaining Cooperation under Anarchy: Hypotheses and Strategies." *World Politics* 38 (1), 1-24.

Rousseau, J.J. (1962). *The Social Contract*. Retrieved fromhttps://www.marxists.org/reference/subject/economics/rousseau/social-contract/ch01.htm#001

Sanchez, J. M. (1987). *The Spanish Civil War As a Religious Tragedy.* Virginia: University Press of Virginia.

Sarkar, B. K. (1921). "The Hindu Theory of State". *Academy of Political Science*, 36 (1), 29-90.

UNESCO.(n.d.). *Nation-State*. Retrieved from http://www.unesco.org/new/en/social-and-human-sciences/themes/international-migration/glossary/nation-state/

Waltz, K. (1959). *Man, the State and War*. New York: Columbia University Press.

Waltz, K. (1979). *Theory of International Politics*. New York: Random House.

WEF (2018). *Opening Plenary with NarendraModi, Prime Minister of India*. Retrieved fromhttps://www.weforum.org/events/world-economic-forum-annual-meeting-2018/sessions/opening-plenary-3b35f029-befa-4892-a2d7-3725a9d94418

Wendt, A. (1992). "Anarchy is What States Make of It: The Social Construction of Power Politics". *International Organization*, 46 (2), 391-425.

5

Area Studies towards the Construction of a New South Asia

Saumya Maniny Sinha

'Theories form the backbone of a discipline.' In the absence of theories, disciplines cease to be disciplines. International relations as a distinct branch of Political Science is no exception to this rule. Such has been the impact of Western thinking in this field, that the discipline is sometimes called as *American Social Science*. A blind reliance on Western discourse to comprehend issues like Nation-Building Process, Foreign Policy Priorities, Politics of Ethno-Nationalism, Party Politics, Regional Migration or the Politics of Political Economy in a particular region does more harm than good, as the understanding which has developed is superficial and inadequate. Area Studies scholarship has now become an integral part of international relations as it helps in the better understanding of a country's relation with others in the region. International Relations is an young discipline that has yet to earn an independent and indigenous status in the South Asian Region. This paper aims to discuss and introspect the state of the art of Indian

Thinking in International Relations. The Paper shall be divided into three sections. In the First Section, the paper highlights the Occidental vs. the Oriental debate and attempts at understanding the tendencies of hegemonising the discipline in the absence of Non-Western Thinking. Most of the universities in this region depend on the Epistemological knowledge and pedagogy of the West to explain this area. The Second Section will basically explore the reasons for the poor theorisation in this field by our scholars. The Third Section showcases the need for Indian Scholarship to strike a consensus among her neighbors on a range of issues. It also aims at providing ambitious suggestions for the construction of new Theories of a New South Asia.

A student approaching the study of International Relations is confounded with the challenge of understanding the increasing complexities of International life. In resolving these difficulties, Theories of International Relations play a very important role.Theories form the backbone of a discipline. All disciplines rely inextricably on Theories for a systematic investigation and holistic understanding of various facets of human behavior. "Theories are general statements that describe and explain the cause or effects of classes of phenomena."[1]

International Relations is no exception to this rule. As a sub-branch of Political Science, it is still regarded as a young discipline.Its genesis was laid down in the Woodrow Wilson Chair in 1919. A life span of approximately 100 years may be long for an individual, but for a discipline as dynamic as international relations, it is still regarded as young by all means. While Political Science basically conducts Research of People, political events, personalities and their behavior, international relations conducts research on issues like War and peace, nuclear arms race, global warming, human security, global migration, power shifts, foreign policy and Diplomacy etc.

According to Quincy Wright, "The study of International Relations contributing to the understanding, prediction, evaluation and control of the relations among states and the conditions of the world community, is at the same time a history, a science, a philosphy and an art."[2] Much water has flown from the river thames and today the changing pattern of international relations is like an express train out of control. Such is the wide arena of subjects covered under International Relations, that it touches our everyday life in a number of ways. Be it global warming, globalisation and world trade, human rights violations, arms race, terrorism and human trafficking, international relations caters to them and also studies other Trans-national crimes or in the words of Shashi Tharoor, "Problems without Passports."The Theory-Building exercise of International Relations literature focuses on developing a co-ordinated approach to solve these problems, as 'Global Problems require Global Solutions'.

Norman Padelford and George Lincoln define international politics as the interaction of state policies within the changing pattern of power relationships.[3] For anybody grappling to understand the structure of States and their power structure, international relations helps to understand the Foreign Policy of states and the role of diplomacy there on. The discipline enables to comprehend the rise and fall of states in the Power Pyramid.

International relations helps in the peace management and conflict resolution in War—ravaged areas or the Conflict zones of the world.

International relations also help in the study of Regional Security Complexes and Area Studies, which provides a holistic understanding of an area from a multi-disciplinary perspective.

The discipline of international relations also helps understand the working of international and regional organisations, study of International Law and its application. Hence, these multi-dimensional roles of international relations are substantiated by relying on Theories. Hence, Theories, no doubt, form the backbone of a discipline.

Theorisation in International Relations

The term "Theory of International Relations" is a misnomer because there is not one single theory, but several competing Theories. Hence, a family of Theories exists in international relations like game theory, bargaining theory, realism, idealism, system theory etc. Right from 'Problem-Solving' to 'Critical Theories', each provides a particular understanding of the global phenomena, but to compartmentalize them on the basis of fixed Paradigms or Perspectives would be a gross Injustice. Couloumbis Wolfe in his 'Introduction to International Relations' in 1978 has clubbed the theories or approaches into two groups as: Traditionalists or classical and behaviouralist or scientist. Be it HansJ. Morgenthau, Raymond Aron, Stanley Hoffman, Reinhold Niebhur, Arnold Wolfers of the Traditionalist School or Karl Deustch, Mortan Kaplan, Rosneau, J. David Singer of the Behavioralist School. Or Richard Ashley, Robert Cox, Andrew Linklalir, Michael Foucault, Christine Sylvester, Jean Elshtain or Ann Tinker of the Critical theorist school, International Relations as a discipline has been infamously "Ethno-Centric" i.e., there is the domination of the White race over the Non- white. Stanley Hoffman in 1977 characterised it as an 'American Social Science'. The academic community has not moved beyond the understanding provided by Samuel Huttington in 'The Clash of Civilisation and the Last Man', or John Hertz's "Security

Dilemma" or Joseph S. Nye's interpretation of Power as hard and soft power. Or for that matter we still feel safe in interpreting the World through Morgenthua's Power Approach. To put it blatantly, there is a Pro-Western and Pro-American strain in the theorisation of international relations. (Hans J. Morganthau, an American is regarded as the father of international relations, not Sun Tzu or Kautilya for that matter)

The perspectives or understandings of international relations which are being inculcated, thus, are only reflecting one side of the spectrum:the global north. The theories of international relations which are being developed are Partial Theories as they reflect a partial Reality i.e., the Western Perspective. In the 18th and 19th Century of Pax- Britainica, it was dominated by British Scholars. In the 20th Century of Pax Americana, it was dominated by American scholars and maybe in the 21st Century, there is possibility of domination by Chinese and Indian Strategic thinking provided we do the necessary ground-work for that. Hence, power and influence not just dominate the State apparatus, but also the academic discourse on International Relations. The domination of Western Thinking in International Relations is not just symbolic of its Hegemonic designs, but is also indicative of the dependence of the Orient on the Occidental in the absence of Non-Western Thinking in International Relations. Unfortunately, our Histories are narrated in their voices and language.Hence, the legacy of Colonial rule further gets institutionalised through their Ideological Domination. A part of the reason for the absence of a Non-Western thinking is the failure of the academic community in not coming up with an Alternative Non-Western perspective.

The Non-Western and Indian Thinking in International Relations

The Non-Western or the Global South i.e., the developing and less developed countries of Latin America, South Africa and Asia have been hesitant in building their own Theories. Amitav Acharya and Barry Buzan in their book "Non-Western International Relations Theory" have highlighted this issue and listed various reasons for the poor Theorization in global south. Many reasons are responsible for the poor theorization as has been discussed below – (1) Western International Relations have acquired a Hegemonic status in the gramscian sense. It becomes difficult for Theories from the global south to make a place for themselves in the International Arena, hence, Colonialism in the ideological and academic field still persists. Hence, this type of Politics is very discouraging and damaging. (2) Growth of International Relations as a discipline has been dwarfed by Political science as a master science. The blending of politics, diplomatic history, Law in the discipline, makes its Theorization even more difficult. (3) Local conditions discriminate against the production of I.R. Theory. Sometimes, it is lack of funding, Non-availability of Resource material, language barrier, poor pedagogy techniques which create obstacles in the path of Theory-Building. (4) Lack of Standard Books and reading material on International Relations affects the Growth of the Discipline. Instead of locally produced good quality text-books, the Indian Universities rely on Indo-scholars (Indian scholars teaching in Foreign Universities) and their Oxford and Cambridge Publications to understand our areas of study. (6) Its study and reach becomes restricted because there is a dearth of books in Hindi, Urdu, Bengali, Tamil, Telugu, Odisi and other Regional languages. (7) In the absence of Standard Theories on the subject, the Central and Private Universities and State Universities have developed their own discourses and literature to understand the concepts, quite oblivious of the other.'Theories of the global south do exist, but they are hidden and need to be interpreted in National Narratives. It is in this sense that Area Studies and the scope for Indian Thinking elicits great curiosity'.[4]

Indian International Relations or Indian Thinking in International Relations refers to the opinions and streams of thought held by Indian scholars studying International Relations in India. Conceptualizing Indian International Relations is no easy task. It is difficult to trace the evolution of Indian Thinking as it is the product of the British Colonial history and Post-Independence India. The foundations of the thinking has inarguably been laid down by Indian Prime Minister Pt. Nehru. The reflections of Indian thinking can be found in the ideas of Panchsheel and Non-Alignment laid down by Jawaharlal Nehru, the ideology of *Vasudaiva Kutumbhakam* and Ahimsa laid down by Mahatama Gandhi, the philosophy of Internationalism suggested by Rabindranath Tagore and the lessons of Diplomacy and Statecraft imbibed from Kautilya's.

It is commonplace view in the academic discourse now that Indians do not have a strategic culture in their Indian Foreign Policy. The Indian Thinking in International Relations has not been recorded in written texts and hardly there have been attempts of Theorising it. Newspapers and Magazines, Journal Publications, Press releases, Commentaries, Speeches and texts of Indian Statesmen on a range of issues help in comprehending India's view-point. Indian scholar Kanti Bajpai is right in observing that there is a considerable degree of 'Resistance to Theory-Building in Indian International Relations' as the general perception among scholars was that 'the State was right in its doing, hence, a critical approach should not be adopted.[5]

The study of International Relations as a separate discipline started in India in 1955 when the School of International Studies was established in Jawaharlal Nehru University. For purpose of convenience, we can divide the Indian thinking in international relations into two phases: First generation of international relation scholarship focuses on the formulation of the philosophy of Indian foreign policy and developing a world-view on different contentious issues. The second generation of I.R. Scholarship starting from 1990's onwards starts paying more attention to India's immediate neighbourhood and the South Asian milieu.

Towards a New South Asia

> ".....the challenge of ethnicity and Nation-Building, operating in a highly complex nexus of society, economy and polity, hinges on issues of access and stakes in the Power structure. In this context, the experiences of South Asian states are instructive as well as illuminating. These polyethnic societies are characterized by greater ethnic diversity than perhaps any other region in the world. However, in terms of boundary delineation, levels of development, content, context, constraints, as well as the potential of varied demands for recognition, power and status, uniformities as well as variations among the ethnic groups across the borders can be discerned."—Urmila Phadnis.[6]

The term "Region" is quite ambiguous in international relations. Conventionally, it is regarded as a permanent and fixed historical entity, but today it is seen as a product of the inter-play of Geo-Strategic compulsions, economic equations, socio-Cultural and ethno-political complexities. Thus, Region is a geographical cluster of states that are proximate to each other and are inter-connected in economic and cultural terms. South Asia as a Regional Sub-system generates more an "Interdependence of Rivalry" than an "Interdependence of Shared Interests."[7] Although most emerged as independent nations in 1940's, the states in the region are facing several –Internal and External Challenges.

"Poor Governance, high poverty, deficient infrastructure, low Literacy, malnutrition, corruption, religious extremism, terrorism and great power involvement"are the varied challenges threatening the geo-strategic salience of the Region.Growth with Inequality has proved disastrous for South Asia. It has performed poorly on most of the Development Indicators.

South Asia, the Southern region of the Asian continent, comprises the Sub-Himalayan countries including the adjoining countries on the West and East. South Asia covers about 5.1 million square km, which is 11.51 percent of the Asian Continent or 3.4 per cent of the World's total land surface area. A quarter of the World's population resides in South Asia. It is a vast area which comprises of India, Pakistan, Bangladesh, Afghanistan, Nepal, Maldives, Bhutan, Iran and Sri Lanka, according to an U.N. definition. Mynammar (Burma) and Tibet are also sometimes defined as part of South Asia.In popular usage, South Asia includes the eight countries mentioned above, excluding Iran.[8]

South Asia is one of the world's most dynamic regions. Its biggest country, India, is the world's largest democracy and second most populated country. Post-2001 World Order regards South Asia as the epicenter of major tectonic and geo-strategic shifts. Unfortunately, the Theorisation of International Relations as a young discipline in South Asia has still not been taken up at the indigenous level. A Country's priority in the field of Higher education is reflective of its Policy priorities with respect to National Security. The future of Area Studies Scholarship not just depends on the countries of that region, but also the International Community as a whole. As far as India is concerned, till the 1990's, she was more concerned with her Indigenous development and resolving contentious issues with her Immediate neighbours, than developing a coherent literature explaining the Historical, Socio-economic and Political affinities between India and her immediate neighbours.

Further, India was regarded as a country of superstitions and Snake-Charmers in the Distant "Far East". Hence, there was very little academic interest of the World in her which was engaged in the Two World Wars and its fallout. However, the Cold war expansion of U.S. interest in the East gave rise to "Area Studies" as now they required Knowledge of New Areas in the 'East' where they could extend their influence. This gave rise to the study of 'South Asian Studies'as an inter-disciplinary study in American colleges and universities. The funds were granted to train scholars, policy-makers and Professionals to understand the polity, history and socio-economic milieu of South Asia as a Region. This emphasis on South Asia as an arena of 'Area Studies Scholarship' became more pronounced with the 9/11 Terrorist Strike in USA and henceforth, the Declaration of "War against Terrorism", US Invasion against Afghanistan (2001) and Iraq (2003). These developments led to an increasing number of students gravitating towards the study of South Asia.

Ironically, the study of South Asia started initially at the University of Pennsylvania. In 1947, 'India: A Program of Regional Studies'was started. It was funded by Carnegie Endowment of International Peace and Rockfeller Foundation. Similar moves were made at University of California, Berkeley, University of Chicago and Columbia University. Similarly, Centers of South Asian Studies were opened at London University and Oxford University.

The study of South Asia as an Area Studies made a late entry in this region, as most of the Young Democracies were still trying to establish themselves and the foundations of their foreign policy and their national priorities was in a nascent stage. In South Asia, the academic space available to the discipline started expanding in 1970's when some of the premier universities in India, Pakistan, Bangladesh, Nepal, Sri Lanka and Bhutan started the study of South Asia in which they were focusing on the study of their history, language, culture, religion as a part of larger South Asia. The approach of the Area Studies was primarily multi-disciplinary, each isolated and secluded from the other. It is but obvious that, hence, the groundwork done by the West on South Asia as a Region had a definitive impact in building its own Academic edifice in the Literature. Hence, the West started playing an important role in theorizing of international relations in South Asia.

Unfortunately, the universities were not giving proper focus and emphasis in the development of a comparative perspective in the study and Theorisation of South Asia. An Iron curtain seems to have descended on the South Asian boundaries; hence, each country has been treating and theorizing its political history, socio-cultural paradigm and foreign policies in such a way that they look distinct from the other.

Lack of poor theorization of South Asia has also contributed to the failure of SAARC as a Regional forum. There is an ardent need for theory construction and building a structural interpretation of the rise and nature of social movements in South Asia, the challenges of Terrorism, global warming, role of religion, ethnicityin South Asia and exploring new areas of economic co-operation. Focusing area studies scholarship in these spheres will not just help this region, but also strengthen SAARC as a regional forum.

There is a profounding impact of India over whole of South Asia. We share a common Hindi-Urdu Tehzeeb. The songs of Lata Mangeshkar, Nusrat Fatehali Khan, Nazia Hasan, Abida Parveen spread their melodious strings across South Asia. The love for Bollywood and its films have transcended all boundaries. Movies like Dabaang, Secret Superstar, Hindi Medium have a popular rating not just in our Immediate Neighbourhood, but also in China. India-Pakistan Match has always been a Thriller and the News of Imran Khan becoming the Prime Minister of Pakistan has been gladly welcomed in India also.

Hence, South Asia one of the busiest laboratories of the Modernization process will immensely benefit from the development of a Non-Western perspective and India as one of the largest country of the region will have to play a pivotal role in this Theorization process.

> "The Indian Elephant cannot transform itself into a mouse. If South Asia is to get itself out of the crippling binds of conflicts and cleavages, the eighth will have to accept the bigness of the Nineth. And the Nineth that is India, will have to prove to the Eighth that big can indeed be beautiful."
>
> — *Bhabhani Sengupta*

Notes

1. Siddarth Mallavarapu, 'Theories of International Relations' in *International Relations : Perspectives from the Global South*, ed., Chimni, S., Bhupinder and Mallavarapu, Siddarth, Ch.1, p. 5, Pearson Publications.
2. Mahendra Kumar, *Theories of International Relations*, Ch 1.
3. Ibid. Pg. 11.
4. Amitav Acharya and Barry Buzan, *Non-Western International Relations Theory*, Routledge (2009), pp. 9-16.

5. Siddarth Mallavarapu, *op. cit.*, Ch. 2, p. 27, Pearson Publications.
6. Urmila Phadnis, *Ethnicity and Nation-Building in South Asia*, Sage Publications, 1989.
7. Barry Buzan, "A Framework for Regional Security Analysis" in *South Asian Insecurity and the Great Powers*. Barry Buzan and Gowher Rizvi (Macmilan, 1986), p. 8.
8. Saumya Sinha, (Eds.) Maniny, "Afghanistan: Prisoners of past or Pioneers of a new future", *World Focus*, Sept. 2017.

6

Assessment of India's Foreign Policy in the Modi Regime

Subhash Kumar Baitha & Kumar Adarsh

Introduction

The foreign policy that India formulated after independence reflected our culture and political tradition. Our foreign policymakers had before them the lessons of Kautilya, the pragmatist who had recognized war as an important instrument of power and foreign policy. They were also impressed by the Buddhist traditions of Ashoka, who advocated peace, freedom and equality. Nehru opted for the later and also incorporated into his foreign policy, the ideals of international peace, and pacifists settlement of disputes, the policy of NAM, Panchsheel and peaceful coexistence.

After him, his daughter Indira Gandhi came to power. She was the supporter of realpolitik and thus helped in the liberation of Bangladesh and furthermore led the India's first atomic test and demonstrated to the world India's power in the region as well as in the world. After her, PV Narasimha Rao came up with the Look East Policy in which he aimed to cultivate economic and strategic relations with South East Asian nations in order to secure India's position as a regional power. After that, I K Gujral through his doctrine tried to give unilateral concessions to immediate neighbors and to fabricate great relations, especially with China and Pakistan. Under the leadership of Vajpayee government, India's foreign policy got elevated to new heights. Friendship and cooperation was promoted with all the major powers of the world. It was during his period only that India became a nuclear weapon state not withstanding a few restricting forces and in this manner he added to a gigantic ascent in India's global profile and prestige.

The Modi government has not exclusively been impacted by the approach of past governments, for example, of PV Narasimha Rao and Vajpayee. However, he has likewise taken it to another skyline. His diplomatic success lies in making an authority that blends and orchestrates with the general thought of India both at the domestic level and globally. The role of the individual in foreign policy implementation of any country is extremely crucial and so is the case with India. PM Modi with his new style of diplomacy has been marked by the symbolism of a deep personal rapport with foreign leaders.

His personal style is a diplomatic asset, which was evident in his recent visits to the Gulf countries. During his visit to Abu Dhabi, the Crown Prince accompanied by his five brothers received the Prime Minister at the airport, a rare honor for any visiting dignitary. Similarly, the King of Jordan offered his personal helicopter for Modi's visit to Palestine. The advancement of national objectives and interests during these visits, including the clear demonstration of India's continued commitment to the cause of Palestine, and the first strategic acquisition of oil fields in the Gulf, were thus facilitated by the personal friendship that he has assiduously cultivated with leaders of West Asia and the Gulf (Chaudhary 2018).

India is not yet completely in a situation to lead or set the rules for the international order. However it is finding a way to look for full participation in the most vital worldwide administration stages. India is as of now a member of the G20, the East Asia Summit, Shanghai Cooperation Organization, Missile Technology Control Regime and the BRICS coalition, a demonstration of its status as an expanding nation with a rapidly developing economy. New Delhi additionally tries consistent way for permanent membership in the UN Security Council. It has likewise been currently campaigning for full participation of the Nuclear Suppliers Group. At the same time, India has been attempting to reinforce its initiatives, regardless of whether through global endeavors are not, as in Yemen and Libya, recognitions of its roles in UN Peacekeeping or popular recognition of its contribution and roles in the two World Wars. The effective result of the COP21 environmental summit in Paris and India's constructive role has additionally paved the way some towards shedding its reputation as a multilateral 'naysayer' and 'obstructionist' (Jaishankar 2016).

India has recently embarked upon institution building of its own. The International Solar Alliance represents one such effort, as do the Indian Ocean Rim Association (IORA) and BBIN. While India will continue to lobby consistently for inclusion in multilateral security institutions, its presence in the evolving international economic and trade order will still require a clearer articulation of its trade policy, one that gives greater priority to India's concerns on services, intellectual property, and labour mobility (Jaishankar 2016).

Some of the major policy initiatives taken by Modi's

government to prove that India is going to be more assertive in his foreign policy are as follows:

1. Look East to Act East
2. Paradiplomacy
3. Indian Ocean Outreach

1. Look East to Act East

The Modi government knew the significance of Southeast Asian countries and Pacific nations and accordingly, he altered the policy from Look East to Act East. The Look East policy of PV Narasimha Rao was not especially intense in light of the fact that it neglected to set up its foundations because of local political variables, from frequent changes with liberalization process, lack of connectivity with ASEAN nations. At that time India was developing and evolving and as a result it had very little to offer to the ASEAN. India's relationship with ASEAN is a key pillar of our foreign policy and the foundation of our Act East Policy. Act East will reinforce the grounds with greater connectivity, the prospect of enhancement of trade and exchange of information. Export-oriented ASEAN will take a glance at India because of India's emerging market and quality services. The 3Cs – Connectivity, Commerce, and Culture are the main focus of the Act East Policy to establish a far deeper relationship with the ASEAN countries (Vishwanath 2018).

India has additionally followed a proactive diplomacy, courting ASEAN members, Vietnam to Myanmar, creating an impact in the ASEAN. India has pushed for the acknowledgment of the 2000 km long India- Myanmar-Thailand trilateral highway. Much of this, as Modi accentuated, has come without India's 'claims' concerning the ASEAN, weather economic or territorial. This again is a powerful message; additionally. The presence of all the

ASEAN heads in the 2018 Republic Day parade was an indication that India is at long last moving with its Act East Policy despite the fact that China strives to build its impact in the region (Vishwanath 2018).

America too wants to have influence in the Asia region and as a result, the present government in USA has been from time to time using the term Indo Pacific, in which India's role is emphasized a lot as America is aware that with the assistance of India it can counter the growing influence of China and therefore the notion of Indo Pacific maybe broad not covering just East Asia and Australia, but also the Middle East where with respect to Pakistan and Afghanistan, India can be a bulwark.

The expanding impact of China in the South China Sea has not been acknowledged by a few ASEAN individuals particularly the Philippines and Vietnam. They have not acknowledged the chronicled claims and the improvement exercises done by China in the South China Sea. A significant part of the claim is quarrelsome and far from being obviously true. In 2016, the Philippines won a case at the Permanent Court of Arbitration in the Hague, that discredited China's claim over the vast majority of the South China Sea and furthermore made it clear that the Reed Bank was inside the Philippine's exclusive economic zone (Viray 2016).

The unprecedented rise of China is a shared concern and so the ASEAN Nations engage India as the alternative to an increasingly assertive China. However, neither side appears to confess this duality of the dependence and discomfort with Beijing. ASEAN has failed to put up a joint front against China's building of artificial Islands across the South China Sea where claimants like Vietnam and Philippines have taken opposite trajectories of accusing Beijing. India's confrontation with China at Doklam last year saw ASEAN wary of taking sides (Vishwanath 2018).

Modi has tried to extend and develop India's politico-security commitment in the Asia Pacific with ASEAN at its center and to take it beyond, into a socio-cultural and civilizational interface that underlines India's points of interest over the world forces. Nearer connections of Buddhism and Ramayana from the first Millennium has been revived to strengthen domestic constituencies for stronger relations (Vishwanath2018).

In the ASEAN-India Free Trade Area (AIFTA, operational since 2010) trade is pegged at $71.6 billion in 2016-17. Though India's deficit with the ASEAN was $9.5 billion in 2016-17, it has decreased from $14.75 billion in 2015-16. This will underscore how India looks at RCEP (Regional Comprehensive Economic Partnership) which includes the ASEAN, India, China, Japan, South Korea, Australia and New Zealand (Vishwanath 2018).

Comparable with Modi's Neighborhood First approach, his Act East Policy saw Assam's Chief Minister Sarbananda Sonowal being invited to join the PM's banquet for the 10 ASEAN leaders. This eagerness is required to assist in synergizing linkages between India's Northeast and Southeast Asia. The introduction of India's Look East arrangement matched with the expansion of ASEAN. The addition of Cambodia, Laos, Myanmar, and Vietnam resulted in ASEAN sharing borders with India. They were, appropriately, conceptualized to be at the focal point of India's Look East policy and their network with the tiger economies was to render financial help to spare them of political unrest. Presently the new spotlight on Act East economies was to bring economic relief to spare them of political turmoil. Now with the new focus on Act East, all eight Northeast states are expected to be connected by rail by 2020 (Singh 2018).

2. Paradiplomacy

The Prime Minister, during his run-up for the office, promised a strong foreign policy with an aim to improve relations with immediate neighbors. He emphasized on the need to increase bilateral trade and cooperation on matters such as counter-terrorism and to secure peace and stability in the South Asian region. Modi also proposed an idea of "para-diplomacy", where every state or city could forge bilateral ties with foreign countries or federal cities, leading, even though theoretically, to a de-centralization of foreign policy (Kumar and VR 2017).

In a country as sizeable as India (a subcontinent), there is a definitive need for decentralization of foreign policy implementation and in selected areas of diplomacy. Second, it can be contended that states are frequently preferable compared to the Central government in attempting strategic measures in zones of exchange of trade and commerce, foreign direct investment, education, cultural exchanges and also outsourcing of business.

Another factor that brings the significance of paradiplomacy to the surface is that there may be situations where the Central government will contrast with state governments on ideological and political grounds, which makes it likely that a few judgments of New Delhi may not be seen to the greatest advantage of states and the other way around. Furthermore, given India's size, provincial governments are regularly better in improving diplomatic relations with different governments in their neighborhood in view of geographical, cultural, historical and economic reasons. For example, West Bengal can have more fruitful paradiplomatic relations with Bangladesh and Bhutan than an MEA official positioned at the Nation's capital. So also, Kerala has personal stakes in taking part in political relations with the Gulf nations as an expansive number of the state's inhabitants discover employment in that nation.

India has seen a sudden boost in its subnational diplomatic activities in the last few years. In early 2015 the Ministry of External Affairs ask the CM of Andhra Pradesh Chandrababu Naidu, to lead a high-profile delegation to China in April of that year, a month before PM Modi's state visit to China. On his visit to Bangladesh in June 2015, PM Modi included Mamata Banerjee Chief Minister of West Bengal in his official delegation though she did not make it and the Teesta water dispute remained unaddressed. But the land boundary issue of India and Bangladesh was finally resolved after a wait of 4 decades. After which the two countries started their successful exchange of 162 adversely held Enclaves. Without the consent of CM of West Bengal, this wouldn't have been possible. The inclusion of chief ministers in Prime Ministers visit overseas or the ministry of external affairs asking a chief minister to lead a overseas delegation in advance of a prime minister's visit is a relatively recent practice in the official conduct of India's foreign relations (Tewari 2017).

In recent years, the term "city diplomacy" has gained increased usage and acceptance, especially as a strand, if not a variant of paradiplomacy and public diplomacy. Town twinning, as it's more commonly called, is a concept where cities develop their own foreign relations based on cooperative agreements. These pairings can be conducted for cultural or economic exchanges, which, in turn, are beneficial to both cities/towns.

Subsequently, town twinning agreements have been signed between Mumbai and Shanghai, Ahmedabad and Guangzhou, Varanasi and Kyoto for their economic development and to build more cooperation between the two cities.

The real challenge for Modi is not just to increase

province-to-province, city-to-city exchanges but to ensure that a larger number of States and their cities and towns – particularly those that are yet to develop as imperative financial center points – take an interest in such trades and derive advantage from them. This is a testing undertaking since the essential challenge is normally financial. In this way, another region from China, Japan or the US will first try to improve ties with States that are monetarily dynamic. However, in numerous recorded occasions recorded, social linkages are too are an imperative factors (Maini2015).

A few states like Maharashtra, Karnataka, Andhra Pradesh, Telangana, and Gujarat are as of now taking long walks in setting up paradiplomatic relations while the Ministry of External Affairs (MEA) has established a State Division. The government must engage in better policy formulation and institute clear guidelines in order to see the fruits of pursuing some National diplomacy (Tewari 2017).

3. Indian Ocean Outreach

The Indian Ocean is perceived to be the current center of the strategic world by many geo-strategists, fulfilling the prophetic words that have erroneously been attributed to AT Mahan, "Whoever controls the Indian Ocean will dominate Asia; the destiny of the world would be decided on its waters". Often regarded by historians as the womb of maritime civilization, globalization has accentuated the maritime security challenges affecting maritime trade in the region (Ghosh 2017).

The Chinese presence in the Indian Ocean Region has undoubtedly created a sense of unease and apprehension, not only within some littorals but also within the security establishment in India. Honestly, a significant number of the littorals have frequently played one against the other and the subsequent China-card against India. However at a more profound level, every one of them is careful about Chinese hegemonistic inclinations, despite the fact that they are forced to bear Chinese financial and on occasion military largesse. This is probably another rationale behind India non-committal attitude towards the Chinese economic initiative of the One Belt One Road (OBOR) and its maritime manifestation in the Maritime Silk Road (MSR) (Ghosh 2017).

While China has been building ports, roads, bridges and power stations across Asia, countries express growing concern about the terms for such infrastructure investment. China's acquisition of Hambantota Port in Sri Lanka in a debt-to-equity swap deal underlined problems with what has been called China's "debt trap diplomacy." Opaque terms and predatory loan practices without social or environmental assessments have entangled some nations in Chinese strategic objectives (Pant 2018). The formulation of the "string of pearls" strategy, furthering China's larger military and commercial ambitions under the guise of economic development, has managed to bait nations out of India's strategic orbit (Mukherjee 2018).

The ongoing ideological move embraced by the Abdulla Yameen administration in the Maldives is an example of this transformation. The change of the island state from a pro-India bastion to a Chinese customer state is a measure of Beijing's prophetic methodology and represents an expression point in Sino-Indian maritime dynamics. Since the Maldives represents a buffer zone surrounding India's maritime strategic space, China's unfaltering infringement there is a genuine aim for concern. To address this, striking arrangement choices are required from New Delhi. And keeping in mind that there are numerous key alternatives for Indian policymakers to counter Chinese control, India's principled position of "strategic autonomy" must also be reformed (Mukherjee 2018).

The Modi government has made the Indian Ocean a priority, and former Foreign Secretary S. Jaishankar has argued in favor of "reviving the Indian Ocean as a geopolitical concept". Modi has also highlighted the value of the "Indian Ocean region, " visiting not only Seychelles, Mauritius and Sri Lanka but also several East African nations along the Indian Ocean littoral. Inviting Seychelles and Mauritius to join the existing maritime security cooperation arrangement among India, the Maldives, and Sri Lanka in 2015, Modi had underlined that New Delhi seeks "a future for Indian Ocean that lives up to the name of SAGAR Security and Growth for All in the Region." He outlined a set of goals that included seeking "a climate of trust and transparency; respect for international maritime rules and norms by all countries; sensitivity to each other's interests; peaceful resolution of maritime security issues; and increase in maritime cooperation" (Pant 2018).

India is sending the message that it isn't simply the Indian Ocean and South Asian power, but one with capacity and intent to shape the wider Indo-Pacific, extending from its proximity to the Indian Ocean to interests in the South China Sea, the Middle East, Africa and the Pacific. What's more, this comprehension of Indian strategic reach is broadly acknowledged. The United States has respected this developing impression and other real powers have additionally reacted decidedly. The re-emergence of the Quad, involving the United States, Japan, Australia, and India on developing regional security strategies, mirrors this growing consensus (Pant 2018).

The Transformed Ministry of External Affairs

The MEA has experienced a gigantic change since 2014 and has become more 'people-oriented', giving priority to rescuing Indian citizens who are stranded abroad for various reasons. Furthermore ever since Sushma Swaraj took charge of the Ministry of External Affairs (MEA), she has proved it to be true by her timely actions and easy accessibility. In fact, it is her accessibility and endeavors that in the past 4years more than 80,000 Indians stuck abroad have been rescued.

Several rescue operations were propelled in the war-torn areas of the world such as Iraq, Libya and Yemen. In Iraq with the rise of ISIL in northern Iraq, where hundreds of thousands of Indian migrant workers live, the security of those overseas Indian came under threat. On 16 June 2014, the MEA set up a 24-hour helpline at the Indian consulate in Baghdad for the assistance of Indian nationals stranded in the conflict cities. It has been reported that 46 Indian nurses were successfully abducted from the Iraqi town of Mosul who was later freed and flown back to India. However, the government was inefficient in saving the life of 39 workers.

A similar situation occurred in Libya and Yemen. In Libya, where many Indian nationals were stranded because of the armed conflict that broke in Benghazi and different parts of the nation, MEA through timely action saved the lives of hundreds of people. In Yemen, after the outbreak of aerial attacks by the Saudi led coalition following the coup by the Houthi rebels, Government of India launched a massive rescue operation called Operation Raahat to save hundreds of non-resident Indians located there. Minister of State for External Affairs General V K Singh himself oversaw the entire rescue operation right from the battleground towns of Sana'a and Aden, with the rescue Indian operations based in Djibouti. The operation was exceptionally effective and gotten enormous acclaim from all over the globe as it protected Indians as well as a large number of nonnatives-stranded in the war-torn nation as well (Chennabasaveshwar 2018).

The MEA has established "Videsh Bhavan" in Maharashtra and the Ministry of Overseas Indian Affairs has set up the Overseas Worker's Resource Centre in Gurgaon. These institutions will counsel Indians who are planning and looking for work abroad. They will help the candidates escape the dubious and fraudulent recruiting agents who take advantage of their limited knowledge about the process and dupe them. And also help them in escaping from the foreign land during the crisis situation (Chakraborty 2018).

Earlier the MEA used to be just a ministry for diplomatic purposes. But today, it is performing the diplomatic role with a difference, ensuring safety of the Indians in trouble abroad, and also generating funds for the development of the country and it is because of the changing role of the MEA, among others, that there has been an increase of 53 percent in the Foreign Direct Investment (FDI) in the country.

Tackling Pakistan and China

With Pakistan, the present Government has been following a two-dimensional approach. From one viewpoint, New Delhi is reliably keen on detaching Islamabad from the international community by mobilizing nations against its evil design to create, nurture and use terror as an instrument of state policy. On the other, in this diplomatic battle, India has also succeeded in cornering Pakistan on the international legal forum a fact that got reflected in Kulbhushan Jadhav's case at the International Court of Justice, where India succeeded in stalling Jhadav's execution till the final order. Similarly, on Kashmir, despite deafening *hullaballoo* by the Azadi gang and their overground 'intellectual' supporters, the Government has not only held ground but, as was seen in the case of rewarding Major Gogoi, it has sent a clear message that the very 'idea of India' cannot be held hostage to anti-India forces, both domestic and global (Mishra and Pandey 2018).

Also, the attack on January 1, 2016, on the Indian airbase at Pathankot has changed the Indian narrative on Pakistan. Prime Minister Modi has since then, repeatedly called on Pakistan to be sanctioned as a state sponsor of terrorism and to be isolated by the international community. The Uri attack of September 18, 2016, and the Indian response through the so-called surgical strikes ten days later on September 28/29 are an indication that India and Pakistan are back to the future. Modi's obsession with "terrorism" from Pakistan is puzzling considering that since 2011 we have not suffered a mass civilian casualty attack. Thus the message is loud and clear: India is determined to assert and claim its rightful position by taking on all its adversaries in the language the situation demands (Mishra and Pandey, 2018).

Indian response to Chinese aggression since the time of Nehru was hazy. With Modi government in power, India took an aggressive and an assertive stance, as was seen in the Doklam issue. India took China by surprise when it conveyed, through its actions, that this is a new India that is ready to retaliate to Chinese aggression not only on its territories but also on behalf of its friendly neighbors in terms of security. This bold and decisive move by India raised India's respectability not only among the global powers but also among its friendly neighbors who now rest assured that India would be a co-partner in protecting their sovereign rights against China. (Mishra and Pandey, 2018) New Delhi has, moreover, firmly refused to endorse Beijing's One Belt, One Road initiative, which seeks, among other things, to connect substantial parts of Pakistan to China via ground transportation (Ganguly 2018).

Increase in Economy

According to the government, Modi's foreign visits have resulted in a sharp rise of Foreign Direct Investment (FDI) into India. The inflow of FDI to India has jumped to $60.08 billion in the last three years of Narendra Modi government. According to a release by Ministry of Commerce and Industry, the FDI inflow to India in the financial year 2016-17 was $60.08 billion, which was around $5 billion more than $55.6 billion recorded in 2015-16. In the financial year ending March 2015, India had received $45.15 billion as FDI as against the $36.05 billion received in 2013-14.

In spite of Modi's dynamic foreign policy, Nepal has turned out to be an abnormally troublesome accomplice, incognizant that its advantages are inseparably connected with India. The Maldives, delicate on fundamentalist inclinations and fanatic to China, is separating itself because of its misguided policy. SAARC, the principal vehicle for regional combination, remains slowed down.

Conclusion

There is no doubt that under Prime Minister Modi, India enjoys a higher profile in international relations than any time in the recent past. The overall strategy underlying Modi's foreign policy is sound and there are strong continuities with the past. The priority accorded to India's neighbourhood, the pursuit of strong economic and security partnerships with the US, Japan, Australia and countries of South-East Asia, managing the China challenge through a mix of competition and cooperation, the sustained and expanding engagement with Africa and the reaching out to the large and influential Indian diaspora are all elements of continuity but there are a new vigour and energy with which these are being pursued by Modi. The challenge of going forward must take into account the changed geopolitical terrain, marked by the relative retreat of US from its global role under Trump, the pursuit by China of a hegemonic role taking advantage of Western disarray and its own accumulation of formidable economic and security capabilities and, as a consequence, its more interventionist role in our own immediate neighbourhood (Saran 2017).

There are two key elements that will decide if India can emerge as a key countervailing power to China's assertion of predominance. One is whether Prime Minister Modi can activate his remarkable political power and popularity to drive the economic reforms and structural transformation of the governance system India needs to start crossing over the yawning power gap with China. It certainly has the potential to do so. The focus must be on the China challenge and not diverted by a distraction with Pakistan. This truly is a sideshow. Secondly, India's quest for power should not just be about muscle and brawn. The late Singapore leader, Lee Kuan Yew used to say that India's rise does not generate the same anxieties that China's does precisely because India is an open, transparent and democratic country. I would add the perception of India as a successful plural democracy, able to handle immense diversity and possess a culture that has universal appeal and resonance. These are invaluable, intangible assets, which must never be devalued in an effort to be seen as tough in comparison to previous governments or in serving short-term electoral gains (ibid).

References

Banerjee, Tuner (2018). "China's Maritime Quest In The Indian Ocean: New Delhi's Options", *The Diplomat*, 24th April 2018.

Chakraborthy, Rimi (2017). "Thanks To Sushma Swaraj, Nearly

80,000indians Struck Abroad Have Been Rescued in 3 Years," *MensXp*, 28th Aug. 2017.

ChanakyaIas Academy "Paradiplomacy And India: Growing Role of States in Foreign Policy" Retrieved on 18th May 2018 from https://www.chanakyaiasacademy.com/images/Article-III-DEC.pdf

Chaudhary, Dhananjay Roy (2018). "Modi's Personal Touch to Diplomacy Furthers India's Interests Worldwide," *The Economic Times*, 26th April 2018.

Chennabesaveshwar (2018). "4 Years of Modi: Going Beyond Borders On Rescue Ops," *Oneindia*, 26th May 2018.

Diplomacy & Defence, "Philippines Identifies Sites In the South China Sea For Potential Joint Exploration with China" 3rd March 2018.

Financial Express (May 19, 2012). 3 Years of Modi Rule: FDI Inflows Jump To $60 Billion in 2016-17 From $ 36 Billion In 2013-14, Retrieved May 23, 2018, fromhttps://www.financialexpress.com/economy/3-years-of-modi-rule-fdi-inflows-jump-to-60-billion-in-2016-17-from-36-billion-in-2013-14/676518/

Ganguly, Sumit (2018). "Modis Foreign Policy Revolution," *Foreign Affairs*, 8th March 2018.

Ghosh, P.K. (2017). "Power Dynamics In The Indian Ocean Region: Indias Maritime Outreach" *IAPS Dialogue*, 5th April 2017.

Jacob, Happymon, (2016). "Losing The Neighbourhood", *The Hindu*, 18th May 2018.

Jaishankar, Dhruva (2016). "India's Five Foreign Policy Goals: Great Strides, Steep Challenges", *The Wire*, 26th May 2017.

Khanna, V.N. (2010). *Foreign Policy of India* (6th Ed.), New Delhi, Vikas.

Kumar, Mohit, and V.R., Anish (2017). "New Foreign Policy Parameters", *The Pioneer*, 12th June 2017.

Maini, Tridivesh S. (2015). "Infusing a New Dynamic to Sister Cities", *The Hindu Centre*, 30th March 2015

Mishra, Mukesh and Pandey, Abhijeet (2017). "New Era in India's Foreign Policy", *The Pioneer*, 26th December 2017.

NDTV (23 Oct, 2016). "External Affairs Ministry Also Contributed To Foreign Investment Growth: Sushma Swaraj", Retrieved May 23, 2018 From https://www.ndtv.com/india-news/external-affairs-ministry-also-contributed-to-foreign-investment-growth-sushma-swaraj-1478032

Pant, Harsh V. (2017). "Three Years of Narendra Modis Foreign Policy", *ORF*, 31st May 2017.

Pant, HarshV. (2018). "As India Tries to Grow its Influence in the Indian Ocean, China Poses Stiff Competition," *Scroll*. In 5th May 2018.

Saran, Shayam (2017), "In Year Four, Modi's Foreign Policy Needs Some Course Correction," *The Wire*, 29th May 2017.

Sibal, Kanwal (2014), "Modis Foreign Policy," *Indian Defence Review*, 2nd April 2014.

Singh, Swaran (2018), "India –Asean Summit: Modi's Act East Policy Has Set New Benchmarks" *Hindustan Times*, 29th January 2018.

Tewari, Falguni (2017) " Paradiplomacy in India: Evolution and Operationalization", *ORF*, August 2017.

The Economic Times (Aug. 27, 2017), "External Affairs Ministry is Now More People Oriented: Sushma Swaraj", Retrieved May 20, 2018 Fromhttps://economictimes.indiatimes.com/news/politics-and-nation/external-affairs-ministry-is-now-more-people-oriented-sushma-swaraj/articleshow/60246595.cms

Viray, Patrica Lourdes (2016) "The Verdict: Philippines Arbitration Case Vs China" *Philstar Global*, 12th July 2016.

Vishwanath, Anurag, (2018), "Why Act East Will Work When Look East Did Not", *Financial Express*, 3rd February 2018.

7

Indo-Thailand Relations
Cultural Connectivity and Role of Buddhism

Alok Kumar Gupta & Vandana Mishra

Introduction

Instrumentalities of conducting foreign policy by different states have been changing with changing world order and security paradigm. With growing primacy of economic diplomacy over military diplomacy, foreign policy of nation-states have come to rely more on extension and expansion of soft power along with increased concentration over hard power. Accordingly smart power i.e. a balanced combination of soft power backed by hard power is the most sought after instrumentality of conducting foreign policy in the contemporary world. Shashi Tharoor, once a Minister of State for External Affairs, Government of India, spoke and wrote, "Hard power without soft power stirs up resentments and enmities; soft power without hard power is a confession of weakness."[1] Soft power thus is an ever-expanding arena with most countries of the world exploring their cultural assets and everything that they could develop and use as leverage to attract the people of other countries of the world.

Cultural connectivity has thus come to play a constructive role and an important instrumentality of enhancing connectivity among countries of the world. This is more relevant for those countries among which there exists civilizational ties and presence of epistemic communities. Gradually cultural connectivity helps towards creation of security communities which leads to cementing and strengthening of ties with strong potentials for exchange in the field of trade and commerce. India is no exception to such change and development in the field of foreign policy instrumentalities. It has started exploring its leverages to exploit them as a source of soft-power which would help towards building relations with relevant countries of the world.

It is in this backdrop that contemporary Indian foreign policy is flooded with hugs, handshakes and hand-holding with various nations when top-level summits takes place. Some scholars have criticized the terms and tactics whereas others have applauded them. Yet one thing that is becoming obvious by now is that India's role in international relations and conduct of foreign policy has grabbed international attention and has helped India to project as a strong international player.There are proven evidences of the facts that India's civilization and culture did spread over in many parts of the world in the past millennia through trade and it struck firm roots in Southeast Asia including many of its dance forms.[2] Southeast Asia region consist of the members of ASEAN[3] that is linked for centuries with India both geographically and culturally. India while facing challenges to reset its relations with the west in the immediate years of the cold war also formulated the foreign policy choice of 'Look East' which was later transformed into 'Act East Policy' (AEP) under the present political dispensation. It is in consonance with this foreign policy choice that India signed a Free Trade Agreement with ASEAN in 2009. India strongly aspires to build relations and renew the partnership with these countries via trade, commerce and business. However, these countries and their economies are better integrated with China, which as a rival of India in South East Asia. Their strong ties with China have been one of the factors that have acted as a bottleneck towards India's fulfilment of AEP aspirations. India is exploring ways and means to achieve its AEP aspirations and full membership of ASEAN towards furtherance of its national interests. Soft power could be one such means which India has come to realise in the recent past and is evident from many of the speeches of Indian leaders in their interactions with ASEAN members on bilateral and multilateral forums. India has already started exploring its leverages with countries with similar culture, artistic traditions, family values, and customs to name but a few.

Another strategy that India has been adopting in the recent past is exploring the mechanism of building ties with each of the members of ASEAN on individual basis with an aim of charting its course for full membership. Thus, India treats Myanmar as a 'Gateway to ASEAN' solely from geographical contiguity point of view. Similarly, it treats Singapore as 'Gateway to ASEAN' solely from economic and development point of view. Therefore, authors in this paper endeavours to treat Thailand as 'Gateway to ASEAN' solely from cultural connectivity point of view. There is adequate and strong commonality between India and Thailand in terms of Buddhism that could help towards building cultural bridges with consequent strong relations in other walks of life. Being the country of origin, India could tap and use Buddhism as its cultural heritage and develop it as soft-power leverage. Accordingly, this paper attempts to explore how Buddhism could play a determining role towards enhancement of cultural connectivity between India and Thailand.

Cultural Connectivity in Foreign Policy

Cultural connectivity is not an alien concept in foreign policy discourse. Since ancient times, culture has remained the linchpin of interactions among the different kingdoms situated in different parts of the world. Culture is taken to be one of the three important elements of a country's soft power. The other two elements of soft power are political values and legitimacy of a country's foreign policy.[4] Cultural diplomacy is though considered as a 'new concept' but is an 'old phenomenon' in the field of foreign policy and international relations. Cultural diplomacy could be defined as the exchange of ideas, information, art and other aspects of traditions and practices as part of culture among nations and their peoples in order to foster mutual understanding.[5] Most of the major powers of the world have already been investing intensely in their efforts to promote cultural diplomacy in spite of their late awakening to role of culture. Still it has greatly paid them diplomatic rewards. Compared to United States and China which are big powers of the world, major countries like India, culture has been for more an important ingredient of its social system and more ancient than other. Cultural diplomacy of India, though not identified in the contemporary context, has always been part of its rich cultural heritage with global outreach. It was the widely prevalent diversified cultural assets of India that prompted the founding Prime Minister Jawaharlal Nehru to conceive Indian Council of Cultural Relations in 1950 so that the civilizational heritage of India could be projected to the outside world. However, the organization may not have been able to live and function in the spirit in which it was created and thus India severely handicapped in tapping a valuable resource that it could have used as an instrument of foreign policy and also for economic benefits. Cultural connectivity has happened for India including the extension of its soft power outreach but not at the behest of Government's rather most of it has happened on account of private initiatives at individual and group levels.

People used to travel long distances just to have a glimpse of other cultures and this resulted in intermixing of different cultures and respect for each other's culture, thereby building long-lasting relationships. The travellers were also gifted with symbols depicting their identity and cultures. However, with the passage of time, cultural aspect received a severe setback when the military might, naval supremacy and air power became the dominant issues on the international platform. In the contemporary phase, the international community is witnessing a revival of cultural aspect. There may be several reasons behind this, firstly the international community is completely exhausted with the consistent acts of terrorism and military might and the quest for peace and construction is more dominant. Thus, displaying the instruments of peace is far relevant than displaying the instruments of mass destruction. Secondly, the international decisions are not the sole domain of the leaders alone and secret diplomacy has given way to public diplomacy, thus the role of people has acquired a greater significance. Gone are the days when the diplomacy was conducted and the decisions were taken only by the prominent leaders of the nation and role of citizens was limited to obedience and obligation. Now the diplomacy, decisions, agreements are open for the people to scrutinize, judge, criticize and applaud. Consequently, public diplomacy has been increasingly gaining a place of primacy in the foreign policy matrix of most nations, with cultural connectivity being the dominant part of it. India cannot be left behind in this endeavour. Thirdly, state alone is no more a direct threat to the security and strategic interest of the country rather many non-state actors have come into existence against which cultural diplomacy is being considered as an important tool of blunting the biting power of such threats. Fourthly, Weapons of Mass Destruction (WMDs) are turning out to be a more show-piece rather than for conflict resolution through deterrence. Moreover, it has given way to 'cultural diplomacy' as 'weapons of mass communication'. It has been the most evident shift in the world diplomacy in the aftermath of the event of 9/11 terrorist attack in US.

Religion has made its way to diplomacy, and since then, a number of diplomatic initiatives have been categorised by experts under the heading of 'faith or religion based diplomacy'. This diplomacy is embedded in religion—its texts, practices and traditions.[6] In the parlance of diplomats, faith-based diplomacy is 'track two', that is, diplomacy practiced by non-state actors, officials of non-governmental organizations (NGOs), religious leaders and private citizens.[7] In this context 'cultural connectivity' as an important tool of foreign policy has tremendous future sense.

Cultural connectivity, however has been so far a supplementary and of secondary importance with other major discourses. Cultural aspect is a domain that involves the people and is easily understandable to people. It is something that connects the people mentally, emotionally and socially giving impulse for people-to-people contact. The leaders have used culture as an instrument to establish relationships with the neighbours.The cultural aspect is important because it provides a common ground for countries and the relationships based on culture are more peaceful, constructive and trustworthy. Though India realised and began late the relevance and utility of the power of cultural connectivity and soft power, yet it must understand that it has tremendous resources to use as cultural heritage. Discussion of the soft power ingredients in India's international relations took off parallel to Nye's evolving views on the subject. C. Raja Mohan argued as early as 2003 that "India could always count itself among the few nations with strong cards in the arena of soft power, asserting that India's biggest instrument of soft power was its diaspora. India's diaspora is certainly an asset, but far from the only one. Beyond its cultural and civilizational riches, its vibrant (if at times chaotic) democracy, its free media, its mostly independent judiciary, its dynamic civil society, and the impressive struggle for human rights since independence all make it attractive to publics in much of world where these characteristics of its national experience are known.[8] It is in this context that the authors wish to explore the role of Buddhism towards building and strengthening ties with Thailand as part of India's Act East Policy. It also seeks to examine India's Buddhist diplomacy towards Thailand vis-à-vis China's attempts to enhance its own brand to nurture its relations with Thailand and other Southeast Asian countries. 'Cultural connectivity' thus, will also have tremendous future sense for Indian foreign policy.

Buddhism as India's Leverage

Gautam Buddha though born in Lumbini in Nepal attained his Nirwana (Enlightenment) and spread his sermons and preaching in India. Thus, India is considered to be the country of its origin. It was founded in the late 6th century BC and then spread to Sri Lanka, Myanmar, Bhutan, most of the Southeast Asian countries, China, South Korea and Japan, often adapting to and blending in with the traditions of its host. Contemporary world has several ramifications of Buddhist practices and followers. China is believed to have the largest number of Buddhist in the world. Most of the populations in Thailand, Cambodia, Myanmar, Bhutan and Sri Lanka follow Buddhism. India though cannot boast of a large Buddhist population[9], but it is the place where the religion was founded. It also upholds the tradition of Buddhist learning and hosts the 14th Dalai Lama, the spiritual leader of Tibet. The important places related to Buddhist heritage like Bodh Gaya (in Bihar), and Sarnath (in Uttar Pradesh) and Kushinagar (in Uttar Pradesh) are situated in India. These places have been prominent pilgrimage centres for Buddhist followers from all over the world. According to estimates, one of every six visitors to India visits Bodh Gaya, and many of them also travel to other sites of Buddhist pilgrimage.[10] It is true that India has great leverage in terms of being the cradle of this philosophy and religion for several reasons.

Firstly, although Buddha was born in Nepal, India is the spiritual birthplace of Buddhism because he received the enlightenment in India. Secondly, the sacred place of Buddha's enlightenment has emerged as an international tourist centre and Buddhists from all parts of the world visit these places. Thirdly, most of the Southeast Asian Nations are Buddhist nations and the relations can be developed on the basis of complementarity that we have large number of Buddhist shrines and the neighbouring nations have large number of followers. The Buddhist population in other parts of the world are thus religious diaspora in limited sense. Fourthly, the global message of Buddhist philosophy took birth in India and was later on patronised by the emperors and then spread to other parts of the world. Fifthly, some of the oldest centres of Buddhist learning such as Nalanda and Takshila exist in India and are once again being revived as modern centres of great learning. Sixthly, most of the

Buddhist nations have been shaped and influenced by India so the intermixing of cultures enables the countries to pave the ground for common cultural connectivity. It will also pave the way for smoother economic relations in future. Seventhly, the philosophy of Gautam Buddha is not limited to suit the needs of a particular nation, but it is universal in spirit. It incorporates a philosophy that is based on interdependence and cooperation. Last but not the least, India can also advance strong neighbourhood policy with the help of Buddhist connectivity as most of the strong followers of Buddhism are there in its immediate and extended neighbourhood.

Indo-Thailand Relations

India and Thailand celebrated 70 years of establishment of bilateral relations in 2017 which were formalised soon after India achieved independence in 1947. It has experienced considerable growth in diverse fields over the last several years. Immense untapped potential still exists which remains to be harnessed.[11] The relationship between India and Thailand thus extends over a great span of time and is rooted in history, cultural and religious interactions. The shared heritage extends to religion, art, architecture, festivals and Buddhism is the linchpin of this interaction. The bond has also been praised by David Thussu in his book *From Buddha to Bollywood* by saying that the "Millennia old relationship between India and rest of Asia has a strong cultural and communication dimension and Buddhism was at the heart of this interaction." Relations between India and Thailand are not of recent origin. Religious, cultural, linguistic, mythological and trade links have existed for over two millennia. References are found in ancient Indian literature characterising Thailand as *Swarnabhumi* or the Golden Land. Buddhist influence reached Thailand over 2000 years ago, soon after senior monks Sona Thera and Uttara Thera were sent by Emperor Ashoka to spread the gospel of Lord Buddha in 3rd Century BCE. Beside Buddhism, Hindu influence is clearly visible in Thailand's religious practices, customs, traditions, deity worship, architecture of palaces and temples (*wats*), in the arts, sculpture, dance, drama, and literature.[12] India took a fresh look in the changing world order in early 1990s and adopted the changed economic and strategic paradigms of international relations. India's 'Look East Policy' (LEP) and Thailand's 'Look West Policy' launched in 1996, converged to bolster economic and trade links. LEP was later transformed into 'Act East Policy' (AEP) under the present political leadership. Since then top level visits of officials and leaders and increased interactions have provided a strong fillip to bilateral partnership.

Accordingly, in the contemporary world and regional order Thailand holds a significant position for India because of several reasons: Firstly, it can be an important gateway for its membership to ASEAN owing to cultural connectivity; Secondly, Thailand has extended a free trade agreement to various nations including India. New challenges to global trade may also open up new possibilities in Indo- Thai trade. According to Somkid Jatusripitak, the deputy PM of Thailand, Trump administration is changing the direction of trade regulation. Trump has already dissociated from the pact that Obama had inked with 11 Pacific rim-countries, four of which were from10-member ASEAN block. UK Brexit from EU has also raised the level of uncertainties. Thai investment in India has increased considerably over the years.[13] India-Thailand bilateral trade rapidly rose to more than US$ 9 billion per annum from 2012-13 to 2014-15. Trade diminished after that to about US$ 8.5 billion in 2015-16 on account of turbulence in the international economy.

Thirdly, an idea of India-Myanmar-Thailand (IMT)

trilateral highway from Moreh (Manipur) in India to Mae Sot in Thailand through Myanmar was conceived at the Trilateral Ministerial Meeting on Transport linkages in Yangon in April 2002.[14] The 1,360-km IMT Highway was initially scheduled to be completed by 2015. According, to an official from India's MEA, the completion of the project is now expected by 2020.[15] IMT will give a boost to the road connectivity in South East Asia. India has also proposed to extend connectivity to other ASEAN nations. It will thus give a boost to trade with all the Southeast Asian nations including Thailand. The Highway also has the potential to evolve into a linear economic excellence zone.

Fourthly, India and Thailand are also linked by sea and share a maritime boundary in the Andaman Sea. The Indian Ocean is one of the most militarised regions in the world. The Chinese are trying to establish a maritime presence in Southeast Asia as well as the Indian Ocean. This might not be necessarily directed against India but still it has considerable geopolitical and strategic ramifications. India is already involved in joint patrolling exercises with Thailand and Indonesia, and has offered to cooperate with the littoral states in the implementation of the 'Eyes in the Sky" programme for patrolling the piracy-infested Straits of Malacca.[16] The cooperation between India and Thailand thus also extends to maritime security cooperation.

Fifthly, Northeast India is being seen as an attractive market for the investors and it will also be linked through the other Asian nations through the IMT trilateral highway. It will also link Northeast India to Thai market.[17] It will help in the overall development of the region by developing infrastructure and turn it into an attractive destination for investment.

Sixthly, the linking of India and Thailand can also help in countering China's "one belt one road initiative" to enhance its influence in the region as the trilateral highway is also planned to be extended to other nations such as Cambodia, Laos and Vietnam and this can pave for further ties with the ASEAN nations.

Last and the most important, in terms of culture, Thailand has a large number of Buddhist followers and they could be treated as religious tourists for India as it has all the places of pilgrimage that are related to life of Buddha. The Buddhist population of Thailand could be lured to visit by facilitating and smoothening their pilgrimage and consequent tourism. This will have potentials to build bridges across population and initiate Track-2 diplomacy which is a sure road to cultural connectivity.

Buddhism in Indo-Thailand Relations—Imperatives for Cultural Connectivity

Thailand has been a meeting ground for the Buddhist and Brahmanical traditions of India. Buddhism spread to the Southeast Asia with the efforts of Kings and Emperors. Presently 94.6 percent of total population of Thailand are the followers of Buddhism.[18] Given this fact Thailand becomes a land of opportunity for India. This creates potentials for tourism and for people-to-people contacts as well as bilateral business and economic exchanges between India and Thailand. Currently, there are more than 150 weekly flights between India and Thailand connecting nine Indian cities. More than 1.1 million Indian tourists visit Thailand annually. On the other hand just about 100,000 tourists from Thailand come to India, mostly to Buddhist sites. This number needs to be enhanced for which India really need to plan and work upon the plan to create tourist opportunities in Indian cities wherever Buddhist heritage are available. To promote larger tourist inflows, India was earlier issuing single entry e-visas. In addition, India has recently approved multi-entry business and tourist visas for five years, in place of one year at a time.[19]

India needs to improve flight and road connectivity as well as infrastructure including hotel accommodation, other relevant local hospitalities, and upkeep of religious sites in general, and Buddhist sites in particular. Most of the Buddhist sites are highly underdeveloped and they are yet to be developed on the level of world class standard with modern facilities in its vicinity. This will help to generate employment, business and many other opportunities on and adjacent cities to these heritage sites.

The efforts of contribution of Nobel Laureate Rabindranath Tagore cannot be ignored towards securing and enhancing cultural connectivity between India and Thailand. The founding of Vishwa Bharti University at Shanti Niketan for the cultural interaction of Asian scholars was an important step towards Asian connectivity. The department of Indology included the study of Buddhist Literature where many Thai students received their education. He also expressed his views on the preservation of Indian culture in Thailand in his poem "To Siam" and recommended the establishment of Thai Bharat cultural lodge. The lodge consisted of library, Indian Yoga experts as well as Hindi classes to promote learning the local language among Thai students.[20] This practice is still going-on and now another Hindi Sansthan at Wardha near Pune is also hosting number of Thailand students who are doing research on Hindu scriptures, mythologies, and many other allied areas alongside learning Hindi language. Certainly, such endeavours are required to be expanded so that cultural connectivity between India and Thailand are taken to new heights.

Renowned universities like Nalanda and Takshila were the centres of higher learning including Buddhism which were later destroyed by Islamic invaders. Although political leadership neglected Buddhism, its remnants were and are still there. This has been attracting a good number of religious tourists to India who visit these shrines for chanting and solace, not only from Thailand but also from many other countries of the world. Foundation stone laying ceremony of Nalanda University on 27th August 2016 was attended by the Thai Ambassador which is one of the most constructive options in the recent years. Undoubtedly, the progress of such universities would promote India's cultural connectivity with other countries of the world and especially with the Southeast Asian nations. Thailand fund for Nalanda University was established on the day of its inception which reveals tremendous potentials towards promotion of cultural linkages between the two countries. Earlier also Thai private sector had contributed US$ 5,000 in 2012 for the same purpose. This fund is expected to be allocated for the scholarship for Thai students pursuing MA programme in the school of Buddhist studies, Philosophy and Comparative Religions at Nalanda University.[21] Thus, this is a clear sign of India's growing soft power and cultural connectivity in particular, which awaits a strong boost from the public and private sectors on a continuous basis.

The relationship between India and Thailand thus extends over a great span of time and is rooted in history, cultural and religious interactions. The shared heritage extends not only to religion, but also to art, architecture andfestivals and Buddhism is the linchpin of this interaction as stated above. Although the high-level exchanges and visits are still continued cultural diplomacy is limited only to gifting statues of Buddha, and holding conferences and therefore no substantial development in the relation is visible on the ground level. The deepening of the relations requiressome different strategies. It is quite surprising such strong relationship existed in past with the efforts of just one or two people. In the contemporary context, if such initiatives are state-sponsored and the programmes are institutionalized through the communication and network linkages, it will boost the relations on all fronts along with economic, political and social relations. Such interactions can be initiated only through "soft power" expansion, which according to Nye is the "power of attraction". Attraction is only possible if we exploit the commonalities of the two nations and respect and accept the diversity and differences. Historical records and literature is replete with soft power resources but everything is on the verge of destruction.

One of the soft power resource and commonality that exist between the two nations is that India has Buddhist shrines and Thailand has large number of Buddhist followers as stated above. India though the birthplace of Buddhism has failed in exploiting its potentials and improving its ties with the neighbours and extended neighbours such as Thailand. India is far behind other Buddhist nations in terms of institutions, leaders, followers, and is also least interested in hosting the Buddhist conferences. No serious steps have been taken by the government of India towards creating awareness and reaching out to the people about the importance and treasure that the philosophy holds. Recently, Prime Minister Narendra Modi has expressed willingness for an intensive phase of foreign policy activism and one of the most surprising features of his diplomacy has been the frequent evocation of Buddhism. Modi while extending his outreach to leaders in the subcontinent and Asia, from Nepal to Japan and China to Myanmar, and Thailand has projected Buddhism as one of India's bridges to these nations. This is indeed a welcome move but requires to be pursued aggressively.

Prima facie some of the religious places that are most

obvious have not been developed in terms of local hospitality and arrangements, building and maintenance of infrastructure. Even the local Buddhist shrines and places are not inter-connected through railways and roadways and are almost neglected since long. India's over-priced sub-par hotels, combined with chaotic local conditions for tourists and unsympathetic state bureaucracies in charge of most tourist sites are hardly the Asian ideals for religious tourism including family holidays. Fact remains that archaeological and other attractions are stupendous which could also be developed as places of tourism which are located within the proximity of Buddhist shrines. The very birthplace of Buddhism and where it got nurtured has been side-lined on the international map to the extent that it is considered alien to its own people. In this way due to utter negligence and underdevelopment of Buddhist heritage India is unable to facilitate such a huge number of Buddhists coming from Thailand. Therefore, India needs to explore the imperatives for itself which would provide a strong boost to its soft power expansion. It is in this sense that once again there lies tremendous future sense in the cultural connectivity of India.

Initiatives Thus Far: Its Strategic Implications and Economic Advantages

Firstly, the revival of Nalanda University which was an important centre for Buddhist philosophy is an important step in this direction. Efforts should be initiated to transform it into international centre of learning. The revival of Buddhist studies will help in creating awareness and appreciation for the cultural legacy. The student exchange programmes can help in building intellectual environment of the state. There are many other Centres of Buddhist Studies and Learning at different State and Central universities and colleges which must be integrated with the upcoming Centre for Buddhist Learning at Nalanda University. In this way the philosophy of Buddhism can be professionalized and the universities can be nurtured on the lines of international universities. Such academic institutions in India can play an important role in mitigating the conflicts by incorporating religious studies and its relevance towards creating peace. This would help towards research and knowledge creations about all good and positive elements of different brands of Buddhism and thereby serve the cause of humanity. India's idealistic image among the comity of nations will further be strengthened with this initiative.

Secondly, India is a secular country as per its constitution. Therefore, state must not promote any religion. However, developing Buddhist heritage sites and extending and expanding communication infrastructure is not about protecting and promoting religion; rather it amount to mere facilitating tourism and further the economic interests of the country. India has already taken a leaf forward in this direction. This is not against the religious tolerance enshrined into Indian Constitution and also not against the spirit of constitutional provisions in any manner. India may turn out to be the Jerusalem and Mecca for Buddhist followers of the world including Thailand. It will further strengthen India's secular credentials in the eyes of international community as also in the minds of most citizens of India. Japan has already pledged to use its Official Development Assistance (ODA) for the renovation of highways leading to the Nalanda University, which only reveals the eagerness of Buddhist following countries to stand by and help India and contribute towards expansion of soft power and cultural connectivity of India. This will further reap strategic benefits in the arena of ideology for India as India will no more be branded as a Hindu *Rashtra* by its adversaries especially under a rightist political party.

Thirdly, construction of IMT trilateral highway as stated above is an important initiative in this direction as it will boost the people-to-people contact, trade and economy. It will link not only these three nations but also north-eastern region and other ASEAN nations. The Mekong sub-region, or what the Indian government calls the CLMV (Cambodia, Laos, Myanmar, Vietnam) countries, forms a major part of mainland Southeast Asia and connects the Bay of Bengal to the South China Sea, by land. For India, the strategic salience of the sub-region lies in the fact that it shares long land and maritime boundaries with one of the CLMV countries, Myanmar, in the Bay of Bengal, and its important strategic partner Vietnam has a maritime territorial disputes with China in the South China Sea—through which about 50 percent of India's trade passes. The direct impact of China's rise has been playing out in the CLMV countries in recent years, with China emerging as either largest, or a major trading and investment partner of all the CLMV countries.[22] The strategic significance of this IMT highway cannot be ignored in the context of the growing cross-border transportation links that China has been building to connect with the Mekong countries. It is therefore imperative to look at this project in totality with an innovative and practical approach for timely completion and smooth running of this strategic communication link. This will be a road leading to expansion of both the soft and hard power of India in near and distant future.

Fourthly, India ASEAN relations celebrated its 25th anniversary in 2017. India still aspires to get the full membership of ASEAN. This shows that India needs to rethink and reconstruct its foreign policy in relation to ASEAN. It needs to encourage engagement at all levels including social, political, cultural and economic relations. Thailand can be an important nation to engage because of the commonality, complementarityand cultural relations. Buddhism is an area where India can actively engage Thailand politically, culturally and economically. 98 per cent of the world's Buddhist population lives in Asia Pacific region, 14 countries in Asia have more than 50 per cent of the Buddhist population and seven of these have 90 per cent population practising Buddhism.[23] It speaks volumes about the tremendous potential that Buddhism holds in creating spiritual connectivity and constructing Asian identity on its own without any efforts of the government. Thus, given the outreach of Buddhism in the whole of Asia, and India being its birthplace India has a greater leverage but having the resources is not enough as it also needs to exploit the resources in the right direction. India thus has a strategic advantage in terms of cultural heritage and cultural community which could act as an epistemic community as well as 'security community' within other countries.

Fifthly, the role of Buddhism also extends to the Act East Policy initiative because most of the ASEAN nations are Buddhist including Thailand which has the largest Buddhist population. Connectivity, commerce and culture are the foundation of India-ASEAN relations.[24] It has rightly been said that "culture builds the stage and economy performs". Therefore, moving ahead in cultural connectivity paves the way for trade, commerce and other relevant exchanges between and among nation-states of the world. Buddhism in ancient times had constructed the spiritual connectivity among the whole of Asia and developed to a level of creating an Asian identity. Buddhism has tremendous potentials to provide greater and enhanced connectivity which will facilitate: tourism, employment, trade and commerce, including cultural exchange at least among the countries with substantial Buddhist followers. Cooperation with Thailand will also mean a gateway to establish relation with other ASEAN nations and will lead to first building of 'Security Community' and then through that will improve and strengthen relation with other members of ASEAN. The institutions like ICCR should also take the concern of Buddhism seriously and formulate programmes and policies to create awareness among the people as Buddhism is a resource with tremendous potentials to build bridges among Buddhist following population and countries with potentials to facilitate exchange in other walks of a nation's life.

Sixthly, spiritual thirst has sharpened over the years because of the intense distress and negativities in the world. Displaying the instruments of peace and construction is far relevant than displaying the instruments of mass destruction. The reason stems from the fact that destructive materials are within the reach of all the nations but peace, feeling of altruism, connectivity, cultural and historical engagements are rarely found. Therefore, it becomes important for nations to set the stage for unravelling the lost cultural and historical connections and make way towards global peace. A closer analysis of foreign policy discourses suggests that a robust, peaceful and progressive domestic environment is essentially important ingredient which paves the way for a strong connectivity among the nations. Instrumentalities such as Yoga, religion, Reiki, art of living, and Ayurveda etc. have been evolved to deliver inner peace and sound health so that peace in the external environment could be attained. Buddhism stands apart and above all such endeavours so far as India's role in delivering inner peace is concerned. Therefore, India with Buddhist heritage and resources could develop paraphernalia to become the spiritual capital of the world in general and Asia in particular. This shall help India reap strategic advantage vis-à-vis China and also in other walks of its hard diplomacy. India could do so through conferences and seminars on the importance of meditation, yoga and the same should be held and invitations can be extended to prominent Buddhist scholars who are well versed in this art both within India and elsewhere.

Seventhly, Ayurveda is an important area which evolved in India thousands of years ago and it was also practised by earlier Buddhist monks. However, although the knowledge of Ayurveda spread to various parts of the world, its scope is severely limited in India itself. Today only a handful number of people practise Ayurveda and meditation that is practised in Buddhism. Thus, government and people should initiate efforts towards utilizing the knowledge and potentials and turn it into a precious resource. Thailand also has various ayurvedic centres, ayurvedic spa therapy and different other modes of treatment. India should make use of its indigenous knowledge and create such medical centres and organize conference on the practise of Ayurveda to disseminate the knowledge. The Ayurveda-oriented massage centres of Kerala and other parts of India could be greater places and centres of attraction of people from Thailand and other parts of the world over massage parlours of Thailand which are notoriously famous in the world. The practice of Ayurveda derived from India has made its place in Thailand also and that also could be promoted with Indian collaboration and its images could be purified. They also practice yoga and it is an excellent way to rejuvenate mind and body. There are various meditation centres in Bodh Gaya such as Dhamma Bodhi Vipassana Centre, International Meditation Centre to name but a few. All these can be an attractive option for Thais. India need to work and exploit these potentials to score strategic advantage over China which has been using Buddhism imported from India in its economy as well as foreign policy.

Eighthly, Thailand has large number of Indian diaspora. The total population of Indians in Thailand stands at 85, 000 which is 0.07 per cent of total Thai population. In this the number of person of Indian origin is 70,000 while there are 15, 000 Non Resident Indians (NRI). They are mostly involved in four sectors of tourism, textiles, service sector and industrial development through big ticket projects. All these have contributed in enhancing the economy of the Thailand.[25] Tourism receipts directly contributing to Thai GDP of 12 trillion Baht range from 9 percent (one trillion Baht) in 2013 to 17.7 percent (2.5 trillion Baht) in 2016. The global average fortourism revenue is 9 percent of GDP of Thailand.[26] Thus, this diaspora could also be tapped by India to spread its business tentacles and spread of soft power among Thais the way Chinese population have been doing for China. India here too has strategic advantage over China which India has largely ignored and has thus been at receiving end.

Ninthly, India also has a vast number of Buddhist shrines and historical places as mentioned above. It has the potential to attract foreign investment, boost tourism, and generate employment. Constructive engagements can also be an instrument of public diplomacy. Therefore, India needs to wield its soft power in a more systematic way and initiate the nation-branding approach to enhance its acceptability among the nations in general and Thailand in particular. France and South Korea alongside many other countries of the world have acquired tremendous edge in their foreign policy through the instrumentality of Nation-Branding.The other tourist places within the vicinity of the Buddhist shrines should also be developed to attract the religious tourists once they decide to visit Buddhist shrines. Buddhism has inspired every aspect of Thai's life of architecture, scripture, painting and literature and therefore has provided

India considerable leverage in this aspect of Thailand's life.

Tenthly, the temples of the Thailand have the scriptures of Yogis inscribed on them. Common cultural heritage is also shared in the major religious festivals. The Thai festivals include Songkran, Loy Krathong, Thai Chinese vegetarian festivals, long boat race share common cultural heritage with Holi, Kartik Purnima and Deepawali, Navratri and Onam. Thai Buddhism comprises of Brahmanistic and Buddhist elements. Even though Buddhism is official religion in Thailand, it has great religious tolerance for other religions as well and many rituals and beliefs are same as Hindu rituals. The national emblem of Thailand is Garuda, vehicle of Lord Vishnu. The walls of the magnificent temple next to Kings grand palace are painted with the stories of Ramayana. Many Gods such as Brahma, Vishnu, Shiva are commonly worshipped by Thais.Thus, India has an adding advantage with Thailand, because along with Buddhism, they also share other cultural and religious heritage. India also has a large number of temples dedicated to these Gods. If such temples are restructured combined with proper hospitality arrangements and they are made accessible with proper transportation facilities along with adequate security arrangements, it will also help in generating employment in the locality and thus in local capacity building. This will help in attracting more people from Thailand. Many office and residential areas in Thailand have spirit house with the statue of Brahma and offerings of God, incense sticks and flowers. *Havana/Hom* is conducted in which HomKund is sanctified by chanting mantras before the fire God Agni is invoked. The great stupa (Phra Pathom Chedi) at Nakom Pathom is identical with Sanchi Stupa in India. Many Thai archaeologists are of the opinion that Shikhara was later addition to pagoda of blending Thai aesthetic sense with Indian architectural art. Therefore, given such huge resource-base in terms of temple, arts and aesthetics India has largely been failing to further strong relations with Thailand. There is no denying the fact that Thailand has greater connectivity with China than with India. It is solely for the reason of slackness and ignorance on part of India. Though, lately realised within the Indian political leadership each of these could be nurtured to secure strategic advantage over China in Southeast Asia.

Gaya airport is just five kilometres away from the main centre and spiritual capital of Buddhism i.e. Bodh Gaya. Thai tourists coming to Bodh Gaya can also make a trip to Sanchi Stupa and other major historical places like Sarnath, Nalanda, Rajgirh, Sravasti etc. India needs to develop Airport and Railway platform with proper connectivity on the lines of international standard. All such places related to Buddhism within India require to be connected with proper communication and other relevant facilities to facilitate smooth tourism of prospective Buddhist tourists. Thailand is the only country where the King coroneted is to be a Buddhist. A comparative study of Indian and Thai tourism industry indicates that in Thailand the traits of behaviour were too good and the major determining factor of politeness, modesty and willingness to help and accept people has promoted their tourism. On the other hand Indian tourism industry needs improvement in terms of behaviour, honesty and other skills that could attract tourists from other countries.[27] Therefore, along with proper infrastructure and hospitality arrangements, the role of local people is also important. These tourists should be seen as an asset for India not only in terms of economic benefits accruing out of it but also in terms of enhancing cultural connectivity with countries which would lead to benefits in other areas of nation's life like trade, commerce and technology.

In 2016, on the visit of Thai minister both the sides had

agreed on cooperation, securing sea lanes of communication and maintaining peace and security in Indian Ocean (signing of white shipping agreement).[28] Both the countries also agreed to boost the defence ties with each other. In the same year India and Thailand signed several key pacts in the field of economy, counter terrorism, cyber security and human trafficking.[29] In 2018, Thailand has agreed to act as an intermediary between India and ASEAN and support constructive cooperation in Indo-Pacific. It also agreed to boost bilateral and multilateral cooperation in ASEAN and Indo-Pacific region both on land and sea route.[30] Bilateral trade multiplied eight times since 2000 to reach US$ 8.6 billion in 2013. Exports from Thailand were US $4.76 billion and exports from India were US$ 2.61 billion.[31] Total trade value between Thailand and India reached US$ 10.38 billion jumping 34 per cent from 2016 in which Thailand has recorded $2.6 billion trade surplus with India.[32] Both the nations have set the target of increasing bilateral trade from $8.5 billion in 2015-2016 to $16 billion by 2021.[33] It thus indicates that although the trade relations between both the nations are consistently increasing, balance of trade is always tilted in favour of Thailand. It is on this count that Indo-Thailand relations need to be explored and policies evolved to maintain the balance of trade and commerce. India has all the potentials yet has not been able to tap it and use it for economic and cultural connectivity. India seriously needs to look into it and work upon it.

Conclusion

Generally there are three factors that shape the foreign policy of most countries: history, geography, and capability. Each of these factors has been an important ingredient of India's foreign policy since ancient days and has decisively influenced India's conduct of foreign policy and international relations at different times and in different ways. India's power of attraction, the foundation of any country's 'soft power', has been derived from each of the above three factors. India's international profile is on the rise and has been able to build an international personality within the comity of nations in manner and might that contemporary world is now paying heed to India's actions and perceptions on matters pertaining to world community. Therefore, it makes it obvious that India's emergence as a major actor on the global stage has been attracting many countries of the world towards it. India's fastest growing economy is an attraction for many countries of the world. It is high time that India should promote its soft power potentials to better integrate the communities and people with itself for all future beneficial purposes. India must do it both at general level with all the countries of the world as its target as well as with individual countries as its target where it has leverage on one or the other count. In case of Thailand it is Buddhism which could be used as leverage for enhancing cultural connectivity. Such an endeavour will help a peaceful environment, would facilitate economic growth, generate employment, and would lead to overall development of the country. It will truly make the oft quoted proverb 'Together we march, together we develop' a meaningful one. The partnership between India and Thailand is awaiting a huge response to this effect. Indeed India has tremendous future sense in its capacity of cultural connectivity.

Notes

1. As quoted in David M. Malone, "Soft Power in Indian Foreign Policy", *Economic and Political Weekly*, Vol. 46, No. 36, September 3-9, 2011, pp. 35-36.
2. Jayshree Sengupta, "India's cultural and civilizational influence on Southeast Asia", *Observer Research Foundation*, 30 August,

2017, http://www.orfonline.org/expert-speaks/indias-cultural-and-civilizational-influence-on-southeast-asia/

3. ASEAN (Association of Southeast Asian Nations) is made-up of eleven members i.e. Myanmar, Thailand, Singapore, Malaysia, Indonesia, Vietnam, Cambodia, Laos, Brunei, the Philippines and the recently added Timor Leste.
4. For details one may see Joseph Nye, "Get Smart: Combining Hard and Soft Power", *Foreign Affairs*, July/August 2009.
5. For details one may look into M.C. Cummings as cited in Melissa Nisbett, "New Perspectives on Instrumentalism: An Empirical Study of Cultural Diplomacy", *International Journal of Cultural Policy*, Vol. 19, No. 5, 2013, p. 557.
6. Rishika Chauhan, "Modi and Buddhism: Between Cultural and Faith-Based Diplomacy", *ORF Occasional Paper*, November 2015, p.4.
7. Joseph Montville, "Transnationalism and the Role of Track-Two Diplomacy", in *Approaches to Peace: An Intellectual* Map, ed. By W. Scott Thompson and Kenneth M. Jensen (Washington, D.C. United States Institutes of Peace, 1991). As quoted in Brian Cox & Daniel Philpott, "Faith-Based Diplomacy: An Ancient Idea Newly Emergent", *The Brandyine Review of Faith & International Affairs*, Published online on 27 April, 2010. Available on www.doi.org
8. Ibid., No. 1, p. 35.
9. There are some 7,955,207 Buddhists, comprising 0.8 percent of the population. The followers of Buddhism are among the six religious minorities which have been accorded the 'National Minority' status.Census 2011, Ministry of Home Affairs, Government of India, available at www.censusindia.gov.in Accessed on 15 March, 2018.
10. Ron Purser, "Reviving Buddhism in India, "*The Huffington Post*, September 2013. As quoted in Rishika Chauhan, Ibid., No. 6, pp. 4-5.
11. Ashok Sajjanhar, "India-Thailand Relations: A 70-Year Partnership", *Raisina Debates*, September 15, 2017, www.orfonline.org
12. Ibid., No. 11,
13. Amiti Sen, "Thailand to India: Speed Up Decision on Free trade Pact", *The Hindu Business Line*, January 13, 2018. http://www.thehindubusinessline.com/news/world/thailand-to-india-speed-up-decision-on-free-trade-pact/article9547331.ece
14. "India-Myanmar-Thailand Joint Task Force Meeting on the

Trilateral Highway Project", *Press Release*, Ministry of External Affairs, Government of India, September 11, 2012. Available at www.mea.gov.in

15. See Transcript of Media Briefing by Secretary (ER), JS (BM) and Official Spokesperson (26August, 2016), Ministry of External Affairs, Government of India, 26 August, 2016. Available at www.mea.gov.in
16. Ibid., No.11,
17. "North East India is an Important Attractive Market: Thailand Minister" *Meghalaya Times*, 3 February, 2018http://www.meghalayatimes.info/index.php/front-page/18617-north-east-india-is-an-important-attractive-market-thailand-minister
18. According to *World Fact Book*, USA, CIA. According to the same source nearly 7.1 percent of total population of the world are followers of Buddhism. However, according to another source nearly 6 percent (376 million) of the total population of the world are followers of Buddhism. http://www.adherents.com/Religions_By_Adherents.html
19. The facts produced here are borrowed from Ashok Sajjanhar, Ibid., No. 11,
20. Sawitree Charoenpong, "Rabindranath Tagore in Thailand: His Visits and Its Impact", *Indian Embassy*, Available at www.indianembassy.in.th/pdf/Rabindranath%20Tagore.pdf Accessed on 19 March, 2018.
21. Patamon Panchavinnin, "Thailand Fund for Nalanda University has been established", *Thai Embassy*, 2 September, 2016, Available at http://newdelhi.thaiembassy.org/en/2016/09/thailand-fund-nalanda-university-established/ Accessed on 15 March, 2017.
22. Naresh Bana & K. Yhome, "The Road to Mekong: The India-Myanmar-Thailand trilateral Highway Project", Issue Briefs and Special Reports, 07 February, 2017, www.orfonline.org
23. P. Stobdan, "Asia's Buddhist Connectivity and India's Role" *Institute of Defence Studies and Analysis*, 19 February, 2016. https://idsa.in/issuebrief/asias-buddhist-connectivity-and-indias-role_pstobdan_190216
24. Manish Chand, "Act East: India's ASEAN Journey" *Ministry of External Affairs, Government of India*. November 10, 2014.http://www.mea.gov.in/in-focus-article.htm?24216/Act+East+Indias+ASEAN+Journey
25. Pranav Kumar, "Indian Diaspora in Thai India Cooperation"

Institute of Peace and Conflict Studies, 27 May, 2008http://www.ipcs.org/article/southeast-asia/indian-diaspora-in-thai-india-cooperation-2578.html

26. "Tourism to Continue Growth Spurt in 2017", 17 February, 2017, *Bangkok Post*, Available at https://www.bangkokpost.com/archive/tourism-to-continue-growth-spurt-in-2017/1199925Accessed on March 19, 2019.
27. Dr. Swapana Patwari & Yamini Sharma, "A Comparative Study of India and Thailand Tourism", *IJMT*, Vol. 19, No. 2, July-December 2011, Available at http://ijmtpublication.com/files/IJMT_volume%2019_2_16.pdfAccessed on March 19, 2018.
28. "India and Thailand to Boost Defence Ties" *The Indian Express*, 18 June, 2016. http://indianexpress.com/article/india/india-news-india/india-thailand-to-boost-defence-ties-2859804/ White shipping means sharing and exchange of advance information regarding identity and movement of non-military commercial vessels. There is a particular colour code for ships, white is the colour code for commercial ships, grey is the colour code for military vessels and illegal ships are coded as black.
29. Ibid., No. 28.
30. Thailand to be ASEAN India's intermediary, "Bangkok Post, 26 January, 2018 https://www.bangkokpost.com/news/general/1401950/thailand-to-be-asean-india-intermediary
31. India Thailand Economic and Commercial Partnership, Embassy of India, Bangkok, Thailand. 3 February, 2018 http://www.indianembassy.in.th/pages.php?id=124
32. Ibid., No. 30.
33. Ibid., No. 13.

8

The Eurasian Region and India in 21st Century

Diplomatic Victory

Gitesh Kumar

Introduction

SCO is an effective regional organization in the Eurasian region with the global interest. It was established in 1997, the members being China, Russia, Kazakhstan, Kyrgyzstan, and Tajikistan, known as the Shanghai-Five. In the year 2001, Uzbekistan joined in SCO as another member. The primary objective of the SCO is to expand cooperation in economic, security and military areas at the regional level and coordination on global issues. From a geopolitical perspective, the SCO is often seen as an active organization established by Beijing and Moscow to jointly coordinate their interest in the Central Asian region. For China, the SCO is initially served as a tool to enter into the Post-Soviet space in Eurasia without disrupting Russia's political and military dominance. From the Russian perspective, the SCO is useful in preventing Beijing's ability to act unilaterally in the region and bounding it by the institutional norms. As far as Central Asian Republics are concerned, the presence of China in the organization counter balances Russia in the region. However, it remains to be seen if the expanded organization would have also equal growth performance in its geostrategic influence in the region. In year 2005, Iran, Mongolia, Belarus, Afghanistan, India, and Pakistan gained observer status in the SCO. On 8-9 June 2017 at the Astana summit, the capital of Kazakhstan, India and Pakistan were made as the permanent members. This is great diplomatic victory of India's foreign policy (Bhattacherjee, 2018, p. 2). It seems that the year 2017 is a milestone in foreign policy because SCO is the first organization in entire Eurasian region in which India became a permanent member. It means India has gained a platform to articulate its desire to play a much more meaningful as well as constrictive role in the region. In other words, an important aspect of its membership is that India can play an important role inthe New Great Game of the Central Asian region. In addition, SCO is a great platform for India to discuss with SCO members new areas like banking and, financial sector, regional connectivity, military exercise, intelligence and development cooperation. It is worth recalling that, Russian diplomat Alexander M. Kadakin remarks seven years before in June 2010, "Our position has all along been that we want India as a full-fledged member of the SCO (Roy, 2011, 3)."The main goals of SCO are as follows: Firstly, to improve the mutual confidence as well as good neighborly relations. Secondly, promoting effective cooperation in the area of trade and commerce, science and technology, tourism, climate change, geostrategy and so on. Third, to maintain regional peace, security and stability. Finally, towards the establishment of a new, democratic, just and rational political and economic international order.

From the strategic point of view, SCO's agenda is also closeto combating "the three evils", namely, terrorism, separatism and extremism. Firstly, terrorism refers to terror causing instability in the country and aboard. Secondly, separatism refers to any action aimed at breaking the territorial integrity of a country including those intended at separation of a part of its territory or disintegration of the state, committed by violence. Third evil, the extremism aimed at a violent removal from power or violently holding on to power, and changing the constitutional order of the state, through violent encroachment on public security, including the group or organization.

The members of SCO established Regional Anti-Terrorist Structure (RATS) on 15 June 2001 with headquarter in Tashkent, Uzbekistan. India would also benefit from the RATS especially, in the security and military activities which would help India to gain from the vast area of intelligence inputs related to terrorism activities, drug-trafficking, cyber security, climate change of the region[1]. Also, the annual joint military exercise among members would help gain valuable new military operational insights.

India's connectivity in Eurasian Region

India has been focusing to promote the geostrategic and economic cooperation through Chabahar and SCO in 21st century on the global politics. The Chabahar port and Shanghai Cooperation Organization (SCO) are the most important part of Indian foreign policy for reasons of accessibility and the connectivity with Central Asia as well as entire Eurasia.

In fact, the SCO's members have been thinking to initiate negotiations for the Free Trade Agreement (FTA) by 2020[2]. India should not miss this great opportunity because

New Delhi can look to use a great platform of SCO for expanding alternative route to the Eurasian region as an important part of New Great Game of Central Asian Region. There are more expectations from Pakistan and India in SCO forum especially, in the area of mutual trust, and effective cooperation in politics, trade, technology, security and military and so on.

Historically, India and Iran have long shared a connection in the area of cultural, commercial as well as linguistic ties since ancient times going back thousands of years. In modern time, both countries established formal diplomatic relations in 1950. However that legacy of Persian influence including the Mughal dynasty is the architecture for Indo-Iran relations, which at the present time or characterized by positive interactions. An example is the development of Chabahar port in Iran with cooperation of India. Overall diplomatic, geostrategic as well as economic activities are a beneficial for regional connectivity. Chabahar is known as the 'trilateral junction' among India, Iran and Afghanistan.

From the regional integrated perspective, Chabahar's role to the International North South Transport Corridor (INSTC) that aims to link up Central Asian Republics and Iran through rail, road and shipping networks gives India access to the much larger engagement in Eurasian market and geostrategic point of view. There are two initiatives regarding the importance of Chabahar port and SCO to India in the 21st century.

Economic Cooperation through New Routes

During a landmark visit of Prime Minister of India, Narendra Modi to Tehran on 23 May, 2016 an agreement was signed with Iran as well as Afghanistan, known as Trilateral Transit Agreement (TTA) that recognised the trade corridor that would connect the Chabahar port to Afghanistan. And also, on 3 December 2017, the first phase namely, Shahid Beheshti as a part of Chabahar port was inaugurated by President of Iran, Hassan Rouhaniin the presence of External Affairs Minister of India, Sushma Swaraj, and delegates from 17 countries. In October 2017, India sent already its first shipment of 15, 000 tonnes of wheat to Kabul through Chabahar port[4]. On the other hand, India joined as the permanent member on 9 June 2017 in SCO whichis considered as a great platform to provide a unique opportunity SCO to discuss with other members areas like banking and financial sector, regional connectivity, and development cooperation. It meets member need for a proper exchange of information related to these areas. This great achievement of Delhi in 2017 marks significant progress, creating furthermore, potential power in the trade and economic terms.

These are new routes for promoting the commercial activities with the multilateral cooperation. This is in addition, tothe multi-modal transport of goods and passengers across the three nations already in existence. These two achievements of Indian foreign policy in the year 2017constitutes historical efforts and strength making it a golden year for creating access for India with Eurasian region in the field of trade as well as commerce. In fact, the need forIndia to push its connectivity with Eurasia for market integration mean India should maintain a proper focus at the regional integration in the coming year.

Geostrategic Perspective: New Directions

The Chabahar port development in South-eastern in Iran with cooperation from India marks a new route and direction for a new geostrategic beginning in Persian Gulf region. New Delhi's strategic calculus in the rising Asian security architecture indicates new directions for participation in term of investment, exchange of intelligence and military engagements with countries especially in Asian. Consequently, this can be a counter to three evils face by SCO platform namely, terrorism, separatism and extremism.

India as a permanent member in SCO since June 2017 representsa new strategic victory for Indian diplomacy as it provides a platform for discussion ofits own complications related to terrorism, security, development, and so on. On 1 December 2017, External Affairs Minister of India, Sushma Swaraj attended the annual summit of SCO at Sochi in Russia. It was the first time that India took part at the annual summit as full-fledged member at SCO. This time, Secretary General Rashid Alimov, highlighted the historic decision of the Astana Summit to expand the organisation opening up new opportunities for development and increasing its potential. With the admission of India and Pakistan as full members, the SCO engine got a new boost. India would also benefit from the RATS in various areas, in the security and military activities which would help gain vital intelligence inputs related to terrorism activities, drug-trafficking, cyber security, and so on. Furthermore, Chabahar port and SCO unique role from the geostrategic perspective in the global politics in the 21st century.

To conclude, from the larger aspect of geostrategic and economic perspective, trilateral cooperation (India, Iran and Afghanistan) and SCO have been working towards an integrated development of connectivity infrastructure including road, ports, rail networks that open up greater opportunities in the 21st century to entire Eurasian market and India through Chabahar port and SCO forum. Thus, these initiative of New Delhi have been great, as they form a new opportunity for expanding the multilateral cooperation bypassing Pakistan in Eurasian region.

Development Programs

There are various initiatives takenby SCO member states since thirty years such as the Multilateral Trade and Development Program, which is permanent body, with its staff doing a greater interaction with the observer members. The primary objective is to improve rehabilitation of infrastructure, amplified interaction regarding the business and banking sectors, energy engagement and associating with the institutionalized in the entire Asian continent. Unfortunately, the SCO's trade programme systematically lacks of a regional strategy for promoting the trade as well as commercial assistance (Norling, & Swanstrom, 2007, p. 432). Within the framework of the SCO interbank cooperation, Russia and China agreedduring Shanghai Summit on a project in the area of energy, agriculture and investment venture with US$ 500 million funds shared between Vnesheconom Bank of Russia and the State Development Bank of China. It agreed on US$ 2 billion worth of contracts with the observer members including India. Thus, this regional organization currently provides a platform for fortifying of the bilateral arrangements with the vision of constructive approach. From this perspective, India'semerging presence in SCO is to be seen at the background of Russia trying to maintain the Central Asian Republics (CARs) within its orbit and China disposed to attract additional states into its strategic interestsin Central Asian region. As long as China and Russia vigorously works against Central Asia's access to South Asia for their own reasons, it will significantly obstruct Central Asia's realization of potential opportunities (Norling, & Swanstrom, 2007, p. 432). Moreover, as long as states in Eurasia are trapped inold thinking and view the regional economics as a zero-sum game, coordination will be hard to achievefor the cooperative engagement among the members.

This organization's focus is to build up the infrastructure. Highways, pipelines to transport energy resources and development of direct connectivity through railway lines to facilitate transportation are underway, deepening of financial cooperation, mining investment, and expansion of energy cooperation. Provision of an important sphere like political as well as legal foundation may help to consolidate mutual trade and commercial integration, with the access to world market and consolidation members in the area of energy potential (Grainger, 2012, p. 15). However, these domains are relevant for connecting entire the global market in the coming years.

From the strategic perspective, SCO's members have taken various initiatives which support the military exercises such as Peace Mission in 2007, Peace Mission 2010, the Tianshan-2 in 2011 exercises, Peace Mission in 2012, Combined Border Activity in 2013, Peaceful Mission in 2014, Xiamen-2015 (the last in which all members participated). In these actions, joint maritime exercises between the Chinese and Russian navies occurred twice in 2016, under SCO framework (Jackson & Steven, 2017, p. 30).

Likewise, the traditionally held counter terrorism exercises "Peace Mission" in 2016 were supported by Tajikistan, Kazakhstan, Kyrgyzstan, China and Russia. It is important to examine that these exercises to maintain the bilateral exchanges between Beijing and Moscow into the SCO framework in just two years (2005-2007). These have become regular as a result of the strengthening of cooperation among the memberstates of the organization particularly after the signing of Dushanbe Declaration in the year 2008 (Jackson & Steven, 2017, p. 30).

Beijing organized to work with all members of the organization in order to accomplishthe peace as well as prosperity in the region and to strengthen the economy, aimed at the development of the members, within the framework of Shanghai Cooperation Organization "Info SCO". This program has been a cooperative approach among the members for the positive relations in the coming year. On the other hand, SCO members existed in favor of the amplification of the organization activities to promote cooperation for the realization of a multipolar world (India and China are main supporter for multipolar world). This may also indicate the desire of the SCO to be one of the new centers of power on the world map. From this perspective, the enlargement of SCO membership including India in global politics has been most important development in this century. Two aspects are more important to India regarding SCO development program. Firstly, India has entered in the Central Asian region through regional organization with direct connectivity, participation in the dialogue and decision has been making, and participating in the program and activities related to non-traditional and traditional issues. Another aspect is that SCO members including India deliberate the programs related to trade and commercial activities (especially, Free Trade Agreement among the members) and the biggest issue in this century like climate change. These areas are open opportunities to build up the development programs which arethe most relevance in the 21st century. There has been a change in the contemporary global politics especially, after American President Donald Trump assumed power on 20 January 2017 which marked a trend from the globalization to anti-globalizations. From this perspective, the economic development program as well as integration of the world, it is important to note that the SCO members require the development program with the coordination and systemic management to face contemporary challenges such as climate change, non-traditional issues and connectivity.

SCO and India: Energy Security Cooperation

Energy component defines India's interactions with oil and gas producers like Kazakhstan, Iran, Russia and Uzbekistan and consumers like Tajikistan, China, Pakistan, Kyrgyzstan and Mongolia. This is as proposed by Russian President Vladimir Putin in the year 2007 while shaping a common energy system in both the regional and global contexts[4]. Within this framework, India and Russia are exploring a possible hydrocarbon pipeline route through International North-South Transport Corridor initiative. From this perspective, energy resources as the basis for continued economic growth constitute highest priority for the greater energy cooperation. But it is most important to know that the cooperation of energy security can be increased through dialogue among the members. Consequently, the integration of national energy engagement assumed significance. Also Russian President Vladimir Putin called for the belt of counter narcotics security around Afghanistan and Central Asian region which seems an aggressive approach for removing the financial roots of the drug trade in Afghanistan. These elements have potential for the improving the multilateral cooperation.

New paradigm shift from west to the east, the main role of Central Asian countries are the geopolitical landscape in which the energy will boostthe opportunities of political and economic weight in its relations with the SCO members. In terms of securing energy supplies from the country to country such as between the European Union and China, SCO is likely to play a role.

It has done memorandum of understanding between the UN and Interpol. Here a question arises whether the EU should explore ways of engaging in a structured dialogue with the SCO on non-traditional threats regarding the security issue. Therefore, various experts proclaimed that suspended NATO and EU cooperation with Russia on Afghanistan could be an opportunity to engage cooperation with the SCO in order to remain a crucial actor in Afghanistan's stabilization process[5]. That is high priority fields like countering terrorism. China has also the potential to become an increasingly important partner. Afghanistan's stability is critical issue. From this perspective, SCO including India should improve to seek a deeper level in the area of political cooperation, intelligence sharing and long-term coordination of economic policy and assistance.

Conclusion

There is recognition of India's membership of SCO of its continuous a dynamic cooperation which is appropriate for the interest of New Delhi. India would be able to make potential platform in order to engage economically and geostrategic engagements with the Central Asian countries through a forum of SCO. At the same time, there will be opportunities to continue interactions with Pakistan during SCO summit. Then, it will be opportunities to discuss with the energy issues, drug trafficking and also terrorist activities in the region. Nevertheless, New Delhi needs to make solid diplomatic efforts with all SCO members to attain own national interests. It is the most important to examine that India has opportunities to develop connectivity in the transportation sector with the SCO members in the entire Asian continent and also across the world. At this great achievement of India in the year 2017 as the permanent membership in SCO may create new models regarding traditional and non-traditional threats, and also to covenant with new challenges in Afghanistan and Central Asian region.

Furthermore, India and China have been raising economically and strategically as powerful country in the world politics. At the same time, trade between both countries is growing at the highest level. They have been also working together in many international as well as regional organizations like BRICS (Brazil Russia India China South Africa), RIC (Russia India and China), and so on. India and China are major countries in these organizations and also provide with new opportunity for closer interaction in the SCO platform which indicated a positive role on the global politics.This provides a stage for India to play an active and cooperative role with the SCO members at the multilateral engagements. From this perspective, India needs a long way of strategy in the area of security, trade and cooperation domain in the 21st century.

Notes

1. Suyash Desai, "India's SCO Challenge", *The diplomat at https://thediplomat.com/2017/12/indias-sco-challenge/. Accessed on 16 April 2018.*
2. Ibid
3. Sabena Siddiqi, "Can the SCO Bring India and Pakistan Together?" *The Diplomat at https://thediplomat.com/2018/02/can-the-sco-bring-india-and-pakistan-together/. Accessed on 3 March 2018.*
4. SCO Energy Club: structure ready for international interaction, not Shanghai Six's elite club, " Retrieved from http: / / infoshos.ru / en / ?idn=13913
5. Sabena Siddiqi, *op.cit.*

9

Afghanistan and China

Political and Strategic Relations in Post 9/11 Period

Jyoti Gupta

Introduction

Afghanistan and China are connected since the ancient times through Silk Route. They are not only linked by the trade and commercial engagements but also cultural exchanges. In the modern times, China established diplomatic relations with Afghanistan in the year 1955. The relationship has been friendly, but remained a low key affair. Afghanistan was not a significant country for China until the Soviet Union intervened (Ludwig, 2013). During the Soviet intervention, China cooperated with US and Pakistan in order to support Afghan Mujahiddin against the Soviet forces. The reason behind Beijing's assistance was that it viewed the Soviet intervention as latter's strategy to encircle China and to get an access to Indian Ocean through Pakistan (Chandra & Behuria, 2013). After the withdrawal of Soviet forces, China maintained its informal relations with Taliban regime to ensure peace in its Xinjiang province. The prime concern of China was the rising drug trafficking and Taliban's assistance to Uyghur militants. During the Cold War, Afghanistan and China relations saw little cooperation in the political, diplomatic and strategic spheres. Afghanistan always tried to establish a close relationship with China, but China ignored deeper engagement with Afghanistan. However, both countries enjoyed friendly relations and signed the Treaty of Friendship and Mutual Non-Aggression (1960) and a boundary agreement (1963) (Iqbal, 2016).

Evolution of Afghanistan-China Relations

The Era of Foundation Building (2001-2011)

The second phase of Afghanistan-China relations started, after the inauguration of Hamid Karzai Government in 2001. However, China reopened its embassy in Kabul in 2002 (Chandra, 2015). New Afghan government needed international assistance to overcome major challenges like establishing peace, stability, security, economic development and reconstruction of infrastructure and so on. Therefore, Afghanistan was willing to strengthen its relations with China. Beijing also found it is important to support newly established government of Afghanistan because it believed that Uyghur militants were trained in Afghanistan and were using Afghanistan's heroin to fund *jihad* in Xinjiang (Singh, 2002). Although, during the Taliban regime, China secured Taliban's assurance not to provide any kind of assistance to Uyghur militants but the Taliban did not keep its words. Therefore, China had a belief that newly formed government would not provide shelter to Uyghur militants (Small, 2016). Consequently, China decided to contribute in Afghanistan's peace and reconstructions process by providing non-lethal humanitarian assistance. Tang Jiaxuan, Chinese Foreign minister, during his visit to Afghanistan in 2002, remarked that, "China has only one goal over the issue of Afghanistan to promote peace and development in Afghanistan. China will, as always, support the peace process and actively participate in reconstruction[1]".

The first attempt to institutionalise the relationship was a multilateral agreement, Kabul Declaration, among South Asian and Central Asian states particularly, China, Afghanistan, Iran, Pakistan, Tajikistan, Turkmenistan, and Uzbekistan on 22 December 2002. Kabul Declaration committed them to the constructive and supportive bilateral relationships based on the principles of territorial integrity, mutual respect, friendly relations, cooperation and non-interference in each other's internal affairs. They shared their determination to defeat terrorism, extremism, and narcotrafficking. The treaty was significant for Afghanistan because its neighbours, particularly Pakistan, China and Iran, had a significant role during the Soviet intervention and the civil war. This treaty was an opportunity to be free from regional interference for Kabul. However, Afghanistan could not realise this opportunity ever.

Afghanistan was in dire need to build up its economy. Hence it was important for Afghanistan to reach to the global market. Being a huge market, China was a good destination for Afghan goods. The 'Treaty on Good-Neighbourliness and Friendly Cooperation', signed between Afghanistan and China in 2006 (Chandra and Behuria, 2013), allowed zero-tariff treatment to 278 Afghan goods exported to China from 1 July 2006 and established China-Afghanistan Joint Economic and Trade committee (Peoples Daily, 2006). Another agreement which strengthened bilateral relations on the issue of aid, tax reduction and personnel training—Economic and Technical Cooperation Agreement—was signed in 2010[2]. All these agreements strengthen Afghanistan-China cooperation on Afghan reconstruction issues.

China's cooperation not only helped Kabul on developmental issues but it was also used as a tool to reduce western influence by the then Afghan government. Afghanistan's President, Hamid Karzai's visit to China in 2010 as a first foreign visit in his second tenure is a good example. Karzai made visits to China and Iran when the West was criticising him for mounting corruption, cronyism and electoral reform. These visits by Karzai were done not only to build relations with the neighbouring states, but also for curtailing dependence on the US and posit him as a regional leader by diverting attention from the corruption and nepotism charges on him. Karzai realised that close relationship with China would not only minimise western pressure but also lessen the possibilities of western interference to set up a particular political system because China was supporting the Afghan government amidst the rising allegations of corruption, nepotism, and electoral issues and was also not imposing its communist model of political setup (D'Souza, 2010).

China's Response to War on Terror

China's relations with Afghanistan had a tendency to be driven by external factors. This time it was USA and its "War on Terror". It initially claimed to support the US war on terror which it confirmed by ratifying UNSC Resolution 1368 and 1373 in favour of counter-terrorism (Chandra, 2015). It shared intelligence regarding the funding of terrorist groups, permitted FBI to establish an office in Beijing and provided mine sweepers (Small, 2015). However, China's support was limited in nature and motivated by its own selfish reasons. Taliban's removal by the US reduced its concern regarding cross-border linkages of Uyghur militants. As well as US attack in Afghanistan minimised China's apprehension of great power rivalry in East Asia (Small,

2016). It brought an opportunity for Beijing to have smooth relations with the US and to avoid possibilities of any future economic restrictions on it (Ludwig, 2013).

However, it refused any direct military involvement at later stage. For example, it rejected US proposal of being a part of Norther Didstribution Network (NDN) (Huasheng, 2012). Although, China cited its foreign policy principle of non-intervention in the internal matters of any country as a reason for its non-cooperation, its reluctance to cooperate with ISAF was motivated by the various reasons. It had serious doubts about the US intentions and considered long term military, economic, political presence near its border as a threat. Chinese scholar Li Li, argued that the real intention of the US was to establish its hegemony (Ludwig, 2013; Sharma, 2010). China had a fear that intensifying US military attacks would drive the extremists towards its border in Wakhan corridor, in search of safe sanctuary which would work like catalysts for Uyghur insurgency. Chinese support to ISAF might antagonizethe Islamic world (Sharma, 2010) and make it a possible target of international terrorist groups. All of these reasons moved China from cooperation to reluctance. However the policy of limited cooperation proved to be an asset for China in maintaining a balanced relation with the major actors of Afghanistan.

This period between 2001- 2011 has not only built a firm foundation through cooperation but also intertwined both countries in various ways in the face of new challenges. In 2011, the political and strategic context of Afghanistan started changing, when the US announced its plan to withdraw its troops from Afghanistan by 2014, along with the mission of the ISAF (Destradi et al. 2012). On the one hand China's worries about internal security intensified with the Urumqi riots which took place in 2009 (Branigan, 2009) and on the other it became concerned about safety of its investment and people in Afghanistan. Afghanistan was also willing to enhance its cooperation with China to ensure its political, economic and strategic interests. Therefore, both countries focussed on promoting bilateral relations that resulted in a paradigm shift in the strategic relationship.

Strategic Partnership in 2012

The changing political and strategic environment promoted bilateral relations to the strategic partnership level. Hamid Karzai's visit to China in 2012 resulted in the signing of a strategic and Cooperative Partnership agreement, which led to development of the relationship "on the basis of the Five Principles of Peaceful Coexistence, in line with the purposes and principles of the Charter of the United Nations and widely recognized norms of international laws, as well as the basic principles for bilateral relations enshrined in the Treaty of Good Neighbourliness and Friendly Cooperation."[3] The purpose of the strategic partnership was to cooperate in mutual interest and establish peace, stability and development in the region. The joint statement issued at the meeting clearly mentioned five major areas of bilateral cooperation: "political, economic, cultural, security and regional and international affairs", and called these five areas as "pillars that will underpin the China-Afghanistan Strategic and Cooperative Partnership" (Ibid).

Strategic cooperation between Afghanistan and China signifies that China wanted to protect its primary security interests and get an assurance from Afghanistan for its sovereignty and territoriality. That's why China clearly mentioned in the agreement that the "Afghan side endorsed that it is committed to the one-China policy and he expressed its firm support for China's positions on the Taiwan, Tibet-related, Xinjiang-related and other major issues concerning China's core interests" (Chandra and Behuria, 2013). This is the clause which China has inserted in almost every agreement or joint statement with Afghanistan. This indicates that China is using its relationship to strengthen its stand on its sovereignty and territorial integrity among the international community.

The strategic partnership agreement was the result of Afghanistan's rising importance for China because of the withdrawal of the international security forces. The growing significance of Afghanistan is reflected by the visit of a senior member of Politburo Standing Committee and Domestic Security Chief, Zhau Yongkang, just after three months of Karzai's visit to China in September 2012. It is the most important visit since 1966 when Chinese President Liu Shaoqui visited Afghanistan. Yongkang signed agreements on the security and economic cooperation, and a deal to "train, fund and equip Afghan police" (Taylor, 2012). This visit symbolises changes in the Chinese approach towards Afghanistan (Small, 2012). The withdrawal of the security forces would create a security vacuum and provide a breeding ground for terror groups to attack not only Afghanistan and the region but also China. Thus, there were possibilities that deteriorating security situation would impact peace, security, stability, sovereignty and the economies of both countries.

The Era of deepening political and strategic cooperation (2014-onwards)

Since 2014, Afghanistan was facing economic and political dynamism. For the first time, Afghanistan saw the democratic transition of power. With the end of Karzai's rule, Afghanistan's leadership marked a change and Ashraf Ghani became the President. The economic condition deteriorated because of the collapse of the war economy. After 13 years, the US and North Atlantic Treaty Organisation (NATO) combat mission also got concluded in 2014 (Destradi, *et al.* 2012). The security conditions in Afghanistan were very vulnerable. In this political, strategic and economic context, it became clear that Afghanistan needs substantial support of rising political and economic power like China. Changes in the approaches of both the countries were clearly reflected in the increasing bilateral exchanges among the leadership and higher level officers (Huasheng, 2016). Although Afghanistan already desired to have deeper engagement with China, the Chinese side never gave preference to Afghanistan prior to 2012. There after a noticeable shift was emerging into China's policy approach towards Afghanistan. Now, China was getting more involved in Afghan security affairs. It was clearly visible by China's Foreign Minister Wang Yi's visit to Kabul in 2014 to discuss issues related to terrorism, extremism and cross border crime.

The Afghan leadership also expected a greater role of China from the security and economic perspective after the NATO withdrawal. Consequently, in October 2014, newly elected Afghan President, Ashraf Ghani paid his first official foreign visit to China, to attend the inauguration ceremony of the Fourth Foreign Ministers' Meeting of the Istanbul Process. President Ghani called China an important "strategic partner in short-term, mid-term, long-term" (Shahir, 2016). He was aware of the fact that China could not only facilitate Kabul in development and reconstruction of the country but also it is the only country which can exert maximum pressure on Pakistan for the peaceful reconciliation process.Both countries agreed to celebrate 2015 as a year of Afghanistan-China Friendship and Cooperation and held the 60th anniversary of the establishment of formal bilateral relations in 1955. Afghanistan again expressed its firm support to China against ETIM (Eastern Turkistan Islamic Movement). China, on the other hand, decided to give training on counter-terrorism as well as counter narcotics to Afghanistan force. Both countries expressed their willingness to enhance their cooperation in the field of intelligence sharing related to border security, joint law enforcement in the region and non-traditional security issues[4]. Before 2014, China had provided limited non-lethal humanitarian aid like training to a limited number of personnel in the security sphere. Therefore, there was huge potential to deepen cooperation in security issues because Afghanistan was not able to maintain its security and stability without outside support. The cooperative and comprehensive bilateral relations of Afghanistan and China were not only crucial for Afghanistan but it was also significant for China. The reason was not only China's interest in economic ties with Afghanistan but also its interest in expanding its influence and status in international politics (Muhammad Khan, 2015). The growing sense of responsibility presented challenges before China, and also provided it with an opportunity to present itself as a responsible power in international politics.

Cooperation in Regional Frameworks

Afghanistan and China not only cooperated bilaterally; they also developed and strengthened their relations in the trilateral, quadrilateral and, multilateral frameworks. China is using the strategy of cooperating with regional countries as a safeguard against the possibilities of becoming the main target of terrorist groups. This strategy can also reduce as well as share its responsibilities with other major stakeholders in Afghanistan. Therefore, under the bilateral framework, China preferred to cooperate with Germany, India, Iran, Pakistan, United Kingdom, and the US. Under the trilateral frameworks, China collaborated in Afghanistan-Pakistan-China, India-China-Russia, China-Russia-Pakistan and Afghanistan-China-US frameworks. It's multilateral strategy reflected in collaboration with Shanghai Cooperation Organisation (SCO), HoA, Quadrilateral Coordination Group (QCG) and Quadrilateral Cooperation Coordination Mechanism (QCCM), 6+1 dialogue. Although China is cooperating with various regional groups, it prefers a greater role of SCO because it helps China in securing its geopolitical interests. The main reason for the huge impact of China over the SCO is that the organisation was initiated by China with the support of other Central Asian countries. However, scholars like Weitz (2011) do not view SCO as a capable actor in Afghanistan. He pointed out that SCO is a narrow approach based organisation which mainly focuses on counter narcotics and has done nothing substantial other than issuing declarations. The conference on Afghanistan of March 2009 complained about the trafficking of Afghanistan based narcotics. However, it did not help the Afghan government in countering the drug dealers by providing financial or other assistance (Aris, 2011). Similarly, during the 18th SCO summit, held in China on 10 June 2018, Chinese President again emphasised for facilitating peace and reconstruction in Afghanistan through Contact Group (Stanzel, 2018). Although China wished to play a major role in Afghan security affairs through the SCO, it could not play a significant role due to its limited capabilities.

Defence Cooperation on Counter Terrorism

Barry Buzan argued that security of a state is heavily influenced by the security of the other states belonging to the same region. He called it a security complex. A state not only gets influenced by the security situations of the other states but also it affects the security of others (Pattanaik, 2013). Although China shares a very small border with Afghanistan, its security is heavily influenced by latter's security. Therefore, Afghanistan and China have been trying to deepen the bilateral strategic cooperation to maintain security, stability and peace of their nations. Both countries have signed various MoUs and agreements of strategic importance to enhance their cooperation in various issues like personnel training, counter narcotics, non - lethal military aid and so on. Since 2012 senior security officials and leadership started visiting Kabul for discussing the rising security threat and to find out the ways to enhance cooperation on strategic issues. First such visit was of senior Politburo Standing Committee and Domestic Security Chief Zhao Yongkang in 2012 (Huasheng, 2015). This visit has opened the door of deeper engagement in strategic affairs. Afghanistan and China signed their first security related MoU during the visit of Afghan Interior Minister Noor-Ul-Haq-Ulomi to China in 2014. Moreover, two agreements, one between Afghan Interior Ministry and Chinese Ministry of Public Security and another between Afghan Border Police and Chinese Border Security Forces were signed. The primary objective of these agreements was cooperation on border security issues like illegal cross-border migration and drug trafficking. China decided to provide "bullet proof jackets, demining equipment, armoured police vehicles, and devices to search automobiles for security threats" to Afghanistan (Khalil, 2016) for enhancing the capacity of the security forces against cross-border crimes. Thus, cooperation on border issues emerged as a significant area of bilateral strategic relations between Afghanistan and China.

The bilateral relations also found an opportunity to promote the strategic ties by developing cooperation between the defence ministries of both countries. Prior to 2014, it was Chinese foreign affairs ministry which drove the bilateral relationship, but later on Chinese military also emerged as a major actor to drive the bilateral relations (Pantucci, 2017). Although Afghanistan's defence officials already visited Beijing with the hope of achieving latter's assistance in the matters of security, China provided only verbal or limited support. Changing strategic dynamics like emergence of ISIS, withdrawal of International Security Assistance Force (ISAF) and feeble condition of Afghan military compelled China to play a larger role in security sphere.The defence cooperation between the two has deepened with Chinese military assistance to Afghanistan. This is an unprecedented development in bilateral strategic relations because it did not provide any large scale military assistance earlier. Whatever limited aid it provided, it waseconomic and humanitarian in nature. Even if it provided military aid, it was in the form of training and general supplies (Tiezzi, 2016). For example, during the visit of President Ashraf Ghani to China in 2014, it committed to provide training to 3000 personnel in the next five years. Other than training, China offered economic aid of 500 million RMB worth of grants for 2014 and 1.5 million RMB for the next three years (2015-2017)[6]. However Chinese military assistance to Afghanistan is rising significantly. General Fang Fenghui, China's CMC member and Chief of CMC General Staff announced about $73 million for Afghan security forces during his visit to Kabul on 29 February, 2016 (Tiezzi, 2016). The aid was very significant because the purpose of it was to counter Taliban and strengthen the bilateral counter-terrorism cooperation. General Fang clearly mentioned the areas of cooperation on counter terrorism issues. He said that China is willing to "deepen counter-terrorism intelligence, joint drills, and personnel training "in order to" jointly protect regional peace, stability and development" (Khalil, 2016). Therefore, China established QCCM, a group consisting of Afghanistan, China, Pakistan and Tajikistan in August 2016. The aim of this initiative is to enhance cooperation on the issues of counter- terrorism such as intelligence sharing, capacity building for counter terrorism and joint personnel training (Kucera, 2016). However, the group is new and hence there are lots of hopes with the group because it involves a great power, China as well as other neighbouring states of Afghanistan which share the common problem. But Pakistan's support to the Taliban raises questions about the success of the group particularly regarding Afghanistan.

Although China is getting more involved in the Afghan security affairs, its official stand regarding non-deployment of its troops remained constant.However, there were reports regarding establishment of China funded military base in Badaksha province (Callahan and Marty, 2018) and its military vehicles were seen on the Afghan soil towards the end of 2016 (Marty, 2017). If the report of military patrolling and establishing a military base is true then it will be a major shift in China's stand regarding Afghanistan. The Chinese and Afghan governments have denied any such patrolling and said that it was border security forces that were patrolling and kept quiet about the base. These reports may be true because recently China has passed a counter terrorism law which enables it to cooperate in counter terrorism operation outside its border. Therefore, officially China remained firm not to deploy troops in Afghanistan. However, Van Der Kley (2014) has analysed the reasons behind China's reluctance for military patrolling. According to him China believes that military aid cannot solve Afghan problem whereas it will present China as the enemy of international terrorist groups. Consequently, it will be more vulnerable to rising security threat. Along with that Chinese military does not possess the capacity to launch any combat mission. However, it has cited its foreign policy principle of 'non-interference' to not sending its troops to another country. Kley argues that rather than 'non-interference' cost-benefit analysis is the chief cause of its stand. Therefore, China is not accepting openly its military role out of the fear that it can influence its security and economic interests not only in Afghanistan but in other parts of the world.

Afghan Peace Process and Role of China

Afghanistan's future depends on its domestic security situation. It understands very well that peace, security, and stability cannot be achieved without negotiations with the insurgent groups. Afghanistan has tried many unfruitful attempts to reach any consensus with various political actors of Afghanistan through different channels. Kabul perceives that Afghanistan crisis has an external dimension that acts as major obstacle. Afghan President Ashraf Ghani argued that "The problem, fundamentally, is not about peace with Taliban; the problem is fundamentally about peace between Pakistan and Afghanistan" (Rupert, 2015). Therefore, Afghanistan perceives China as an important factor in establishing peace with Pakistan because it is the only country which can persuade latter to bring Taliban to the negotiation table and play a positive role. China is the trustworthy country by all the actors, Afghanistan, Pakistan and the Taliban. Thus, it raises the prospects of successful reconciliation process. This acknowledgement has motivated Afghanistanto approach China in 2014 during President Ghani's first official visit to Beijing to seek a mediatory role. China assured Afghanistan for its constructive role in Afghanistan's future reconstruction and 'Afghan led, Afghan owned' peace process (Pantucci, 2015). China perceives that the reconciliation process should be driven solely by Afghanistan; no external power should interrupt it because external intervention could hurt Chinese interests especially if it is a rival power like India and the US. Therefore, Beijing believes that only 'Afghan led and Afghan owned' peace process is the viable and long-term solution to the Afghan crisis. China considers that comprehensive and politically more inclusive reconciliation process will bring peace. Consequently, in December 2017, Beijing hosted the first China-Afghanistan-Pakistan Foreign Ministers' Dialogue to mend broken ties between Afghanistan and Pakistan (Zhai, 2017). The mutual interest in Afghanistan's peace and stability has created an opportunity for bilateral cooperation to establish peace.

China offered to mediate in the peace process by providing a neutral venue for the talks in November 2014 (Tiezzi, 2015). Thus, China held secret peace talks between Afghanistan and Taliban at Urumqi in May 2015. The Urumqi meeting was facilitated by Pakistani officials to open the possibilities of direct peace talks with the Afghanistan government (Wong and Mashal, 2015). Urumqi meeting resulted in the first round of the direct negotiations between Afghanistan and the Taliban held on 29 July 2015 in Murree, Pakistan. Therefore, the new series of direct peace talks became known as Murree Peace Talks (Shalizi, 2015). Despite the presence of China and the US, no concrete result occurred by the meeting than scheduling the second round of meeting to be held in Urumqi, China on 30 July 2015 (ibid). However, confirmation of Mullah Omar's death back that in 2013 derailed the peace process prior to the second round of talks (Wong and Jolly, 2016). That ended the hope for a successful reconciliation through the Murree process.

After this failure, China further expressed its support for peace talks in November 2015. Chinese special envoy to Afghanistan, Deng Xijun said that "We've already facilitated [the peace process]. We will offer facilitation again. And if the two sides agree, we will be ready to offer a venue. But we will not mediate" (Tahir Khan, 2015). Its negative response on mediation may be driven by that Beijing understand that it can hurt its neutral image and the Taliban may consider it tilting towards Kabul which will serve no good to peace process as well as its own interests and relations with the Taliban. China's another effort was to cooperate with the QCG, consisting of Afghanistan, China, Pakistan and the US formed in December 2015. It held five rounds of meetings in 2016, but Taliban refused to be a part of the talk until their demands were met. It demanded "the withdrawal of all foreign troops from the Afghanistan, official recognition of the Qatar office, the removal of the Taliban from the UN sanctions list, a halt to the "arrest and elimination" of Taliban fighters, the release of Taliban inmates from prisons, and a stop to what they call "anti-Taliban propaganda," including labelling them as "terrorists" (Ruttig, 2016). While China may be willing to play a role, it is hesitant to play the role expected in the constructive peace process. It has two reasons for not fully supporting the peace talks: First reason, China is concerned about stability in Afghanistan but the balance between its Afghanistan and Pakistan policy is equally important. However, Pakistan is the most significant country for China in South Asia but rising importance of Afghanistan also cannot be ignored. Second reason, China has an equally good relationship with the Taliban and views Taliban as a means to balance the US and ISIS presence. China perceives that given the US presence in the QCG, it could not play such a vital role. This may be the reason why China lost interest in the QCG. Therefore, it became increasingly sceptical about its effective role in the peace talks. QCG cannot garner any positive result not only because of the non-cooperation of the Taliban, but also due to the reason that the states interests do not extend beyond the Taliban (Kousary, 2016). Therefore, till now China could not lead Afghanistan on the path of peace.

Conclusion

The foregoing analysis brings out the fact that there has been expansion in bilateral cooperation between Afghanistan and China on regional politics. It has a greater focus on peace, development, security and cooperative approach between both countries. From this perspective, Afghanistan-China relations in the field of security cooperation have been steadily growing since 2012. The agreement on Strategic and Cooperative Partnership of 2012, provided to maintain a hope of greater support of China in the wake of improving the international support. Afghanistan not only enhanced its interactions bilaterally but also in tri-lateral, quadrilateral and multilateral framework with China on the regional as well as international platform.

Afghanistan expects a strong support from China for the reconciliation process. In contrast, the Murree Peace Process and *Quadrilateral Coordination Group* (QCG) could not produce anything constructive engagements in Afghanistan. Despite creating doubts about Pakistan's role in combating the Uyghur militancy, China did not effectively put pressure to on the Taliban accept the peace process in the region. However, Afghanistan got Chinese various type of assistance and support like financial, technology and so on, but it did not result in any solution to the conflict. Despite the failure of peace talks, Afghanistan is still looking towards China's supportive role. Therefore, Beijing and Kabul need further the cooperative approach for strengthen the bilateral relations.

Notes

1. Government of China (2001), Ministry of Foreign Affairs, Report. Accessed on 24 June, 2017.
2. Government of Afghanistan (2012), Ministry of Foreign Affairs, *Joint Declaration between The People's Republic of China and The Islamic Republic of Afghanistan on Establishing Strategic and Cooperative Partnership*. Accessed on 9 August 2018.
3. Government of Peoples Republic of China (2014), Ministry of Foreign Affairs, *China-Afghanistan joint statement on deepening strategic and cooperative partnership*.
4. Ibid.

10

Locating Nehru's Approach Towards Regionalism

A Challenge to Western Hegemony

Niraj Kumar

Introduction

The origin and development of regionalism have been historically rooted in western phenomena. Therefore regionalisms as well as international system have been shaped through western prism of theory. As a result, non-western academia has been institutionalized by the western theory and its contents. After the sixty years of decolonization, non-western scholars are still struggling for the recognition of their theory due to hegemonic nature of colonial mindset. The west has control over the non-western curriculum, language, text and the whole academic thought process of non-western as well as Indian scholarship. But, it doesn't mean that non-western academia failed to counter the west and its ideology. During the colonial period, most of the non-western leaders opposed the political control of the west and after the decolonization some of the non-western scholars are highly critical towards the western mode of knowledge production such as Edward Said, Frantz Fanon, Ashis Nandy, Dipesh Chakrabarty, Gayatri Chakravorty Spivak and Homi Bhabha. Similarly, in international relations theory, Appadorai, Mallavarapu, AmitavAcharya and Kanti Bajpeyi are trying to establish the non-western forms of international relations theory by differentiating their history from the West.

Since 1947, India has been advocating the inclusive model of regional as well as international organization. Thus, it supported the UN and its bodies for achieving the peace at the international level. This inclusive model of regionalism has been deeply rooted in Indian history, philosophy as well as in the freedom struggle. For India, regionalism is a policy for propagating its ideology across the world such as development, disarmament, democracy and decolonization. On the other hand, the founder of Indian foreign policy Nehru has better perception about world history, therefore, he was critical towards western ideology. In the early age, Nehru understood the strength of India in terms of its size, resources and image and this image of India has contributed to play a leadership role among the third world countries. Nehru advocated the policy of Non-Alignment Movement (NAM) for unity among the third world countries in which they can protect their autonomy for pursuing the development. He has also advocated the Panchsheel formula for making a friendship relationship with his neighbors in which a state can protect their border without spending more money on the production of arms. For Nehru, regionalism should be based on dynamic institutions and rules rather than bodies static in nature. He has advocated that regionalism is more a function of norms and this normative claim of Nehru can be captured through the sociological process of norm localization. He also opposed those types of regionalism whish were based on balance of power. Thus, Appadorai stated that "The major contribution of Nehru is non-alignment".[1] By adopting the policy of non-alignment, Nehru wanted to attain and retain the sovereignty, territorial integrity, security and national interest of the third world countries in bipolar international system. Rana rightly pointed out that non-alignment is an innovative idea of Nehru and it can help the non-western scholar to construct an alternative theory for refuting the western monopoly of balance of power discourse.[2]

Regionalism at a Glance

The emergence of regionalism as a political process is not a new phenomenon but it has linked to the expansion of colonial ideology. Therefore, the British definethe region as an empire and America called it as a sphere of influence in its Monroe Doctrine. Later on, Woodrow Wilson proposed his principle of region as a union of states by developing the League of Nations. But, the spirit of regionalism is understood and studied after the Second World War as the subsystem of international relations. In the mid decade of 1940s, world politics has entered into new phases which were different from past events and developments. Because, in this era the dynamics of world politics has changed by the end of Second World War, with the emergence of newly independent states mainly from Asia and Africa, increasing the tension between East and West bloc and the question of restructuring the Europe which was destabilize through the two World Wars. These are the events that forced the international actors for the creation of regional institutions which helps to make a peaceful world which is also called as a first wave of regionalism[3]. In the first wave of regionalism, mostly three types of regional institutions have emerged such as multipurpose, security alliance and the subordinate of multipurpose regional organizations. The first type of organizations were United Nations, The Organization of American States and Organizations of African Unity and the objectives of the these organizations have to fulfill economic as well as security interest of member states. The second type of regional organizations was setup for achieving the security interest of member countries like North Atlantic Treaty Organization (NATO), The Warsaw Pact, South East Asia Treaty Organization and the Central Treaty Organization. These organizations have been offensive or defensive alliances, established in order to expand sphere of influence and to counter the attack of each other groups. The last type of organization have been economic in nature, defined in terms of economic interest of western countries such as International Monetary Fund, World Bank and the General Agreement on Tariffs and Trade etc.

Similarly, a new wave of regionalism started from mid decades of 1960s which is called the second wave of regionalism. Like the first wave, it was also inspired through the multipurpose interests. But, these organizations have been established in developing countries such as Association for South East Asian Nations, The Economic Community of Western African States, The South African Development Community, The Caribbean Community and the South Asian Association for Regional Cooperation etc[4]. In the Post Cold War era, a new wave has been started which is characterized through its complexity and the driving force of this wave is the false promise of World Bank and IMF which is structural Adjustment Program which have been defined as a development partner of Third World Countries. On the other hand, the end of Cold War and emergence of global market through the ideas of liberalization, privatization and globalization did help third world countries to establish such types of organizations which fulfill their own interest such as North American Free Trade Agreement, Commonwealth of Independent States, Shanghai Cooperation Organization, BRICS, IBSA and Asian Regional Forum and MERCOSUR etc.[5] In this way it is found that all of the waves of regionalism can be differentiated through its content, context, approaches and agencies. The contextual differences indicates the location of regionalism in which it emerges and the approaches tell that how regionalism has been adopted top-down and bottom-up approaches for achieving its interest. Thus, Soderbaum stated that "Regionalism can be distinguished from temporal, spatial and theoretical senses".[6]

Defining Regionalism

To define regionalism is a difficult task for scholars who are working on international relations as well as international political economy from relatively a long time. The difficulty comes from the changing nature of international relations along with the emergence of new approach towards theorizing the world order. Somehow most of the scholars from the different discipline agree that it is the sub system of international relations through which can be seen the different approaches of international relations such as realism, liberalism, Marxism and constructivism. But, another question arises from the debate that what are the factors for differentiating it from two other concepts such as region and regionalization. Therefore, Edward in his article, 'The New Wave of Regionalism' defines region as a group of countries located in the same geographically specified area and it has two essential components namely close physical proximity and sharing of cultural ties[7]. On the other hand, Louise Fawcett counters it by highlighting that "The world is not structured in such a neat manner; to the contrary, regions disappear and reappear as they are transformed by various economic and political factors"[8]. Therefore, region has been described by the static school in which it defines region works as a territorial, military and economic space controlled primarily by states. In contrast to static school, functionalist has advocated that the function of the economy, environment and culture are the main driving forces of a region. But, Castells adopts a holistic approach for defining the region. In his views, he stated that "Region is space of places and space of flows, where former denoting the territorial region and the latter the material organization of the time sharing social practices that work through flows"[9].Whereas, regionalization is a process in which economic variables play a major role, such as free flow of goods and services, tariff reduction, and mergers and acquisition etc. It means a geographical area is regionalized through the autonomous and empirical process that leads to increasing regional economic interdependence and regionalized patterns of economic transactions. Therefore, Haveem had seen regionalization as purely economic phenomena. According to him "Regionalization refers to that process which actually builds concrete patterns of economic transactions within an identified geographical space"[10]. Therefore, it can be said that the process of becoming a region depends upon the intertwined relationship between state and market.

For theorizing the regionalism in world politics, contribution comes from mainly two schools realism and liberalism. First school advocates that for any state regionalism is a tool for maximizing its power to achieve its national interest. Therefore, Joseph Grieco stated that "Institutional co-operation involves the voluntary adjustment by states of their policies in such a way as to help each other reach a mutually desired goal"[11]. For realist there are four conditions in which states go for regionalism firstly, a regional organization is formed to react by weaker states against the major power's man oeuvres. Secondly, regionalism is a tool for countering the hegemony. Third is called as bandwagoning means that small state joined the regional organization for their security purpose. Lastly, strong states go for regional cooperation for status quo or creating hegemony. In contrast to realist, liberals oppose the basic tenets of realism by saying that the market is the main driving forces of regionalism rather than state, it is market that forces state to go for regionalism. According to liberal thinker Krasner "States promote the creation of formal and informal institutions in order to facilitate the solution of common problems and to coordinate action and this cooperation is called as a regime".[12] Apart from these two schools, some of the scholars highlight the role of idea and identity for adopting the regionalism as an ideology through the process of regionalization within the region. Thus regionalism has been defined as a political process characterized by economic policy, cooperation and coordination among states. But, all these definitions have its own limitation such as the objective of these schools is to introduce a number of concepts to be utilized in the analytical framework of this study. They have been adopting the exclusionary forms of theorizing in it represents a specific production of knowledge and it has located only in European history.

Constructing the Western Dominance

In international relations, mostly the non-western scholars have been recognized that the theory of regionalism is constructed through the western ideas, experiences and practices. It can be understood that there are two types of dominance one is physical dominance means that weaker is subjugated by stronger and other is hegemony. Hegemony can be reflected in two forms material as well as ideational and it is sustained through the coercion and consent. Thus western dominance over theory of regionalism has been shaped through the multiple forms such as exclusion, ethnocentrism, marginalization, oppression, contempt and ignorance etc. Thus, Robert Cox stated that "Theory is always for someone and for some purpose and international relation theory can be generally understood as serving the purpose of the dominant western actors".[13] Generally western scholars established its hegemony by adopting the four strategies such as auto-centrism, universalism, and disjuncture and agency denial.[14] Firstly, western scholars have tendency to theorize the tradition of world order from its ideas, culture, politics and historical experiences through the exclusion of non-western tradition of world order. After that they universalize it by subjugating the ideas and identity of non-western textual forms of principles which is prevailed from long time in non-western world. Thus, Steve Walt says that "International relations scholars have long relied on historical cases and quantitative data drawn from European diplomatic history"[15]. They also claimed that the tradition of non-western history does not fit into what passes for international relation theory. Lastly, they absolutely denied the contributions of non-western scholars for making a theory of states, regional institutions and world order by saying that the non-western countries are the consumers of knowledge rather than producer.

It is the politics of knowledge where non-western theory and thinkers have been marginalized thus all the western theories are political in nature. Because, none of the theories and methodologies have detached the scholars from the circumstances of life, of his involvement with a class, a set of belief and a social position where they belong to. The Europeans not only universalize their own way of idea but also institutionalize the non-western text, languages and education system by adopting the two way process.[16] Before generating their own institutionalizes knowledge system they attacked and degraded the non-western intellectual and its spiritual traditions. After that they completely replaced the indigenous forms of knowledge system through the exercise of its power during colonial time for an example Macaulay established the western modes of knowledge in India but before establishing the system he asserted that "It is, I believe, no exaggeration to say that all the historical information which has been collected from all the books written in the Sanskrit language is less valuable than preparatory school of England".[17] Macaulay has intention to setup those types of institution who fulfill his own colonial interest for a long time. He advocated that "We have to create a class who are Indians in color and blood, but English in tastes, opinions, morals and in intellect".[18] In this way western scholars explore a cultural supremacy that can annihilates non-western people's beliefs, names, languages, environment and heritage of struggle. It is the politics of knowledge production of the West which still continuing since imperialism to new imperialism thus they controls the text, trade and the selective promotion of scholars and suppression of indigenous forms of knowledge for its hegemony. Thus Loomba wrote that "The European supremacist domination depends for it continues maintenance and expansion, even its survival, upon the reproduction of its own intellectual paradigms".[19]

Challenges to Western Hegemony

The challenges to the western world started from in decade of 1950 when the process of decolonization and democratization have been started and the non-western scholars especially from history, economics and sociology focused their research on their own regions. They explored that how western scholars have created a dichotomy between East and West through the meta-narrative of western theory and these non-western intellectuals have been posing some questions to the western academia. Ania Loomba rightly pointed out that "The representation of the orient in European literary texts, travelogue and other writing contributed to the creation of a dichotomy between the west and east".[20] These intellectuals not only criticize the work of western scholar about the non-western countries but also highlight the dark side of European history. As Dipesh Chakravarty in his theory, 'provincialization of Europe' is questioning the European history for universaliza-tion of its culture and civilization[21]. These intellectuals have been explored the effect of colonial norms over non-western peoples. They find out that the ways of representation and modes of perception that are used as fundamental weapons of colonial power to keep colonized people subservient to colonial rules. They claimed that the control of west over non-western comes through the two ways. Firstly, west conquered the physical territory later on through the civilizational superiority which was based on rationalists, modernists and scientific thoughts. Asish Nandy wrote that "The west is now everywhere, within the west and outsides; in structures and in minds".[22] They find that the western knowledge system has its own limitations because it lacking the objective analysis of western history, philosophy and culture. They claimed that the western institutions as well as knowledge system have been interpreted by themselves and glorified it. Thus, Gayatri Spivak criticized Foucault for treating "Europe as a self-enclosed and self generating entity, by neglecting the central role of imperialism in the very making of Europe".[23] After criticizing the western mode of concepts, non-western scholars have been advocated the representation of non-western theory in each and every discipline. According to Aditya Mukharjee "The academic elite in the developing countries who are migrating or trying to migrate to the west reproduce their own paradigms of acceptability".[24]

Locating Nehru

Apart from these academicians, non-western leaders like Nehru, Sukarno and Nassir had strongly advocated the peaceful coexistence in a bipolar world through Non Alignment Movement (NAM). For them, non-western countries have to develop without joining any block and they tried to restrict the western doctrine of military alliance and counter alliance. Thus most of the third world countries avoided joining these regional alliances in order to focus on their economy as well as social development. Nehru had played a crucial role for the creation of NAM thus Amitav Acharya highlighted in his statement that "The case of Nehru is very interesting and relevant, because Nehru was recognized both within India and in the world as a thinker in his own right"[25]. For Nehru's idea of regionalism is different from western forms of regionalism because he was the ardent supporters of inclusive notion of regionalism based upon equitable rules. Nehru has been admired the promotion of regional culture as well as local sociological norms by adopting the third world identity oriented regionalism. Appadorai praised the Nehru's modal of regionalism in his views "Nehru advocated the theory of Non-Alignment when world is polarized between the two power blocs. It was a counter discourse to the western notion of balance of power and a strategy to protect the third world national interests, sovereignty and territorial integrity".[26]

By adopting the rule based regionalism Nehru had wanted to democratization, development, complete disarmament and decolonization in non-western countries. He had tried to explore a new strategy for international relation rather than to follows the western model of international theory which is based upon power politics, balance of power, armament and a narrow meaning of nationalism that led to war in world politics. Thus he wrote that "Moves with new desires; for where we used to build and love; is no man land, and only ghosts can live; between two fires".[27] He had wished to put an end to mad world system which breeds war and conflict and which crushes millions; to abolish poverty and unemployment and releases the energies of vast numbers of people and utilize them for progress and betterment of humanity; to build where today we destroy.[28] But mostly western scholars have been labeled that Nehruvian idea of world is an ideal and utopian whereas contemporary world order follows the approaches of realism. While, Anirudh Deshpadey has been supported the idea of Nehruvian regionalism by saying that it old style of west to neglect the non-western thinkers thus he documented that "Dreams and ideals have always been pursued to make the world a better place and there is no reason to believe that this should not happen today or tomorrow".[29] Similarly, Amratya Sen has same observation that "The world has always been divided between those who want to interpret and change it and who seek practical accommodation with it most of the time".[30] When, we look the Nehruvian idea of world order than find that it was not a theory of single man who interprets it by his own way. But, the origin of this theory has been deeply rooted in ancient civilization of India, basically in Buddhist philosophy that advocates the Madhyammarg (middle path) and counters the extreme approach. Thus, Nehru has been rejected the extreme forms power oriented foreign policy rather than he had appreciated the values such as justice, fairness and tolerance etc. Nehru had also dismissed the geopolitical theory of west that promotes the colonial expansion and empire and he wrote about the Lipman theory of geopolitics "Such a proposal looks very clever, yet it supremely foolish".[31]

Nehruvian regionalism has two basic pillars Non-Alignment and Panchsheel. Non-Alignment has some basic principles such as; respect for fundamental human rights and for the purpose and principles of the charters of United Nations, respect for the sovereignty and territorial integrity of all nations, recognition of the movement for national independence; recognition of the equality of all races refraining from acts or threats of aggression and the settlement of all international disputes by peaceful means[32]. The policy of non-alignment was the demand of time when the word politics had polarized between two block one led by capitalistic ideology other socialistic pattern of mode. In this scenario newly independent countries have a priority to development without joining any of two block and both are power hunger and imperialistic in nature. The aim of two blocks is to establish their own empire throughout the world thus Nehru had warned that "Those who desire peace for the world must know once for all that there can be no equilibrium or stability for either the east or the west unless all aggression, all imperialist domination, all forced interference in other countries".[33] For Nehru non-alignment and Panchsheel are complimentary to each other without adopting the Panchsheel policy the objectives of non alignment cannot be achieved. The Panchsheel has five principles such as mutual respect for each other's territorial integrity and sovereignty; mutual non aggression; mutual non-interference in each other's internal affairs; mutual benefit and peaceful coexistence.[34] Nehru must be aware of the importance of these principles for the establishment of a peaceful world order. According to Nehru "If these principles are applied not only between various states but also in international relations generally, they would form a solid foundation for peace and security and the fears and apprehensions that exist today world a place for feelings of confidence".[35] In sum up, regionalism for Nehru is a tool for achieving human security and justice with a new discourse of international theory. Nehru claimed that his idea of regionalism based on non-alignment and Panchsheel are the way of non-western thought and culture thus it has naturally followed. He stated that "We should keep ourselves free from military alliance and have not joined any of the great power groups that dominate the world".[36] There for Nehruvian idea of regionalism is inclusiveness in which non-western countries have achieve its economic interest by sharing the ideas and it is a soft balancing to the west. His ideas crossed the boundaries by the awareness of regional self consciousness and it would help non-western countries to face many challenges. Lastly his idea of regionalism is open for all by sharing of equal partners not only with its members but also unconditional support of other non-western countries.

Nehru in a New World Order

The Nehruvian approach of regionalism is still relevant after the fifty four years of his death. Because, the dramatic changes at the global level initiated a process of reorientation of the power distribution in international politics. After the decline of cold war, the disintegration of USSR and the unification of Europe for the construction of single European identity have been changed the world order. On the other hand security scenario of world politics has been changed due to power transition like, the decline of communism, the sudden rise of Asian countries mainly, India, China and ASEAN bloc, emergence of resurgent Russia and the establishment of new economic bloc such as BRICS and G-20. In the post cold war era USA has emerged as a sole super power and its global war on terrorism have changed the old discourse of international politics. These existing phenomena of world politics have given a new opportunities, new speculations and new consideration regarding power distribution. History tells us that global shifts happen rarely and are even less often peaceful. There are many challenges in front of world community such as USA is still penetrating its power in the making of decision making and actions through the dominance over the international institutions; the presence of its trans-national corporation in developing countries and the exercise of its military power, coercion and cooperation[37]. The contemporary international system has highly imbalance in terms of inclusive development, access to technology, representation in international institution, various export control regimes and unfair rules of international arms control organization etc. For some time, there are pressures on developing countries to take such types of decisions which serve the interest of developed world. Developed countries seek to control the natural resources such as oil, natural gas and minerals of developing countries. The developing countries objectives are not fulfilled without a rule based WTO, reforms in UN and the agenda of climate changed.[38]

In this new world India has to change its goal and objectives to protect its national interest across the world. The India is not only a nations but a subcontinent in terms of its size, population, and skilled labor, large size of market, arms strength and geopolitical location. India is between two super power countries China as well as Russia and it has also interest with USA and South East Asian Nations. India is depends upon a West Asia for its energy resources which is a turmoil region. Therefore, India should adopt Nehruvian routes of regionalism in which it can maintain cordial relationship with all the emerging power. India should raise the voice of developing countries by highlighting the different rules in different spheres, such as missing the rules of global macroeconomic management, international financial structure, cross-border movement of people and international public good. By adopting the Nehruvian policy not-only India can improve its relation with neighboring countries but also it may make a distance among China, Russia and USA without building the alliance or counter alliance. In this way India will achieve its emerging power status by peaceful means.

Notes

1. A. Appadorai, (1981). "Non-Alignment Some Important Issues". *International Studies*, Vol. 20, (02) pp. 3-11.
2. A.P. Rana, (1969). "The Intellectual Dimension of Non-alignment". *Journal of Asian Studies*, Vol. 28(02) pp. 299-312.
3. A. Hurrel, (2009). "Explaining the Resurgence of Regionalism in World Politics". *Review of International Studies*, 21(4), 331-58.
4. B. Hettne, (2006). "Beyond the New, Regionalism". *New Political Economy*, 10(4), 543-71.
5. H. Haveem, (1997). *Political Economy and the Changing Global Order*. New Delhi: Oxford University Press.
6. F. Soderbaum, & Hettne, P. (2010). "Theorizing the Rise of Regioness". *New Political Economy*, 5(3), 457-72.
7. D. Edward, (2010). "The New Wave of Regionalism". *World Quarterly*, 19(6), 47-64.
8. Louise Fawcett, (2004). "Exploring Regional Domains: A Comparative History of Regionalism". *International Affairs*, 80(3), 429-46.
9. M. Castells, (2005). "Communication, Power and Counter-

Power in the Network Society". *International Journal of Communica-tion*, 9(2), 238-66.

10. H. Haveem, (1997). *op.cit.*
11. J. Grieco, (1988). "Realist Theory and the Problem of International Cooperation: Analysis with an Amended Prisioner's Dilemma Model". *The Journal of Politics*, 50(3), 60024.
12. D. S. Krasner, (2006). "Sharing Sovereignty: New Institutions for Collapsed and Failing States". *International Security*, 29(2), 85-120.
13. W.R. Cox, (1933). "Gramsci, Hegemony and International Relations: An Essay in Method". *Millennium-Journal of International Studies*, 12(6), 162-75.
14. A. Acharya & Buzan, B. (2009). *Non-Western International Relations Theory: Perspective on and Beyond Asia*. New York: Routledge Publication.
15. M.S. Walt, (1983). *International Relations: One World Many Theories. Foreign Policy*. Retrieved from http://www.jstor.org/stable/1149275?seq=1#page_scan_tab_contents.
16. C. Alvares, (2011). "A Critique of Eurocentric Social Science and the Question of Alternatives". *Economic and Political Weekly*, xlv(22), 72-81.
17. A. Mukherjee, (2013). "Challenges to the Social Sciences in the 21st Century: Some Perspective from South". *Economic and Political Weekly*, XL(37), 1-9.
18. Ibid.
19. A. Loomba, (2005). *Colonialism/Post colonialism*. New York: Routledge.
20. Ibid.
21. D. Chakrabarty, (2008). *Provencializing Europe: Postcolonial Thought and Historical Differences*. Princeton: Princeton University Press.
22. A. Nandi, (1988). *The Intimate Enemy: Loss and Recovery of Self under Colonialism*. Oxford: Oxford University Press.
23. G.C. Spivak, (2005). "Scattered Speculation on the Subaltern and the Popular", *Postcolonial Studies*, 8(4), 475-81.
24. Ibid.
25. Ibid.
26. A. Appadorai, (1985). *India's Foreign Policy and Relations*. New Delhi: South Asian Publication.
27. J. Nehru, (1946). *The Discovery of India*. New York: The John Day Company.
28. M. Pilgrim, (1980). "The Origins of Third World Alliance". *Third*

World Quarterly, 2(2), 366-74.

29. A. Deshpande, (2006). "Revisiting Nehruvian Idealism in the Context of Contemporary Imprealism". *Economic and Political Weekly*, XLV(52), 5405-13.
30. A. Sen, (2005). *The Idea of Justice*. London: Penguin.
31. S. Seth, (2011). "Postcolonial Theory and the Critique of International Relations". *Journal of International Studies*, 40(1), 167-83.
32. S. Tharoor, (2012). *Pax Indica: India and the World of 21st Century*. New Delhi: Penguin.
33. Ibid.
34. Ibid.
35. V. Paul, (2005). "Soft Balancing in the Age of U.S. Primacy", *International Security*, 30(1), 46-71.
36. Ibid.
37. D. Nayyar, (2014). "The West and The Rest in the World Economy: the Next Transformation". *Economic and Political Weekly*, L(5), 1-11.
38. Ibid.

11

Analyzing India and Central Asia Relations

Challenges and Opportunities

Mohammad Janesar

Introduction

Central Asiahas including the five erstwhile Soviet Union countries namely Kazakhstan, Turkmenistan, Uzbekistan, Tajikistan and Kyrgyzstan has emerged as a new area of studies after the end of the cold war. Its geographical location, mineral resources, oil and natural gas, potential to generate hydroelectricity, and so on make this region a battle ground for major powers like the USA, Russia, China and some adjoining states. Since its independence, India is also struggled to take advantage of this resource rich region. Since then, India is seen to have made notable efforts to engage with Central Asia. During the decade of 1990's, India initiated pragmatic and coherent foreign policy strategy to tap the opportunities provided by these regions. The "Look North Policy" (LNP) of India in the 1990's is the standing example of this. During a visit to Turkmenistan in September 1995, the then Prime Minister, P.V. Narasimha Rao, made it amply clear that 'for India', Central Asia is an area 'of high priority, where we aim to stay engaged far into the future.

Source- http://www.civilsdaily.com/blog/india-central-asia-relations/

We are an independent partner with no selfish motives. We only desire honest and open friendship and to promote stability and cooperation without causing harm to any third country.[1] Ironically, despite that India did not give much priority to this strategic neighbor as compared to other regions. In fact when the world powers were engaged and fighting for their interest in Central Asian Republics (CAR), India keeps away from the region under the guise of economic downturn facing the nation at that time. Once again, in 1997 India laid down a new foreign policy, popularly called as "Gujral Doctrine", with neighbors and extended neighbors on the top of India's agenda which also assimilated the Central Asian Republics (CAR). CAR are India's extended neighbors. Still Indian government and diplomats failed to keep their footprint in this region. Although, the Indian Government under UPA regime took the initiative to remain engaged with CAR through its

"Connect Central Asia" policy, it had literally no strategy and vision to work out that policy to realize it in practice.

However, India's contemporary engagement with the region is through Connect Central Asia policy. In fact, since the Independence of these countries, India is steadily growing their relations and tries to increase its interest in CAR. Central Asian countries, for their part have provided ample opportunities for India in the field of market, economy, trade and energy security. Now it is time for India to plan how to grab these opportunities. Notwithstanding the opportunities, Central Asian region is also a challenge for India's security and interests. Its neighboring countries Afghanistan and also Pakistan are considered as most unstable and vulnerable countries in the world. Pakistan (fourth globally) and Afghanistan (sixth) are considered as highest risk countries in the world according to the "Human Rights Risk Atlas 2014" released by a global analytical organization.[2] India firmly believed that peace and stability in Afghanistan is the primary objective to constructively engage with CAR.

India's Foreign Policy towards Central Asia

India keeps good, warm and friendly relations with these newly independent countries since antiquity. India has developed strong cultural, historical and trade ties which is now called as India's strong soft power presence in these regions. India's relations got momentum after the end of cold war that is when Central Asian countries secededfrom the erstwhile Soviet Union in 1991. India was among the first countries to recognize these five countries as sovereign and independent. India instantly established diplomatic relations with all of the five Central Asian Republics. Earlier in the decade of 1990s India faced a lot of problems in the field of economic front. Hence India did not give much importance to Central Asia as compared to other regions like South East Asia (Look East Policy) and Middle East. After middle of 1990s, India increasing economic growth due to liberalization, privatization and their consequences as a Globalization policy (LPG) pushed India to search for new marketto fulfill her energy demand. Since then, India has been considering Central Asiaas a valuable place in this field. As a result, India initiates several coherent and imperative policies towards CARs such as India's Look North Policy towards Central Asia and extended neighborhood policy, later developed into Connect Central Asia Policy. Extended Neighborhood policy has become an umbrella policy for India to engage North, East, South and Westward countries apart from her immediate neighbors. The region beyond South Asia or immediate neighborhood, considered as India's extended neighbor, stretches from the Suez Canal to the South China Sea and includes within it West Asia, the Gulf, Central Asia, South East Asia, East Asia, the Asia Pacific and the Indian Ocean Region. This strategic and comprehensive policy was pushed by NDA (National Democratic Alliance) regime under Atal Bihari Vajpayee's government of 1998-2004, which quickly announced "Our concerns and interactions go well beyond South Asia. They include other neighbor and countries immediately adjoining this region- our extended neighborhood".[3]

Later, in 2012 India took an assiduous policy towards Central Asia and unveiled it in the name of "Connect Central Asia policy". This comprehensive policy was led by UPA-II (United Progressive Alliance) government steered by Prime Minister Dr. Manmohan Singh, and announced by former Minister of State for External Affairs late Edappakath Ahmad (E. Ahmad) in June, 2012 during first Track II meeting of the India-Central Asia Dialogue in Bishkek, the Kyrgyz capital[4]. Contemporary Relation between India and Central Asia is based on these broad based and multidimensional approaches which include various elements to strengthen the cooperation with Central Asian region. It covers relation on Security, Economic, Strategic and cultural fronts. Its salient features include—

- High level visits in each other countries;
- Comprehensive economic engagement;
- Strategic partnership between India and Central Asian countries;
- Partnership in the development of energy and natural resources;
- Cooperation in the field of education;
- Land connectivity
- Development of potential in medical fields and
- E-networks

Despite this comprehensive foreign policy, India's trade volume with CAR countries are very low as compared to other countries. In fact Connect Central Asia Policy focused on and calls for setting up universities, hospitals, IT centers, e-network in telemedicine, joint commercial ventures, improving connectivity to boost trade and tourism, defense and strategic cooperation and joint scientific research, but India is still far away from China in Central Asia in all fronts. China has built roads, railways, and pipelines across the Central Asia through its massive One Belt One Road (OBOR) project. However, India has now become a full member of SCO which we have to see as to how India uses this platform to gain deeper access to Central Asia.

India's Opportunities in Central Asia

Relations with Central Asia for India pose great challenges and opportunities. India has great opportunity to link with these energy and natural resources rich countries.

Central Asia Republics have Uranium, Oil and Gas and other natural resources. Central Asia has also great strategic importance for India due to its geographical location. Central Asia is a buffer zone between two nuclear power states, Russia and China and two extended nuclear power states India and Pakistan. These five countries are also situated between great civilizations and it is a linchpin between Asia and Europe. They are landlocked and some countries are double land landlocked. They are also important in terms of security because of its neighbor Afghanistan is a victim of terrorists and some of the banned terrorist organization using Central Asia as a hiding place. These situations provided great opportunities as well as challenges for India to engage with these regions.

India's Opportunity in the Field of Energy Security

Economic developments of countries are largely dependent on an adequate and constant supply of energy resources. Most of the countries are facing these problems and lack of energy turn a nation into poverty and underprivileged status. Hence, energy security is the lifeline of economic development. The International Energy Agency (IEA) defines energy security as "the uninterrupted availability of energy sources at an affordable price." In fact lack of energy is thus linked to negative economic growth and social impacts.

It was energy during the decade of 1990s that pushed India to focus on Central Asia the neglected region (CAR) in the world. Central Asia has abundance of energy in terms of oil, gas, uranium and hydroelectricity. Conversely, India is energy hungry and energy deficit country and facing energy crisis due to fast rate of economic growth and growing population. India is the fourth largest energy consumer in the world after China, USA and Russia.[5] India is amongst the top ten biggest energy consuming countries account for over 60 per cent of world's total primary energy consumption based on annual consumption 2013.[6] The importance of India's energy demand is reflected in an interview of former Prime Minister of India Dr. Manmohan Singh with *Financial Times* in 2004, "Energy security is second only in our scheme of things to food security." Indian economy is fastest-growing economy in the world. GDP (Gross Domestic Product) annual growth rate in India averaged 6.2 per cent from 1951 until 2017, reaching an all time high of 11.40 percent in the first quarter of 2010 and a record low of -5.20 percent in the fourth quarter of 1979.[7]

India GDP Annual Growth Rate

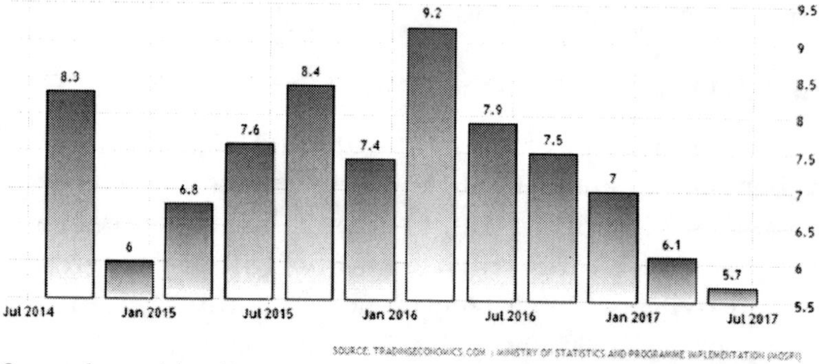

Source: https://tradingeconomics.com/india/gdp-growth-annual

India is the sixth largest economy by nominal GDP and third largest economy in terms of purchasing power parity (PPP) after USA and China. Indian economy is booming and expected to grow fast in coming years and depends on the energy which is an essential to maintain economic growth. Therefore, in this scenario it is obligatory for India to search and diversify their energy policy to maintain momentum of economic growth high. Approximately 70 to 80 percent of India's energy demand is based on the import from other countries and mostly from the Middle East. Middle East is a most volatile region in the world which led India to think of new areas for their energy demand and Central Asia can play a significant role in India's energy requirement. Kazakhstan, the largest and most developed country in Central Asia is largest producer of Uranium. According to the world nuclear organization, over two-thirds of the world's production of uranium from mines is from Kazakhstan, Canada and Australia. Kazakhstan produces the largest share of uranium from mines (39% of world supply from mines in 2016), followed by Canada (22%) and Australia (10%).[8] Uranium is used as a fuel to generate nuclear energy, the most powerful energy in the world. India produces scanty nuclear energy as compared to other developed countries with a shareof only 3 per cent in India's energy basket. India keeps target to supply 25 per cent of electricity from nuclear power by 2050.[9] As of 2016, India has 22 nuclear reactors in operation at eight sites and five more nuclear reactors are under construction.[10] To fulfill India's energy demand and to achieve 25 per cent electricity production from nuclear power by 2050, it needs to purchase more uranium from other countries. Hence, India signed a number of nuclear agreements to purchase uranium and Kazakhstan is among those countries. Despite India's being outside of NPT (Nuclear Non Proliferation Treaty), a number of countries signed a nuclear deal with India because of its credibility in non-proliferation and expertise in the field of nuclear technology.

India and Kazakhstan signed a nuclear deal in Kazakhstan capital Astana during an official visit to Kazakhstan by former Indian Prime Minister Dr. Manmohan Singh in 2011. It was based on the Memorandum of Understanding (MoU) signed in 2009 by two the leaders, former PM of India Dr. Manmohan Singh and President of Kazakhstan Nursultan Nazarbayev during a visit by

Nazarbayev as chief guest on India's Republic Day. This agreement was signed between Kaz Atomprom (Kazakhstan uranium mining company) with Nuclear Power Corporation of India Limited (NPCIL). Their agreement came to an end in 2014 and further both countries extended the agreement when Indian Prime Minister Narendra Modi visited Kazakhstan in 2015 and signed five contracts including a contract with uranium mining company Kaz Atom Prom with India's Department of Atomic Energy to supply 5000 tons of uranium over the next four years (2015-2019).

Apart from nuclear deal, India has also opportunities for ties with these regions in the field of gas, hydroelectricity and shale gas technology. Hence, India signs a quadrilateral agreement with Tajikistan, which is called as TAPI projects referring to Turkmenistan, Afghanistan, Pakistan and India. TAPI will transport natural gas from the Caspian Sea via Turkmenistan through Afghanistan to Pakistan and finally India. Initially it was signed between Pakistan and Turkmenistan in 1995, India joined later while India-Pakistan-Afghanistan signed an agreement to buy natural gas from Turkmenistan. It is supported by Asian Development Bank (ADB) and expected to export about 33 billion cubic meters of natural gas per year up to 30 years. Unfortunately this long route pipeline (estimated to cover 18, 000km) project did not materialize due to several security and reluctant policy of participating countries. Security is a prime hurdle which delayed this project. TAPI gas pipeline will pass through a high risk area wherenumber of districts in Afghanistan are prone to terrorist attacks. The gas pipeline passes through both Pashtun and Baloch dominated regions where the drug trafficking is widespread. The strained relations between India and Pakistan isalso a factor to delay this project. Pakistan is also considered a "very high risk "country according to Aon Risk Maps (AON) report 2017, a risk management services provider company.[11]

India has also developed a cordial and warm relation with Uzbekistan, Tajikistan and Kyrgyzstan in the field of energy sector. Uzbekistan which is rich in gas, invites GAIL (Gas Authority of India Limited) to explore oil and shale gas. During the former Prime Minister of India Dr. Manmohan Singh's State visit to Uzbekistan in May, 2011, 34 agreements were signed on different and wide of range issues. Uzbekistan also offered shale gas technology to India for prospecting in Assam, Gujarat, and some coastal areas.[12] GAIL, the largest public sector natural gas processing and distribution company with Maharatna status also is working and has established an LPG plant in Uzbekistan in 2006. GAIL set up LPG plant along with Uzbek nefte gaz (UNG), which is Uzbekistan's largest public sector natural gas company. India is also engaged with Tajikistan and Kyrgyzstan since their break up from Soviet Union. Both countries are underdeveloped in the Central Asian region, but keep potential for generating hydroelectricity. Tajikistan possesses 4 percent of the world's hydro-power resources. India has strong incentives to engage with these countries particularly Tajikistan, which is vital for India in terms of energy as well as security due to its geographical proximity. In 2009 Tajikistan President Emomali Rahmon invites Indian businessman and express the readiness to open for India businessmen to explore possibilities of investing in hydro-power projects. During the visits of Tajikistan President Emomali Rahmon to India in August 2006, India committed approximately $20 million grants for the modernization of Varzob-1 hydropower station through Indian companies Bharat Heavy Electricals Limited (BHEL), which was built in 1936.This project was completed in 2013 and the plant now generates hydroelectricity.[13] In 2012 BHEL signed Memorandum of Understanding (MoU) with Tajikistan to set up a 100MW hydro electric power project plant on Zeravshan River in Tajikistan. In Tajikistan BHEL has earlier commissioned a hydro generator for Pamir-1 project in Khorog.[14] India's led project has been established mostly in the district of Varzob, Khojent and Kulyab in Tajikistan.

Kyrgyzstan has also rich potential to generate hydroelectricity. Kyrgyzstan is also rich in unexplored natural resources like coal, gold, rare earth metals etc. India is trying to strengthen the ties and cooperation with Kyrgyzstan for energy security.

India's Opportunities in the Field of Economic, Trade and Commercial Sector

In fact Central Asia provides great opportunities in the field of energy security but apart from energy resources these regions also provide great opportunities in the field of economy, trade, commerce and more important as a market. We know that India is a fastest growing country and has largest human resources in the world. Central Asian countries are also growing and now these regions opened their markets for external powers as well. India and Central Asia's trade, commercial and economic ties had existed since ancient times. It was the region through which traders passed on their way from India, China and vice-versa. In spite of India's greater historical or traditional engagement with these regions in the field of culture, trade and commerce, in contemporary era, India is lagging behind as compared to other countries in the field of economic and trade with Central Asia. India's current economic footprint is lagging behind with China (competitor of India) as well as Russia. India's current trade with Central Asia is estimated at a modest $2 billion, which pales in comparison with China's $50 billion.[15] Hence, it is time for India to expand or enhance their economic footprints in Central Asia, were India is ignored since long time.

India needs to increase their investment in Central Asia, which needs a coherent and pragmatic approach and it could be also increased through proper institutional mechanism. In particular, Indian coffee, tea, spices and pharmaceutical industries have acquired a strong grip in Central Asian untapped market. There are a great potential and demand of Indian Information Technology Industries, services mostly education and training, banking, constructions, and food processing industries as well as Indian small and medium enterprises in Central Asia. Although, some of the banks have set up their branch in Kazakhstan like Indian Bank and Punjab National Bank (PNB) subsidiary,[16] but there is need to open branches of the Indian Bank at least in the capital city of each Central Asian Countries.

Former Vice-President of India, Hamid Ansari on his visit in April, 2013 to Tajikistan agreements were signed to saw the shining of the deals to enlarge bilateral cooperation in IT, Energy, Health, Education, Trade, Commerce, Mining and Agriculture. The Indian Vice-President also inaugurated India-Tajikistan modern engineering workshop in Tajik Technical University for creation of a centre of IT excellence.[17] Recently, in July 2015, Indian Prime Minister visited all five Central Asian Countries. During this visits Prime Minister signed five agreements with Kazakhstan that include sectors such as defence, railways and uranium supply.[18] Kazakhstan is the largest economic partner of India in Central Asia and provide huge potential in the field energy and defense sector which India has great demand.

Some of the other potential areas of cooperation for India could be the mining sector, vehicles, electronic machinery and equipments, cotton production and textile industries, seeing that the Central Asian regions have abundant of mineral resources such as copper, gold, uranium and silver. India has great domestic demand of gold as well as other mining resources. Further, cotton and textile industries are also assets for Indian investment, particularly in Uzbekistan, which is the world's 6th largest cotton producer and the second largest exporter of cotton after the United States.[19] In addition, Tajikistan acquires more than 4 per cent of world's hydropower generation, which provides profitable area of investment for Indian electrical companies.

Challenges for India in Central Asia

In fact, Central Asian countries provide lots of opportunities and the region is full of energy as well as mineral resources and their geographical location offers to a large extent grounds for wide-ranging engagement with the region. But the region also poses some numerous challenges for India such as connectivity, security and strategic environment, which need to be addressed.

Connectivity Challenges

Central Asian countries are landlocked and some of them are doubly landlocked countries. As usual it seems that those countries which are near the seas get favorable conditions for trade and commerce. But in spite of being land locked countries, Central Asian Republics (CARs) managed to develop their economy smoothly by constructing roads, highways, railways, gas and oil pipelines. These infrastructure developments link Central Asian markets with East to West and South to North.

The fact of being landlocked condition of the Central Asia poses a challenge for India in integrating its economy with these emerging markets. Additionally, China and Pakistan which are immediate neighbors of Central Asia create a connectivity barrier for India. Both countries are India's immediate adversary, who consistently strives to push India out of Central Asia. Notwithstanding this, Indian government has taken an alternative route via Iran to develop its economy with these countries as well as some of the Eurasian economies such as Azerbaijan. For this reason, India, Iran and Russia signed a multimodal connectivity (ship, rail and road) transport project, International North-South Transport Corridor (INSTC) in 2000. The project was signed by these three nations in St. Petersburg which later expanded to include eleven new members including Kazakhstan, Kyrgyzstan, Tajikistan, Azerbaijan, Armenia, Turkey, Ukraine, Belarus, Oman, Syria and Bulgaria (observer).[20] The INSTC project provide great opportunity for India to link its economy with these countries. The INSTC project will reduce the transporting cost from India to Eurasia and adjoining nations, for the reason that it provides shorter route than the existing route.

In spite of INSTC project, India is also developing Chabahar port in Iran. India and Iran have signed this long-standing agreement in 2000 along with INSTC project. It is seen as a strategic port to counter Chinese development of Gwadar port in Pakistan while India is developing it with benign intentions as it will bypass Pakistan route towards Central Asia and Afghanistan. It is a crucial project as Pakistan does not allow India to send goods to Afghanistan and Iran through its territory by land. In view of that, Iran and India inaugurated first phase of this strategic port in December, 2017.

Security and Strategic Challenges

Central Asia is significant and crucial for India not only in terms of energy security, economic and market access but also for national security as well. It is located next to the world's most unstable region. These regions are situated on the brink of areas extremism and terrorism and India sees the region as a source of religious extremism and terrorism and concerned about it seriously. Some of the banned terrorist organizations are much more active in the regions such as Hizbut-Tahrir and Islamic Movement of Uzbekistan. The region faces a number of internal as well as external threat due to its proximity with war-torn Afghanistan and state sponsored terrorism from Pakistan. Hence, any destabilization situation in Afghanistan could spill over in the vast hinter land, which could jeopardize India's security calculus in the region. Hence, India is much concerned about the situation in Afghanistan. Since the disintegration of Soviet Union, Central Asian region has become a fertile ground for terrorist groups. The transnational nature of these groups, including links with the Taliban and other militant groups in neighboring countries has generated a high degree of insecurity for India. The fear is that if the emergences of *jihadist* groups are not checked, they will eventually pose a serious threat to India's security, especially in the state of Kashmir.[21] Hence, peace and stability in Central Asia as well as in Afghanistan are the prime objectives to India and for that India is ardent to play a bigger role on Central Asia's security chess board. India has striven to prevent these real and perceived threats to its national security. In view of that, India and Tajikistan, which are closest to each other, signed a counter terrorism agreement in December, 2008 and both countries agreed to deepen their engagement to deal with the threat of terrorism and radicalism in the neighborhood especially in Afghanistan and called to end sponsorship, support and provision of safe havens and sanctuaries to terrorists.[22] India and Kazakhstan committed to follow the secular policies and to counter the dividing forces such as fundamentalism, extremism and terrorism.

India also endeavors to drive out these common threats through SCO (Shanghai Cooperation Organization). SCO is a regional or intergovernmental organization, the creation of which was announced on 15th June, 2001 in Shanghai (China) by the Kazakhstan, China, Kyrgyzstan, Russia, Tajikistan and Uzbekistan. It was preceded by the Shanghai Five mechanism. SCO has comprehensive goals and objectives fight against three evils—terrorism, separatism and extremism. It is among the first intergovernmental organizations to explicitly advocate the fight against these three evil forces in the region. On 15 June 2001, on the day which the SCO was constituted, the Shanghai Convention on Combating Terrorism, Separatism and Extremism was signed. Subsequently, the Regional Anti-Terrorist Structure (RATS) was established by the member states, based in Tashkent (the capital of Uzbekistan). India along with Pakistan became a full member of it in June, 2017. Highlighting India's concerns, Prime Minister Narendra Modi said India's arrival into the organization would boost the fight against terrorism. He said, "Terrorism is a major threat to humanity. I have full confidence that the India-SCO cooperation will give a new direction and strength to the fight against terrorism."[24]

Central Asia is also victim of drug trafficking and high rampant corruption which make more complicated the security dynamics and challenges for world powers as well as India to prevent this condition. The regions face serious threat from illegal drug trade emanating from Afghanistan. In fact corruption is everywhere and Central Asia is no exception. There is a direct nexus between corruption, drug trafficking and terrorism. Week border management and failure to prevent drug trafficking and its production in Afghanistan have made drug trafficking an extremely lucrative industry. The money generated by this industry provides a vital source of funding for terrorist groups. It raises money for militant activities, small time criminals and organized crimes. Central Asian countries are situated on the cross roads of "Golden Crescent". This is also called the silk route of drugs. This is a mountainous area of Iran, Afghanistan and Pakistan where opium has been grown for hundreds of years.[25] This area is also a main source of supply of heroin into Russia and Europe. This is the route through which drugs are making their way into northern Indian mostly in Punjab, Haryana and Rajasthan. Heroin, poppy husk, opium and synthetic drugs are the four kinds of drugs entering India. [26]

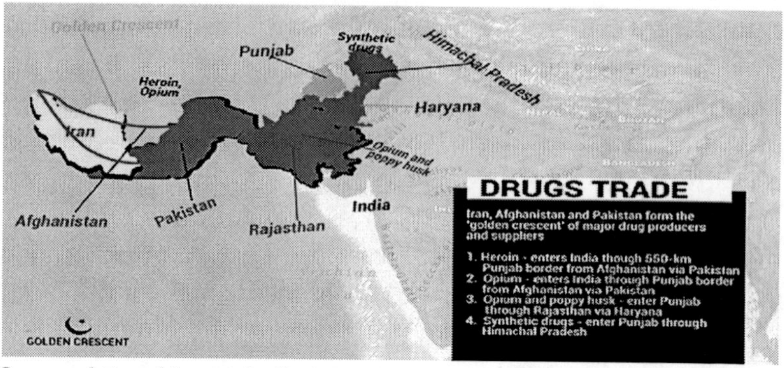

Source- https://www.indiatimes.com

That is a reason, India is impatient to play firm role in Central Asia security chessboard and prevent perceived and real threat to its national security.

Proliferation of Weapons of Mass Destruction (WMD) is another challenge for world powers as well as India in Central Asia. The location of Central Asia is unique. Due to its location between two immediate nuclear power states, China and Russia and then after two other nuclear power states, India and Pakistan make it unique and gives a special strategic position in the world. Earlier, Central Asia was an important instrument of raw material base for the Soviet Union weapons program. Kazakhstan has 12% of the world's uranium resources. It is among the world leading producer country in the world.[27] Kyrgyzstan has sizeable amount of nuclear waste scattered around. Further, Uzbekistan and Tajikistan have substantial amount of uranium reserves. Due to the high corruption, lack of political will, weak border management and absence of special detective equipment, the region have become a lucrative route for smuggling fissile material. The security implication is critical as there is latent danger of proliferation of WMD into the hands of not just states antagonistic to India, but also non state actors like Al-queda, Taliban and IMU. It possess a potential thereat for international community as well as India, which requires multilateral response to prevent this acute and perceived threat.[28]

Conclusion

Central Asia is strategically located as an access between Europe and Asia. The regions provide extensive potential for trade, investment and economic growth. The region is also endowed with ample natural resources such as oil and gas, uranium, gold, cotton and so on. Hence, there is a great opportunity for India to engage with these regions, although, region has been also considered as unstable and vulnerable due to its borders with Afghanistan and immediate neighbor Pakistan. Afghanistan shares boundaries with Tajikistan, Uzbekistan and Turkmenistan. As a result, India's security interests have stakes in the region. Hence, security and stability of a region is prime objective of India.

Shanghai Cooperation Organization (SCO) led by China is a main security providing institution in the region. India has become a full member of this organization in 2015 along with Pakistan. India should need to use this platform diplomatically to fight against its biggest and perceived threat posed by terrorist and extremist groups in that region.

This is a common challenge for all the members of these groups. Interestingly, Pakistan has also become a full member despite its role to play a proxy war against India. Furthermore, China is attempting to project its power in the region through the conduct of joint military exercises with CAR under the SCO platform. This has not gone unnoticed by India. Although, as far as security challenge is concerned, India has taken it seriously in the last few years and established Joint Working Group (JWG) on combating international terrorism with Uzbekistan, JWG with Tajikistan on counter-terrorism and a JWG on international terrorism and other types of crimes with Kazakhstan.[29]

To cope with security threats emanating from the Central Asian Region, India should develop strategic and defense cooperation with all of the countries in Central Asia. Contemporary India has developed strategic relations with only Kazakhstan but other countries like Tajikistan are also strategically important for India due to geographical location. India has developed defense and military cooperation with Uzbekistan, Kazakhstan and Tajikistan. India also signed an agreement on training and exchange program of military personnel with CAR. India has purchased six Uzbek manufactured IL-78 air-to-air refueling aircraft in 2003 for use by the Indian Air Force.[30] Interestingly India is growing in indigenous defense industry but still CAR regions remain a relatively untapped for indigenous defense industry of India. India should need to focus on those issues.

The realization of various policies taken by Indian government in the past, demands not only heavy investment in this area but also long-term and sustained implementation of various ongoing projects. On the trade and economic fronts, India should focus and convince private sector to invest in Central Asian market, which has so far not been viewed by Indian business group as very attractive market.

For that India should frame coherent and specific policies. India has largest software industry in the world and is among economically growing counties hence India should utilized its strength in information technology, banking and small and medium-scale enterprises to strengthen its relations with Central Asia.

Notes

1. Ramakrushna Pradhan, (2015, July 11). "India's Soft Power in Central Asia: Why it Must Act on the Look North Policy". *Mainstream Weekly*, LIII (29).
2. (2013, December 5). "HR: Pakistan placed among 'high risk' countries". *Dawn*. Retrieved from http://www.down.com/news
3. David Scott, (2009). "India's 'Extended Neighborhood' Concept: Power Projection for a Rising Power", *India Review*, 8:2, 107-143, https://doi.org/10.1080/14736480902901038
4. M. Feyaz. (2016, December 23). "Is India Finally Getting Serious About Its Connect Central Asia Plans?" *The Wire*. Retrieved from https://thewire.in
5. Praveen Daddu. (2014, November). *Energy gluttons- the world's top 10 energy consumers*. Retrieved from https://www.hydrocarbons-technology.com
6. Ibid.
7. Joana Taborda. (2017, November 30). *India GDP Annual Growth Rate*. Retrieved from https://tradingeconomics.com/india/gdp-growth-annual
8. World Nuclear Association. (2017, July). *World Uranium Mining Production*. Retrieved from https://www.world-nuclear.org/information-liberary/nuclear-fual-cycle/mining-of-uranium/world-uranium-mining-production.aspx
9. Ibid.
10. European Nuclear Society. (n.d). *Nuclear power plants, world-wide*. Retrieved from https://www.euronuclear.org/info/encyclopedia/n/nuclear-power-plant-world-wide.htm
11. Aon Risk Solution. (n.d). *2017 Risk Maps Aon's guide to Political Risk, Terrorism & Political Violance*. Retrieved from https://www.aon.com/2017-political-risk-terrorism-and-political-

violance-maps/pdfs/2017-Aon-Risk-Maps-Report.pdf

12. Sandeep Dikshit, (2011, May 18). "India to Prospect for oil, gas in Uzbekistan". *The Hindu*. Retrieved from https://www.thehindu.com/news/national
13. Avaz Yuldoshev, (2013, January 11). *Modernization of Varzob-1 HPP completed. Asia-Plus.* Retrieved from https://www.news.tj/en/news
14. Siddhartha P. Saikia. (2017, November 17). "BHEL to set up 100-MW hydro power station in Tajikistan". *Business Line*. Retrieved from https://www.thehindubusinessline.com
15. T.K. Vineeth, (2017, December 4). "India set to tap central Asian market via Chabahar". *The New Indian Express*. Retrieved from https://www.thenewindianexpress.com/business
16. Dr. Athar Zafar. (2015, July 9). *India-Central Asia: Finding New Synergies for Greater Engagment*. Indian Council of World Affairs. Retrieved from https://www.icwa.in/pdfs/
17. Jitesh. (2013, April 18). Vice-President of India, Hamid Ansari visited Tajikistan. *Jagran Josh*. Retrieved from https://www.jagranjosh.com/current-affairs/vicepresident-of-india-hamid-ansari-visited-tajikistan
18. Elizabeth Roche. (2015, July 15). Narendra Modi's visit brings Central Asia back in focus. *Livemint*. Retrieved from https://www.livemint.com/Politics/
19. Facts and Details. (n.d). *Cotton in Uzbekistan*. Retrieved from https://www.factsanddetails.com/central-asia/Uzbekistan
20. International North South Transport Corridor. (n.d). *INSTC*. Retrieved from https://www.instc-org.in/Pages/Home Page. aspx
21. Stephen Blank. (2003). "India's Rising Profile in Central Asia". *Journal of Comparative Strategy*, 22:2, 139-157. https://doi.org/10.1080/
22. *General Knowledge Today*. (2016, December 18). *India, Tajikistan ink four agreements*. Retrieved from https://www. currentaffairs. gktoday.in/tags/india-tajikistan
23. The Shanghai Cooperation Organisation. (n.d). Retrieved from https://www.eng.sectsco.org/about_sco/
24. Kallol Bhattacherjee. (2017, June 9). "India, Pakistan become full members of SCO". *The Hindu*. Retrieved from https://www.thehindu.com/news/national
25. Drug Wise. (n.d). *Golden Crescent*. Retrieved from https://www.drugwise.org.uk/golden-crescent/
26. Maninder Dabas. (2016, June 10). "Golden Crescent – The Route Through Which Drugs Are Making Their Way Into Punjab"

Indiatimes. Retrieved from https://www.indiatimes.com/news/india/

27. World Nuclear Association. (2017, January). *Uranium and Nuclear Power in Kazakhstan*. Retrieved from https://www.world-nuclear.org/information-liberary/country-profiles/countries-g-n/kazakhstan.aspx
28. Sophie Henderson. (2017, April 6). "Central Asia: A Nuclear-Terrorism Nexus?" *RUSI*. Retrieved from https://www.rusi.org/commentary/central-asia-nuclear-terrorism-nexus
29. Ministry of External Affairs. GoI. (2017, May 3). 4th meeting of India-Kazakhstan Joint Working Group on Counter Terrorism, New Delhi. Retrieved from https://www.mea.gov.in/press-release.htm
30. Rollie Lal, (2006). *Central Asia and its Asian Neighbors: Security and Commerce at the Crossroads*. RAND Publication.

12

Democratic Assistance

Emerging Dimension of India's Foreign Policy in South Asia

Salma Zafar

Introduction

India is one of the largest, unique and most successful democratic countries. It is unique in the sense that it lacks the structural variables such as class structure, extent of ethnic diversity, level of income, and education—to predict the prospects of a country instituting and remaining a democracy.[1] Even the longevity and strengthening of democracy in India has been admired. Groucho Marx said about India: "It looks like democracy. It talks like a democracy. But don't be fooled by that. It really is a democracy."[2] Therefore, it can be said that "there is a potential for India to become a beacon for democracy, not only through the power of its example but also of the values that it espouses."[3] Through its foreign policy agenda, India can spread its uniqueness of democracy in non-western world by sharing its assistance with other nation-states.

Promoting democratic form of government abroad has always been one of the fundamental objectives of foreign policy of Western powers. India despite being the largest and arguably oldest democracy in the world has kept itself aloof from accepting the role of democracy promoter in its neighborhood as its foreign policy has been guided by respecting sovereignty and autonomy of other states. However, in recent times through its constructive engagement, India has started promoting democracy in its neighboring countries owing to mainly two reasons. Firstly, the change in orientation of leadership; and secondly, perceived threat to its security from political instability in its vicinity. Bhutan, Afghanistan, Nepal and Maldives are some of the few nation states of South Asia which transformed themself into parliamentary democracy from non-democratic regime and wherein India has been assisting them in its democratization process. India has been assisting its neighbors to democratize themselves in various ways such as helping them in formation of new constitution, in conducting elections and so on. These cases are suggestive enough to indicate a shift in India's foreign policy.

India's Foreign Policy: A Reluctant Democracy Promoter

Samuel Huntington in three waves of democratization talks of the spread of democracy among the different regions of the world. The major role of promoting democracy has been the responsibility of western powers namely USA, Britain and France and so on. In the backdrop of cold war, the world was divided into the two parts—one, democratic or capitalist group led by USA and other, communist group led by USSR. Beside this, the western powers through the international institutions such as IMF and World Bank started promoting democracy. Shifting the focus to South Asia, India has been called as 'big brother' by its neighboring countries, where it has been unequivocally identified as the 'regional power'[4] (given its size in terms of its geography, demography and military and economic power). In this regard, the burden lies on the shoulder of India to spread democracy in South Asia. Therefore, where the western powers with the similar situations have most aggressively adopted the principle of promoting and protecting the democracy beyond their national boundary in their foreign policy, India on the other hand has always been the reluctant democracy promoter. It is often said that India has played a marginal role in the recent 'wave' of democratization processes in the South Asian region.[5] The reason behind this are[6]:

Firstly, India who gained independence in 1947 was reluctant to join either communist bloc or capitalist bloc. India's first Prime Minister while framing the "non-alignment" policy (NAM) decided to stay away from either bloc and thus, lays down the principle of India's foreign policy. India hesitated to take part in West's effort of promoting democracy because Indian leaders view it as the extension of the neo-colonial project. It believed that under the guise of promoting democracy western countries intervene into the internal affairs of non-western countries.

Secondly, in order to unite third world countries, India accepted the other forms of government, be it autocratic or monarchy rule in and around its region. It overtly supported the undemocratic regimes of Myanmar and Bhutan. Simultaneously, it compromised on the issues of human rights and democratic freedoms in Sri Lanka in 2009.[7] Besides this, lays the tradition of Indian foreign policy of upholding the principle of non-interference in internal matters in order to help to create the vision of South Asia as an integrated region. This Nehruvian idea was again reinstated by 'Gujaral doctrine' which once again recognized the idea of non-interference in internal matters in their neighboring countries. The undemocratic regime was accepted by India to promote friendly relations with South Asian countries. This can be linked to the next reason that is upholding the principle of non-intervention.

Thirdly, India upholding the principle of sovereignty and non-intervention in the internal affairs of the other countries, demonstrated that promoting democracy beyond its border is not a priority in its foreign policy. The Indian government has not formulated anything like an official democracy-promotion policy.[8] Besides this, there are no prominent actors in India contributing for promoting democracy abroad.

Fourthly, geostrategic and economics interests allowed India to prevent itself from directly supporting democracy. For example in order to ensure smooth access to natural resources led India to completely eschew any kind of statements or actions that may be seen as supporting democracy in West Asian countries.[9] In order to secure its national objectives, India was reluctant to become the beacon of democracy.

Fifthly, democracy within the country is not functioning in a proper way. There has been internal attacks on India's democracy such as case of emergency, Kashmir issues, North-East issues, Khalistan issues and more recently, the restriction on food habits, attack on citizen's right to dissent with government and continued inequality in socio-economic field and continued attack on democratic institutions and so on. All these require India to pay more attention in strengthening democracy at home rather than abroad. Therefore India's limited participation in democracy promotion activities abroad is also explained both in its desire to focus on internal challenges as well as lack of capacity. India is not in a position to 'proselytize' regarding democracy.[10] This internal weakness prevents India from being an active democracy promoter.

Sixthly, India believed that process of democratic transition is never smooth and is best received and accepted when it is initiated by locals. The democratic transformation through the military is injurious to that nation state. Rather than promoting democracy militarily, the world community should assist the pro-democracy supporters by offering statement of support or the financial assistance.[11]

Seventhly, unlike many western countries, India does not have an institutional mechanism that facilitates the task of promoting and supporting democracy abroad.[12] For example there is United States Agency for International Development (USAID), UK's Department for International Development (DFID), and the Canadian International Development Agency (CIDA), while India has no such equivalent agency. Similarly, India has also no civil society organizations and think-tanks like the National Endowment for Democracy (NED), the Carnegie Endowment for International Peace (CEIP) and Freedom House which are devoted to studying and researching democracy worldwide and lobbying for democracy promotion abroad.[13]Absence of such institutional framework hampers the Indian capacity of promoting democracy to other countries.

Eighth, many scholars have highlighted the institutional shortcomings of India's Ministry of External Affairs (MEA) and the Indian Foreign Service (IFS).[14] The problems include the lack of human resources and expertise. Moreover, democracy promotion abroad was not seen as a strong contributor to national security and was not identified as the major foreign policy goals.

Shift in India's Foreign Policy

Since the end of cold war, there has been the major shift

in India's foreign policy. From being the reluctant democracy promoter, India is now taking up the role of assisting democracy. The statements given by some of the Indian leaders and policy makershighlight this shift in foreign policy. Such as[15]—

> "Liberal democracy is the natural order of political organization in today's world. All alternative systems, authoritarian and majoritarian in varying degrees, are an aberration."—Manmohan Singh, Prime Minister (2004-14), Government of India.

> "India is ready to assist in the great transformation of the regional political landscape that are currently evolving in Pakistan, Bangladesh, Nepal, Sri Lanka and Myanmar, and share its experiences on creating a democratic society...."—Jairam Ramesh, Minister of State for Commerce and Industry (2006-2009); Minister of State for Power (2008-2009), Government of India.

> "We don't believe in the imposition of democracy or democratic values of any country. But if there is any interest in any country about our democratic institutions or in the institutions....we are ready to share these...."—Shyam Saran, Foreign Secretary (2004-2006), Government of India.

These statements highlight that India is now being actively involved in supporting and promoting democracy. It hosted the World Movement for Democracy conference in New Delhi in 1999, to support pro-democracy groups in non-democratic countries and to foster transnational links between them and other pro-democracy groups worldwide.[16] India was also a founding member of the Community of Democracies, an inter-governmental organization established in 2000 with the goal of strengthening democracy worldwide by providing support to emerging democracies and civil society.[17] Later on in 2004, countries belonging to the Community of Democracies, organized themselves into the UN Democracy Caucas which aims at promoting a democratic agenda in the UN.[18] It is supported by NGOs who are involved in promoting democracy. In 2005, Global Democracy Initiative (GDI) was launched by India and US with the aim of promoting democracy and development. Both the countries also pledged to encourage and support the UN in its electoral assistance programs, through national capacity building, constitution drafting and providing electoral expertise for transition democracies.[19] Beside this, India and US also launched UN Democracy Fund, which aims at financing those projects that aims at building and strengthening democratic institutions, promoting human rights and ensuring the participation of all groups in democratic processes. [20]

Apart from participating in multilateral efforts, India has also taken the effort to voice its opinion regarding democracy. Such as India along with Australia condemned the 2000 military coup in Fiji and pushed for the British Commonwealth and the Association of Southeast Asian Nations (ASEAN) to suspend bilateral relations until democracy was restored.[21] Fiji, in turn, sought India's help to reinstitute democracy, including assistance with electoral reform.[22] Simultaneously, India supported the ASEAN Regional Forum in recognizing Cambodia's controversial elections in 1998 "as an important step towards enhancing peace and stability in Cambodia."[23] Beside this, India also supported the Commonwealth Ministerial Action Group's decision to suspend Zimbabwe's membership in the intergovernmental organization known as the Commonwealth of Nations due to electoral violence.[24]

All these efforts reflect the shift in India's foreign policy, though still it has not been accepted as the fundamental objective in its foreign policy as has been accepted by Western powers. This is largely because; India has undertaken the role of assisting democracy rather than promoting democracy. It assists the nation state when it is called by country for its assistance.

India's Democratic Assistance in South Asia

South Asiais a region comprising of eight nation states namely—India, Pakistan, Nepal, Bhutan, Afghanistan, Maldives, Bangladesh and Sri Lanka. Out of these eight countries, India is the only stable and democratic country, while all the other nation states are either witnessing a wave of political change or struggling to strengthen their democracy. Except India, almost every country has witnessed the political crisis related to the process of democratization.[25] Analyzing this event of change, S. D. Muni says that "there are different sorts of evolution taking place, but underneath there is a common thread—the search for democracy. People in the region have become far more aware and aspirational. The states are realizing this."[26] These political transformations in its just neighbors have enabled India to take up the new role—that is of assisting democracy.

India, in recent years is not only supporting democracy around the world, rather it has started providing democratic assistance in its neighborhood and largely in its region. India being the largest democracy in the world and oldest in its region and having the vast experience of conducting election at national, state and local level is now ready to disseminate its experience to its neighbors in an indirect form. In countries like Afghanistan, Nepal and Bhutan, India's democratic assistance of India can be witnessed. This is because—

Firstly, the stable and peaceful region will help in the development of the nation states and will bring prosperity in the region. In regard to this, Stephen Cohen said that "India has used to try to manage relations with its neighbors has been 'political transformation'—in other words—

'making them more perfect neighbors' by applauding and, at times, encouraging political reforms seen to enhance stability in the region".[27]

Secondly, it can be stated as of economic development, dynamism, and collective prosperity in the region as a whole.[28] This aims at creating interdependence among the nation states of South Asia.

Thirdly, there is an explicit goal of India, that is, "the limitation of external powers' involvement in what India considers to be its sphere of influence: India wants to have its say in the region".[29]

In case of Afghanistan, India is not only helping the reconstruction of the war destroyed country, but it is also helping the country in creating the condition that will help in facilitating the growth of democracy. India has assisted Afghanistan in construction of its parliament building, training parliamentary members and providing material support during elections, in the form of supplying Electronic Voting Machines (EVMs) and indelible ink (which is applied on voters forefinger to prevent them from multiple voting).[30] Beside this India has also expressed its willingness to share its experience with federalism, village-level administration, affirmative action policies, and women's rights and so on if requested by Afghanistan.[31]

In Bhutan, democracy process was a top-down approach, where the King Jigme Singye Wanchuk put the Bhutan on the path of democracy. Later on in 2006, he gave up his power to his son King Jigme Khessar Namgyel Wangchuk, under whose guidance election to upper house (National Council) of Bhutan's parliament was held in 2007. Later in 2008, an election for lower house (National Assembly) was held and in 2011, local government elections were held. In 2013, another national election was held and Tshering Tobgay, leader of People's Democratic Party (PDP) became the second Prime Minister of Bhutan. This transition of Bhutan has been well assisted by Indian constitutional experts and election commission. India provided assistance such as—conduct of a series of mock elections to prepare electorate for democracy, sending about four thousand EVMs to Bhutan in 2006, inviting Bhutanese election officials by Election Commission of India to witness the conduct of state assembly elections in India and lastly, election related study tours by Bhutanese electoral officers, security officers and observers.[32] Besides this, Bhutan also sought the help of Indian legal experts during the task of drafting a new constitution for the country and a new election bill.[33]

After a long internal struggle, democracy was established in Nepal and India played a substantial role in it. India assisted Nepal in its democratization process between 2005 and 2008. At the informal level, India actively contributed to Nepal's return to democracy and, accordingly, to the abolition of the monarchy. Between 2004 and 2005, India assumed a facilitation role, which allowed for the initiation of a dialogue between Maoist leaders and the SPA, against King Gyanendra.[34] Since 2006, India renders the direct support to Nepal in the establishment of democracy. India also played an important role in promoting the early execution of elections which had been repeatedly postponed.[35]

In Maldives too India helped in assisting democracy. Maldives accepted democracy in 2008 and its Foreign Minister Ahmed Shaheed demanding India's help said that "We want to get India involved in the democratic reform process. India has immense expertise in building of democratic institutions and we want to tap this expertise."[36] Accepting this request, India tripled its aid to the Maldives from $1 million to $3 million in the fiscal year 2007/08 budget and provided training and material assistance.[37]

5. Stake of India

It is a widely held notion that India is a reluctant democracy promoter. Owing to India's reluctance to promote democracy, even western observers worry about the extent to which it will defend and extend the liberal international order.[38] Even some go on to argue that "despite India's growing economic, political and military power, New Delhi is reluctant to take on greater responsibility for upholding that order and for providing global public goods.[39] This has been largely because of its commitment to the principle of non-interference and non-intervention. However, since mid-2000s it has found itself to be widely involved in "democracy assistance" and since then its approach in this area has been growing and evolving.[40] There is the growing consensus among the Indian scholars and policy makers to provide democratic support to a country only after getting invitation by state. Even scholars Mazumdar and Statz are of the opinion that democracy should be delivered under multilateral auspices or under formal state-to-state agreements.[41] Therefore, owing to all these, India's approach towards democracy is called as 'democratic assistance'.

Unlike US and EU, India is not directly involved in promoting democracy. It does this through its NGOs. India's financial contributions to UNDEF have helped to fund 66 NGO-led projects across South Asia (including Afghanistan, Bangladesh, Bhutan, Myanmar, Maldives, and Nepal).[42] Similarly, Indian International Institute of Democracy and Election Management (IIDEM), founded in 2011 with support of United Nations and Commonwealth of Nations highlights the approach taken by India. It includes providing the training to electoral officials on administering voter education and registration, particular voting technologies, and different electoral systems.[43]

This highlights the wider shift in the strategy of India. This is because—

Firstly, it can be said to neutralize the growing influence of China in South Asia. Scholars even argue that India's "new found sympathy for democracy in the region was shaped by concerns about China's growing influence in its neighborhood, reflecting the view that democratic governments may be more capable of withstanding Beijing's entreaties"[44].

Secondly, forming of the strategic partnership with the Western power, particularly US can be the reason. Establishing the strong partnership between Indian policymakers & US helped facilitate the official dialogue on democracy promotion. In the changing scenario of world politics, US and India laid the groundwork for multilateral democracy promotion projects like the Global Democracy Initiative (GDI) announced during the George W. Bush and Manmohan Singh summit.[45] In this regard it is also said that "India's multilateral engagement for democracy as an instrumental attempt to improve its relations with the USA.....rather than a move driven by the genuine endorsement of democracy promotion as a policy.[46]

Thirdly, it views that this will help in strengthening the relationship with the particular country and will give way to India's economic and security concern. The shift in the region of South Asia also helped India to shift its foreign policy. Gradually, India came to believe that a democratic government can better serve its economic and security concerns than non-democratic ones assaid by Muni.[47] Cartwright is also of the view that "India's apparent increasing support for democracy is predicated more on 'realist' political concerns about the country's strategic and economic interests, rather than an idealistic predisposition to supporting the spread of democracy as a goal in and of itself".[48]

Fourthly, it will help India to enhance its status as an emerging power. India participated into the Global Democracy Initiative (GDI) and began to make contribution to the newly formed UN Democracy Fund (UNDEF). In its first year of operation, the contribution of India was even higher than that of the US.[49]

Fifthly, few scholars argued that partial engagement of India to promote democracy is an effort to build and expand its soft power and thereby, to reinvigorate its capacity to act as a kind of "normative power" in international relations.[50] Indian democratic model presents an example before the developing countries of how to manage a large, economically, linguistically and religiously diverse polity. Manmohan Singh, former Prime Minister of India, has once said that liberal democracy is the natural order of political organization in today's world and that India has obligation to history and mankind to show that pluralism works.[51] It reflects the use of democracy as a soft power to attract other nation-states.

6. Conclusion

India is still reluctant to use its democratic model because the Indian policy-makers do not yet see their democracy as a model for other states and therefore, regard democracy promotion as an inadequate tool for generating soft power in competition with China.[52] However, India has adopted a great technique for delivering technical democracy assistance that goes beyond far-fetched interpretations such as those associated with Indian sectoral support in Afghanistan.[53] India's reluctance in establishing democracy promotion as a policy, Destradi is of the opinion that "India has not become a major new actor in democracy promotion". Simultaneously, he also said that "New Delhi's approach to democracy promotion in the future is thus likely to remain characterized by a high degree of restraint and by the primacy of pragmatism in dealing with undemocratic regimes".[54] India is making the effort to support and strengthen the democracy around its region when they are called by neighbors to assist them. Though sometimes, India's democratic assistance has been criticized as based on realist ground as where its national interest collide, it tries to exclude itself from supporting democracy. Despite of all this, it can be said that India continues to provide its democratic assistance to non-democratic countries without accepting democracy promotion an important principle in its foreign policy agenda.

Notes

1. N.G. Jayal & P.B. Mehta, (2010). "Introduction". *The Oxford Companion to Politics in India*. New Delhi: Oxford University Press.
2. Ibid.
3. P.B. Mehta, (2011). "Reluctant India". *Journal of Democracy*, 47(10).
4. Sandra Destradi, (2012). "India as a democracy promoter? New Delhi involvement in Nepal's return to democracy". *Democratization*, 19(2), 286-311.
5. Ibid.
6. Reason are taken from Siddharth Mallavarapu—"Democracy promotion circa 2010: An Indian perspective" in *Contemporary Politics*, Vol. 16, No. 1 (March 2010), pp. 49-61; Pratap Bhanu Mehta, "Reluctant India" in *Journal of Democracy*, Vol. 22, No. 4 (October 2011), pp. 97-109; and C. Raja Mohan, "Balancing Interests and Values: India's Struggle with Democracy Promotion" in *The Washington Quarterly*, Vol. 30, No. 3 (Summer 2007) pp. 99-115.
7. Sandra Destradi, (2012). *op. cit.*
8. Ibid.
9. A. Mazumdar & E. Statz, (2015). "Democracy Promotion in India's Foreign Policy: Emerging Trends and Developments". *Asian Affairs: An American Review*, 42(2), 77-98.

10. Ibid.
11. Ibid.
12. C. Wagner, (2009). *Promotion of Democracy and Foreign Policy in India*. SWP.
13. A. Mazumdar & E. Statz, (2015), *op. cit.*
14. Ibid.
15. Ibid.
16. Ibid.
17. Ibid.
18. Wagner, C. (2009). *op. cit.*
19. A. Mazumdar & E. Statz, (2015). *op. cit.*
20. Ibid.
21. J. Cartwright, (2009). "India's regional and international support for democracy: Rhetoric or reality?". *Asian Survey, 49*(3), 403-428, pp. 417.
22. Ibid.
23. Ibid.
24. Ibid.
25. Ibid.
26. Ibid.
27. Ibid.
28. Sandra Destradi, (2012). *op. cit.*
29. Ibid.
30. A. Mazumdar & E. Statz, (2015). *op. cit.*
31. Ibid.
32. Ibid.
33. Sarin Ritu, (2007). "Thimphu thank-you for India's democracy gift hamper: From poll experts to EVMs". *Indian Express*. See http://archive.indianexpress.com/news/thimphu-thankyou-for-india-s-democracy-gifthamper-from-poll-experts-to-evms/22707/, accessed 10 Feb. 2014. From Mazumdar, A., & Statz, E. (2015). Democracy Promotion in India's Foreign Policy: Emerging Trends and Developments. *Asian Affairs: An American Review, 42*(2), 77-98.
34. Sandra Destradi, (2012). *op. cit.*
35. Ibid.
36. J. Cartwright, (2009). *op. cit.*
37. Ibid.
38. I. Hall, (2017). "Not Promoting, Not Exporting: India's Democracy Assistance". *Occasional Papers*. See http://www.orfonline.org/research/not-promoting-exporting-india-democracy-assistance/#_edn1

39. Ibid.
40. Ibid.
41. Ibid.
42. Ibid.
43. Ibid.
44. Ibid.
45. Ibid.
46. Reference no. 8. From India as a democracy promoter? New Delhi involvement in Nepal's return to democracy by Sandra Destradi
47. I. Hall, (2017). *op. cit.*
48. J. Cartwright, (2009). *op. cit.*
49. I. Hall, (2017). *op. cit.*
50. Ibid.
51. Ibid.
52. J. Faust & C. Wagner, (2010). "India: A New Partner in Democracy Promotion". *Bonn: DIE (Briefing Paper 3/2010).*
53. Ibid.
54. Sandra Destradi, (2012). *op. cit.*

13

Construct of Peace and Security System in Indian Perspective

Sanchana Srivastava

Before 1919, maintaining peace and security was predicated on the world's countries maintaining a balance of power, forming alliances and engaging in individual self defense. Sustenance and maintenance of peace and security has been one in all the chief fundamental issues of human progress since time out of brain. This worry has exaggerated intercalary centrality and desperation inside the a la mode thermo-atomic age, once the men have gained the capacity to crush the globe inside a minute. Not incredibly, this issue has pulled in the eye of peacekeeping scholars. United Nations office has made an enormous writing this respect. Incredibly, be that as it may, they require an open examination into accounts the contemplations of antiquated Indian scholars amid this exchange. This is notwithstanding the very reality that Indian diviners have done profound research into this subject and their reasoning consolidates a decent link for addressing to a la mode issues with respect to every national and universal peace and security. The present paper looks at the association of old Indian information for achieving peace and security at national also at global levels. Before throughing light on old Indian read, it's yet useful to talk briefly about the contemporary discourse with respect to national security.

In this new era as well, collective security has come to mean something more tha Simply the defense of the community against an internal or external aggression. Needless to add, this Indian emphasis on peace has more relevance to day than any time in the past, as there is an overwhelming evidence to show that any kind of nuclear war would not only shatter human civilization as we know it, it would also poison the air and the oceans and render Earth virtually uninhabitable, a charred and ravaged planet, incapable of supporting more than extremely primitive life-forms.

Contemporary dialogue concerning national security typically focuses on transformation of the concept of national security from a slender prism of territorial security to a wider canvas of human security. It is argued that students throughout the conflict perceived the State as associate in international politics with a definite territorial base and sovereign authority while not giving abundant attention to the peoples residing among a State; the tip of the conflict over a decade past publicised a seminal amendment concerning the construct of national security. On the hand, ethnic, linguistic, religious and communal tensions, that were dormant and overlaid with Cold War rivalries and also the earlier colonial dominance over the accumulation, got a bonus by the 'decompression' result of the top of the conflict. At the same time, many newer sources of threat to national security such as population explosion, unplanned urbanisation, disparities in economic opportunities, proliferation of small arms, drug trade, terrorist act and money laundering, migration pressures and environment degradation surfaced once the conflict is over. Finally, the shrinking of the world and data explosion because of the revolution in information technology and globalisation of economy, weakened the boundaries of State and its sovereignty, "ignited identity as a supply of conflict" and increased sub-State teams and their operations.[1] Since the normal idea of security failed to address these new dimensions of security, it is argued that their is necessity for widening the idea of security. Consequently, several students began to move away from the State-centric Realist approach to Liberal theory of negotiation that stresses on imperatives and opportunities of international and regional cooperation. A unilateralist notion of security must take into consideration cooperative security during this study. As threat to national security will come not entirely from a different state, for example conjointly from non-state actors and natural calamities, a much wider notion of security that broadens the character and sources of threat which might referred to as composite or comprehensive security, gained currency during the Cold War.[2]

Certain critiques of the classical Western notion of security went more to suggest that security cannot be restricted to the well-being of the State and should aim at protection and well-being of people and voters normally residing in the State. This idea of security that is centred particularly on the legitimacy of the individual, is understood as human security. The idea of human security or the safety of the individual and humane governance, have gained wide currency, as economic condition and deprivation enlarged the problem of human security within the developing world. Consequently, growing attention is now paid to human dimensions of security. Whereas the list of threats to human security is long, most will be thought-about below seven major categories, namely, economic security, food security, health security, environmental security, personal security, community security, and political security. Cluster identity, security and recognition of personal space or singled out as basic human desires notably in post-colonial Asia and Africa. It is thus argued that the shift from the 'national security' to 'human security' paradigm is of historic importance.

India is one of the world's oldest civilizations. Its society, way of life and thinking has evolved over thousands of years. *Arthashastra* spelt out the strategy for governance and war in 3rd Century BC, long before any civilization had formed a cohesive thought on war and its strategy. There exist wide-ranging concepts and traditions in the realm of strategic and security affairs from ancient times. These include "the realism of Kautiya's *Arthashastra*, the pacifism of Ashoka, the benevolent and enlightened rule of the Guptas and Akbar, which combined power with tolerance, good governance, the creation of friendly neighbourhoods and the hard realism of Aurangzeb and the British colonial rulers." In modern times, India's post-independence strategic thought was influenced by the Nehruvian world view – which was mainly 'cooperative' in nature.

India conjointly faces a variety of non-traditional security issues. One among the key security challenges facing is that of energy security. This basically involves guaranteeing uninterrupted supply of energy to support the economic and industrial activities necessary for sustained economic process. As so much as Asian nation cares, the necessity for energy security emanates from the growing imbalance between the demand for energy and its availability from native sources, leading to accumulated import dependence. Highlight the problem, the former President A.P.J. Abdul Kalam said, "Energy independence needs to be our nations' initial and highest priority".[3] At the moment, India is the sixth largest energy client within the world and was projected to emerge as the fourth largest client after the United States, China and Japan by 2010. Its economy is projected to grow, from 7 to 8 percent over successive 20 years, and in its wake is going to be a considerable increase in demand for oil. For quite a decade, India's energy consumption has moved at a quicker pace than its economy and it seems this trend can continue. Moreover, although India reduces the utilization of oil in its power sector, the demand for oil within the transport sector shows no sign of subsiding. Thanks to stagnating domestic crude production, India imports just about 70 per cent of its oil. Its dependence on oil is growing quickly. The Planet Energy Outlook, printed by the International Energy Agency (IEA), says that India's dependence on oil imports can grow to 91 per cent by the year 2020. Within the last decade, India has emerged as the fourth largest economy of the planet within the purchasing power parity terms. Thus energy security is crucial for sustaining the present growth rates. Within the short term, there seems very little chance of reducing its energy imports. Currently, around 65 per cent of its fossil oil imports are from West Asia and the rest from numerous components of the planet. It has conjointly made efforts to secure oil and gas assets in various parts of the world, from Sudan to Sakhalin.

Recently, the country's Oil and Natural Gas Commission (ONGC) has invested in twenty two countries to pursue exploration, production, pipeline transportation and also the refinening of hydrocarbons. In the long run, India can expect to shift its energy sources from fossil fuels to renewable energy sources like bio fuels, wind, sun and atomic energy. Another crucial security challenge that India faces these days is terrorism. Whereas economic process has resulted in the softening of borders, it's additionally, sadly, enabled several security issues to create dangerous dimensions. The spectre of terrorism is one such development. Post 9/11, terrorist act has moved centre stage within the security discourse. The shadowy non-state actor is currently the new threat, a threat that has gone worldwide. Indians have suffered cross-border terrorist acts for many years. In Jammu and Kashmir, the Pakistan-sponsored terrorist act has paralysed traditional life since the1980s. Consistent with Indian estimates, terrorist acts have claimed 34,000 lives since as well as over 12000 civilans and 18000 terrorists[4]. India has additionally been been concerned with arms and money supply to Naxalites and separatist teams active in India. In addition to India, Liberation Tigers of Tamil Eelam (LTTE) is understood to have trained the United Liberation Front of Assam (ULFA) and Maoists in India and Nepal. Similarly, it's has been reported that Maoists in Nepal additionally work closely with the People's War Group (PWG) of Andhra Pradesh. Coupled to the present issue is the issue of multinational crime networks. Several of those networks aren't strictly criminal however become concerned in Indian politics, providing them with some amount of immunity from Indian enforcement. Further, India is the principal target, and it's tough for it to form common-cause with international partners to handle them, although a number of these networks are prohibited as a result of the 'war on terror'. The most effective identified of those teams is that of Dawood Ibrahim network. Originally a Bombay based criminal enterprise, these days concerned in everything from extortion to terrorist act in India. The network receives active support from Pakistan's disreputable Directorate for Inter-Services Intelligence (ISI), and Dawood Ibrahim himself is understood to be based mostly in urban center and travel on a Pakistani passport. However,

Ibrahim's activities became so widespread that he's currently on North America and United Nations lists of wanted 'global terrorists' for his role in funding and supporting al-Qaeda. All the same, Ibrahim stays in Pakistan and his network is intact. The ancient and non-traditional threats in an exceedingly dynamic world order are coupled to a variety of trans-national criminal enterprises appreciate small arms, narco traffic and money-laundering and are used by the A.Q. Khan network. Small arms trafficking within the region began as a blowback from the civil war in Afghanistan, the most tragic Asian country. However is currently changing into a widespread drawback.[5] This proliferation of small arms is the dynamic character of insurgencies in India, creating additional violence and lesser possibility to resolution. This development, more or less, additionally explains the expansion within the variety of violent rebellions in various parts of the country. The marketplace for weapons is massive and accessible, and has inspired a resurgence of left political theory, that is currently coupled to Nepali Maoists. These networks also are connected to drug-trafficking. India is bracketed by 2 of the world's 3 largest narcotics producing—exporting regions in what is euphemistically named as the 'Golden Triangle' encompassing Myanmar-Thailand-Laos, constituting the foremost supply of illicit diacetyl morphine and narcotic, though it is shown as declining in recent years. India became a transit country (directly and via Nepal) and some, if not the most, of the crime and violence in India's North-eastern region is coupled to the present issue. South Asia is nowadays a transit point for drugs, instead of being a market. However, as India and different South Asian countries prosper, there is a potential for this prosperity to be affected negatively by the illicit trade and governments within the region are ignoring this risk at their peril. Concealment is another activity coupled to those criminal teams. Although originally serving as a means for poor migrant international labour of South Asian origin in West Asia, the alleged *'hawala'* networks became extraordinarily powerful and dangerous. However in contrast to the assorted different trans-national criminal enterprises mentioned earlier, banking system networks came under the scanner of the international community as a result of their links in funding or supporting world terrorist act. Although this is not to suggests that the threat is eliminated, there is bigger international cooperation in fighting these networks. A number of these criminal networks also are thought to have been employed by the Pakistani government and its agencies, particularly the A.Q. Khan network, for Weapons of Mass Destruction (WMD) trafficking. This link between criminal enterprises and arm proliferation makes it notably necessary to develop international cooperation on these problems. Illegal immigration is among the foremost serious non-traditional challenges grappling India. Illegal immigration into the country happens through its large porous border. Bangladesh especially, poses a threat for India, with huge number of immigrating and major difficulties in controlling the flow. Although the seriousness of this drawback is well recognised, it's all the same tough to tackle as a result of it's entanglement in domestic political problems. Consistent with official Indian estimates, there are estimates of fifteen million illegitimate Bangladesh voters in India. Bangladesh after all, refuses to accept the immigrants as Bangladeshi voters. Half-dozen illegal Bangladeshi immigrants could be a vital cause for ethnic conflicts in north-eastern India. Wherever the illegal immigrants shifted they caused the imbalance of ethnic communities, setting off inter-ethnic violence. Illegal immigration has originally become a supply of trans-national criminal enterprises. Indian police and security agencies believe that they are coupled to terrorist acts. However Bangladesh is not the sole problem in India's neighbours. Tens of thousands of Sri Lankan Tamils have fled the fighting in troubled island and settled in India (though, in contrast to the Bangladeshi migrants, the overwhelming majority of those are formally registered as refugees). According to the India's Home Ministry, 278, 480 refugees have entered Indian territory from Sri Lanka since 1983. Because the fighting in Nepal between the Maoists and the government has picked up, many thousands of Nepalese have additionally shifted to India. Should the situation in either of those two countries worsen, India can expect another bout of unwanted population flows into it. The increasing non-traditional maritime threats within the Indian Ocean region also are in the realm of concern. India has a coastal line of 7600kms with an associated exclusive economic zone (EEZ) of over two million km.[6] The island territories fall within the east area, 300 km away from the mainland. The Indian maritime history provides signs of the rising security threats. Piracy notably has been on the increase. The Indonesian waters, Bay of Bengal and Horn of Africa are among the worst affected areas of the globe. The employment of stealthy weapons and increasing violence is especially distressing. Additional worry is that the news that numerous terrorist teams have resorted to maritime terror in the style of hijacking industrial vehicles. The LTTE, especially, has been perpetrator of such acts in the past. Moreover, the suppuration of Al-Qaida operatives in an exceedingly affective operation by January 2002 has diminished the threat from Al-Qaida. On the other hand the use of sea for terror attacks has increased their outreach. The US-launched global Security Initiative (CSI) could be a welcome initiative. Additionally, several of the terrorist organizations have merchant fleet of their own. These ships are registered under the Flags of Convenience (e.g. those registered in Panama, Republic of Liberia or Cyprus) making it nearly impossible to trace them down. To compound it all, the Indian Ocean region has become another theatre for trafficking of drugs from the Golden Crescent and Golden Triangle region in Asia. Most significantly, natural disasters like Tsunami and Hurricanes like Katarina, has brought the disaster management to the forefront of the world, leading us to currently shift gear to a problem that is seldom considered as a security challenge for India, although it is becoming a common occurrence. Over the last 20 years, India's HIV/AIDS infected population has shot up from 2 per cent to 5.1 million. According to the official figures, nearly 100 of India's adult population are currently carrying the deadly virus. The country's aspirations for the long run are going to be severely constraints by the epidemic. The most important negative impact would on demographic. By 2020, it is calculated that 64 per cent of the entire population would be in economically active. However, the common age of the HIV-positive population in India is presently between 25-30 years. A severe epidemic would imply one hundred forty million new HIV cases. Severe infections of HIV cases might result in the country losing virtually a hundred million of its personnel. The socio-cultural impact of such occurrence is going to be vast, while there is no comprehensive knowledge available on the extent of the infection in the military.

Conclusion

The overall construct of peace and security in the Indian perspective has been discussed in the article. A democratic India, with valuable experiences in building a federal multi-ethnic union and with the accompanying security challenges, has to work with other like-minded states to build an equitable, prosperous and secure future through the deepening of multilateral framework even as it takes independent steps to safeguard its security. Traditionally, national security is defined in terms of the ability of a state to protect its interests from external threats. Those interests are broadly defined as territorial integrity, sovereignty and independence of the nation. However in this web of international relations, the threat to security is not necessarily from one nation to another but also from various non-state sources of insecurity. There is a growing debate on the need to expand the traditional notions of security to address the non- traditional threats and so to develop a more comprehensive approach to security. This is mainly because the traditional security paradigm does not address the rapidly growing non- traditional threats to security like, "the struggle for resources embedded in the pursuit of energy, security, environmental degradation, forced migration, international terrorism, insurgency ascendancy of non-state actors in drugs, arms, money laundering and financial crime organization." The main questions that are being asked today are security from what, when, where and how?

Notes

1. Barry Buzan, "Rethinking Security after the Cold War," *Cooperation and Conflict*, Vol. 32, No. 1, 1997, pp. 5-8. 2 Nalini Kant Jha, "Comprehensive Security: A View from South India," in V. R. Raghavan, ed., *Comprehensive Security: Perspectives from India's Regions* (New Delhi: Delhi Policy Group, 2002), pp. 96-100.

   Victor D. Cha, "Globalisation and the Study of International Security," *Journal of Peace Research*, Vol. 37, No. 3, May 2000, pp. 391-403.
2. Muthiah Alagappa, "Asian Practice of Security: Key Features and Explanations," in his, ed., *Asian Security Practice: Material and Ideational Influences* (Stanford, 1998), pp. 624-29.

3. "Address to the nation on the eve of the 59th independenceday-2005"at http://presidentofindia.nic.in/scripts/independence detail.jsp?id=6.
4. *The Financial Express,* August 11, 2005.
   Afsar Karim, "Terrorism and Indian Response" in N.S. Sisodia and C. Uday Bhaskar in *Emerging India, Security and Foreign Policy Perspective*. (IDSA, 2005) p. 332.
5. David Albright and Corey Henderson, "Unravelling the AQ Khan and Future Proliferation", *Third World Quarterly,* Spring 2005.
6. Indian Maritime Doctrine Integrated Defence headquarters, Ministry of Defence, 2004.

14

New India and Legacies of Indira Gandhi

A Critical Analysis of her Contributions

Shaily

Introduction

Idea of "New India" undoubtedly has been floated by the present political dispensation at the Center. It is yet another 'Idea of India' that we have been debating in the recent past. 'Idea of India' is traced since the days of freedom movement and one that emerged from it acquired some shape during the Constituent Assembly debates. However, there are different views about the contemporary view of 'New India' that has emerged in the current climate. According to some it has not come across as one born out of a historical consensus. Rather, it seems to signal a philosophical schism. Those who are on the other side of the spectrum argue that the results of the 2014 elections were not only reflective of the 'anti-incumbency factor' as cycle of electoral fortunes but it was representing a triumph of the real India over the externally imposed 'left-liberal ideal of India'. Overall this newly born idea of 'New India' has contributed more to unsettling than settling many of the age-old problems of India like: hiatus between the rich and the poor, poverty, unemployment, genuine education, crime, criminalization of politics, and politicization of society, community and crime to name but a few.

India is a land of oddities, puzzles, and paradoxes. It is a land of fettered and unfettered capitalism with current system of inheritance which allows those who manage to become rich and to keep their wealth for their progenies. Accordingly, on the one hand children in India are born into wealth with plentiful opportunities for prospering and amassing wealth; whereas on the other hand millions are born into poverty with their chances, for all practical purpose, blighted at birth. Studies have tried to project that the hiatus between the rich and the poor is reducing at a faster rate as a consequence of economic growth of India. However, when one travels across nook and corner of the country the face of real India presents a very bleak picture and at times they are frightening too.

Two important instruments for climbing out of extreme poverty are education (for producing quality human resource) and health (which enables one to work hard and be productive). For education, lesser said is better. Something that can engineer human nature and deliver quality citizen in the service of the state, has been a victim of State's Nelson's eye with a mere 3.8 per cent of GDP allocated for the same. Educational institutions range from "Bakri Niketan", "St. Boris" (ironically expressed where students go with their sacks (bora) to sit in schools) to five star schools (that of Scindhia, Ambani, and other business houses). Health centres are again no different from our 'temples of learning'. Oddities are also there with rich states and financial capital to BIMARU states within the same territorial unit called India.

Poor economic and social development coincided for years with a keenly democratic tradition. Given its social backwardness, the preservation of democracy was a puzzle. Given democracy, its poor economic performance was equally puzzling. Its puzzling again that a country with prolonged subjugation and plunder yet aspiring to be a knowledge society publishes more than 45, 000 newspapers (of which 7, 500 in English language) with nearly 60 percent of literate people; on the other hand China in its proximity with 90 percent of literate population publishes a meagre 2000 newspapers; and America far from it publishes only 1, 500 newspapers having nearly universal literacy. Therefore, India, despite its poverty and illiteracy, is a nation of exceptional readers. Therefore, there must not be any dearth of 'awareness' on part of the common men. It is a unique contradiction and presents a paradox which cannot be explained.

India is again a land of not one but many paradoxes. Its economy is sizzling with revolution in the field of telecommunication industries, growing size and depth of software which are as sophisticated as any other country; on the other hand almost every election is mired with violence, money and muscle, yet democracy is not only thriving but is also getting entrenched and marching forward; it is surrounded by neighbours where democracy deficit is the order of the day, yet India continues to be mother of all democracies. India always aspires to work for restoring democracy in those countries where there is democracy deficit.

It is in this backdrop that Prime Minister Narendra Modi envisioned his 'New India' the meaning of which he made clear in many of his speeches that it is not about reforming India, rather it is about transforming India. This is not new to Indian people as every change in political regime and successive elections for Lok Sabah has flooded the Indian media with many such slogans for mass consumption. Each of these slogans have raised the expectations of people to the hilt as if their 'good days' are in the offing. Later it has only frustrated them. Such high sounding slogans have ranged from 'Garibi Hatao', to 'Shining India', to 'Arriving India' to 'New India'. All these slogans had the same meaning or objectives of transforming India into a 'sovereign, socialist, secular, democratic, republic' where social, economic and political justice prevails, irrespective of caste, creed, religion and gender. However, governance has hardly ever matched political rhetoric. Social cleavages have always remained politician's paradise which they have been exploiting to nurture and nurse their vote bank politics; to put it more precisely power politics.

Undoubtedly, Modi's idea of 'New India' is inherently an antithesis to the Nehruvian 'Idea of India'.[1] It is in sharp contrast to Nehruvian consensus and would cause more harm than benefits if it is a mere façade for transforming India as an economic giant and a developed country. The 'Idea of India' that was based on twin principles of diversity and democracy may suffer an irreversible damage under the idea of 'New India' under such circumstances as it is being claimed by many within the Indian academia and thinking beings. Therefore, it makes it imperative to understand the real meaning and advocacy of Modi's dispensation regarding their idea of 'New India' and then put the things in right perspective as to whether it aims at 'change with continuity' or a complete break with the past? Whether it aims at carrying the legacy of some other Prime Minster if not Nehru; with a new face? This paper is an attempt by author to present the meaning of 'New India' according to present regime and then explore its legacy if any.

Idea of 'New India': Its' Meaning

Immediately after assuming Prime Minister's office Narendra Modi transformed Yojna Ayog (the Planing Commission) into National Institution for Transforming India (NITI Aayog), which he said is a collaborative federal body whose strength is in its ideas rather than in administrative or financial control. The Chief Ministers do not have to come to NITI Aayog for approval of budgets or plans.[2] He took pledge to transform India into 'New India' and spelled out his vision of the same while delivering speech to the governing council of the NITI Aayog. He expressed his opinion that the vision can propel country's economy on a fast-paced track and it could only be realized through the combined effort and cooperation of all States and Chief Ministers. His speech was well in line with his oft-quoted slogan "*sabkasaath, sabkavikas*". He formulated the narrative of 'Team India' to give meaning to this slogan and reiterated that it is collective responsibility of this gathering to envision the India of 2022—the 75th anniversary of independence and see how swiftly they can move forward to achieve the goals.

NITI Aayog has formulated a "15-year vision" to realize the vision of 'New India'—"India 2021-32: Vision, Strategy and Action Agenda" which is a three-tier action plan comprising of a seven-year medium-term strategy and a three-year action agenda as well. It also includes 300 specific action points or 'mantras'.[3] This agenda for the 'New India' has been prepared by the NITI Aayog with inputs from the states. It has generated new hope among the people and that was also articulated by the then Deputy Chairman of NITI Aayog, Arvind Panagaria, that people expect: housing with toilets, electricity and digital connectivity for all; access to two wheelers or cars, air conditioning and other white goods for nearly all; a fully literate population with universal access to healthcare; a much larger and modern network of roads, railways, waterways and air connectivity; a clean India with clear air and water, clean cities and villages.[4]

The range of stories like Resurgent India, Digital India, Inclusive India, Incorruptible India, Investor friendly India, Transformational India, Clean India, Skill India, Transparent India, Transforming India, Emerging India, Caring India and Communicating India are in the process of shaping India as a 'New India' in the Nation-building process.[5] Prime Minister Modi on the occasion of India's 70th Independence Day delivered a short 56 minute addressand urged the citizen of India to sacrifice in different walks of life to create New India. Team India was expected to run for 'New India' by 2022 by which time he promised, the poor shall have pucca houses, access to electricity, healthcare, sanitation and education; farmers income shall double; and there will be ample opportunities for the youth and women and India would be free of scourges such as communalism, casteism and terrorism.[6] The concept of 'New India'is based on the morality along with the Prime Minister's exhortation of shunning the '*Chalta Hai*' attitude and cynicism and adopting New Hope to build 'New India'. He made a remark that "*tantra se loknahin, lok se tantra chahiye*" (Democracy will be driven by people, not the other way round).[8] In order to achieve the goals of 'New India', India needs not only a strong leadership but also responsible citizenry who are committed to the ideals of the constitution. Prime Minister reiterated to citizensthat it is the time for the country to transform from a Positive India to Progressive India. Prime Minister also talked about Lok Shiksha and deepening the bond between people and democracy. Thus the strength of the poor and the aspiration of the middle class will take India to a New Height. The idea of New India is also about equality of opportunity and the decline of feudalism. The Idea of New India is also about confidence in the Indian way. The period 2017-22 will be for creating a 'New India' with same collective will. The Prime Minister said if Quit India slogan was "*Bharat Chhodo*". The sentiment in India should now be 'Bharat Jodo', this makes it quite obvious that Narendra Modi's slogan of 'New India' seems to be a panacea for all ills that erstwhile India has been suffering from. If the promises of 'New India' are realized even to an extent of 50 percent India will be the State where even citizens from developed countries would wish to make their home; and for Indians it would be next to heaven on earth itself. However, the experience so far has been that slogans and rhetoric have been the fate of Indian politics and promises have always been made by political parties only not to fulfill. Moreover it becomes obvious from the fact that there is hardly anything new in 'New India' as it amounts to presenting the same old wine in a new bottle in a new economic, social and political context.

Legacy of Indira Gandhi

The legacy that Indira Gandhi bestowed upon India and the Indians are remarkable and are imprinted in its political history and on Indian psyche. Indira Gandhi was a truly an international leader. As a Prime Minister of India and member of NAM she exercised a profound influence on international affairs and made tremendous effort for international peace, prosperity and equity among nations. She was the first and has been the only female Prime Minister of our diverse and largely patriarchal society so far. Hercharismatic and epoch making personality left her imprint not only in affairs of her own country but also in international affairs. By virtue of being Prime Minister of India the largest democracy in the world, she was able to make a significant contribution to the practice of international relations. She used the platforms of the Commonwealth, NAM and UN effectively in the furtherance of national interests. She not only preserved the rich heritage of Nehru but also made her own contributions which are unparalleled. Her contributions promoted India's national interest with independent decision-making in international affairs, economic development at home and the immunization of India and its neighborhood in Southern Asia from either of Superpower's sphere of influence.[9] Her politics were pragmatic, and her dealing with foreign leaders were unsentimental. She had clear cut perception of India's strategic and national interests. She was committed to freedom and peace. She played a dynamic role as a leader of mankind in the international arena. Indira Gandhi symbolized the third world regeneration. By refusing to sign NPT, she gained political credit for upholding India's independence and for taking a principled stand against a discriminatory treaty. As Henry Kissinger admits in his memoirs, Indira Gandhi outclassed and outmaneuvered Nixon and Kissinger. Atal Bihari Vajpayee called her "Durga". Another opposition leader remarked in parliament: "Madam you have created not only history but a new geography as well." She put India on the international scientific map by exploding first underground nuclear device at Pokharan in 1974. She demonstrated her diplomatic prowess by developing close ties with the Arab World. Therefore, given her political actions, diplomatic acumen, unique style of governance, and decision-making capacity it becomes quite obvious that her legacies too are unparalleled and has become a foundation-stone for all the later Prime Ministers of the country. It was her sheer personality and decision-making style that she contributed towards the making of India's strong international personality among the comity of nations. The personality of Mrs. Gandhi's dynamism, combativeness and assertiveness only became evident when she began to feel threatened by fears that the Syndicate within the Congress party was trying to control and displace her from power.

The story of Prime Minister Indira Gandhi's ascent in politics begins in 1967 election, when she campaigned for the party across the country. Indira Gandhi has been and still is India's best known politician and leader both inside the country and in the international arena. She was the most dedicated lady having a commendable personality and leadership qualities. She served for fifteen years continuously. As a Prime Minister in between 1971-77 two important happenings marked her term as the Prime Minister. She went around the world to explain the ghastly condition of refugees that India had to sustain in the wake of crisis in East Pakistan (now Bangladesh). She was always in favor of peace. She had firm belief in secularism. She made great contributions towards wellbeing of weaker sections with her oft-quoted slogan "*Garibi Hatao*". Some of her major contributions as the Prime Minister of Nation are: Refusal to bow down to the Hegemony of America; the Green Revolution, the seeds for which were already sown by her predecessor. During 1969, the nationalization of 14 major private sectors banks was a landmark decision. The move to nationalize private sector Banks was a vital step in freeing the economic growth of the country from the clutches of a few vested interests& throwing open the Banking facilities to the common people.Towards the end of 1971, she was thrust upon the war with Pakistan in which she successfully led the liberation of Bangladesh. The sentimental and sensational victory raised the stock of

Indira Gandhi to the cult status and she was hailed as 'Godess Durga.' Again in 1972 she went extra miles to have Peace with Pakistan and inked Shimla Agreement. This helped to mollify the distrust of the Western Powers about India's hegemonic intensions in the region, and improved Indira Gandhi's image as a statesman in the international arena. During 1980-84 which was her last innings of life as Prime Minister of the country, of which she never knew, she was assassinated, for her dare devil decision of purging the extremists from the Akal Takht of Golden Temple at Amritsar. Her feat was further maximized when she put an Indian, Captain Rakesh Sharma, in outer space with Soviet support in April 1984. Sikkim was incorporated as an Indian State in 1975, through a referendum. Introduced clauses in the Indian Constitution related to wages and achieved equal pay for equal work to both men and women. Indira Gandhi positioned herself firmly for the poor which has beena politically significant factor in Indian politics. She directly appealed to this section of Indians, deploying dexterously the slogan "*Garibi Hatao*" (Remove Poverty). She was a great companion of Mahatma Gandhi who was seen as the savior of the poor, and later she was being addressed as Mother India for her efforts at poverty eradication. Following distinctively pro-poor policies, she nationalized 14 commercial banks in 1969, and abolished the privy purse of erstwhile royals. The *Garibi Hatao* slogan was first time used in Indian Politics to directly address the concern of poor people. Under her leadership India secured food self-sufficiency, and made gigantic strides in developing nuclear and space technology. Indira Gandhi deserves to be remembered for redefining democratic politics of the country and building a strong international personality of the country.

Indira Gandhi's Decision-Making: A Critical Analysis

Indira Gandhi was never an ideal subject for critical evaluation.[10] There was also a famous slogan given by Dev Kant Barooah (the then Congress President) "Indira is India, India is Indira". During the two decades she dominated Indian politics, she left a mixed legacy of highly controversial actions and policies some of them long lasting other short lived.[11] In International relations she departed from Nehru's policy of Non Alignment, and moved towards an alliance with Soviet Union, formalized in the treaty of 1971. She heralded a new phase in the history of India. She was its product as well as an architect. It is simplistic to explain it exclusively in terms of her psychological make or to explain her political role and convictions exclusively in terms of her power urge. Her psychological make is further sought to be explained by the fact that she was—Lonely, insecure, suspicious, self-centered and ambitious. These are traits of personality which answer the description of an authoritarian personality given by person like T.W. Adorno.[12] She did not succeed merely because she wanted to succeed. Her success depended on the correlation between her qualities of leadership, attitudes, beliefs on the one hand and socio-economic conditions at the other hand. As it is said by someone, Indira Gandhi was neither a moral giant like Gandhi nor an intellectual giant like Nehru. She failed to get much appreciation for her action in Kashmir and centralized power, and was criticized always for moral and undemocratic way she governed. She convicted herself not only of her indispensability but also of the undependability of the persons, the party and institution.[13] During the days of Indira Gandhi everything was dependent upon a single leader. The Indian politics during that period revolved around the single leader principle which was actively entrenched and at many levels. In Indira's period, poverty was widely rampant therefore she took loan for the government from commercial banks. By taking loans she invested in policy implementation for the poor in which the small farmers, the cottage industries, the small entrepreneurs and self-employed were greatly benefited. The downfall of Indira Gandhi began after India won the war against Pakistan in 1971. She was implicated in court cases and decisions went against her in which she was convicted and later she imposed emergency in the country which spoiled her image indelibly. However, she again made a comeback in 1980 and again adopted number of policies as discussed above which were landmark and had great contributions towards transforming India.

Conclusion

India today is at the cusp of a changing society which is a witness to: a society that is becoming 'tech-savvy' at an unprecedented speed; a country which has highest population of youth unlike any other time in its history; a country with second largest population where human is not a resource but a huge burden; a country where politics is all about capturing power at all costs rather than serving the people and making the population a quality human resource; a country where there is simultaneous growth of traditional media (such as newspaper and television) and internet; a country where the 'digital space' is growing at an ever faster rate and is available in vernacular languages rather than in English alone; a country where 'freedom of speech' has stormed the social media and is turning destructive to social coherence and fabric. These are mere glimpses of the complexity and paradoxes that India is a unique example of.

Idea of 'New India' is not at all new rather it is continuation of the same old phrases by way of which policies are being given a facelift. India does not require new policies rather genuine implementation of the existing policies. The 'New India' has hardly anything new in its basket. The same Idea of India is now being present to the population as 'New India'. It is basically the legacy of Pandit Nehru, Indira Gandhi, and P.V. Narasimha Rao. Narendra Modi is trying to step into the shoes of Indira Gandhi but in different attires, both in terms of her policies and in the style of her functioning Modi is getting more into Indira mode. However, he is doing it carefully by attacking Nehru so that academia and people be engaged in comparing him to Nehru rather than Indira; whereas the fact remains that he is following Indira and trying to carry forward her legacies.

During the two decades in which Indira Gandhi dominated Indian politics, she left a mixed legacy of highly controversial actions and policies; some of them long lasting and other short lived. Indira in life and death was the most controversial political personality of her times. Modi has the same disregard for the institutions and similar tendency to over centralize. For all her imperiousness and ruthlessness Gandhi was totally devoted with compassion towards the poor and downtrodden. Those measures and Gandhi's slogan "Garibi Hatao" have been major steps to promote the interests of poor. She left behind shaky legacy, on the one hand with personalization of power on the other with diminished institutional capacity. Modi is crafty and smart towards taking that legacy forward. He is doing it by pointing hisdouble-barreled gun towards the Congress; one barrel of which is towards Nehru and the second one on Rahul Gandhi or the present Congress dispensation. He is attacking both the past and the present with an avowed aim of destroying the Congress for all time to come; whereas the fact remains he is carrying the legacy of Indira Gandhi, the strongest personality of the Congress that emerged so far.

Notes

1. "The Problem", *Seminar*, November 2017, No. 699.
2. "At NITI Aayog meet, PM Narendra Modi presents New India vision, Arvind Kejriwal, Mamta Banerjee not interested", *India Today*, www.indiatoday.in
3. "300 mantras for 'New India': Here's how Niti Aayog plans to realise PM Modi's vision by 2032", April 24, 2017, *FE Online*.
4. "300 mantras for 'New India': Here's how Niti Aayog plans to realise PM Modi's vision by 2032", April 24, 2017, *FE Online*.
5. Show collective will to build a "New India", *The Hindu*, August 2017, New Delhi.
6. Manjula Srinivas (2018), Book Review "Indira Gandhi—A Personal and Political Biography". http://www.dnaindia.com/lifestyle/review-book-review-indira-gandhi-a-personal-and-political-biography-1967930
7. Independence Day 2017 : 70 "Indian Independence day Celebrations special", *Hindustan Times*, 15 August, 2017, *Indo Asian News Sources*, New Delhi.
8. S.M. Kidwai, "Indira Gandhi: An Outstanding International Leader", *Mainstream Weekly*, Vol. XLV, No. 45.
9. Balraj Puri, (1985), "Era of Indira Gandhi" *Economic and Political Weekly*, Vol. 20, No. 4.
10. Sidharth Bhatia, (2016), "Is Narendra Modi the New Indira Gandhi? Not Really", *The Wire*.
11. Balraj Puri, (1985), "Era of Indira Gandhi", *Economic and Political Weekly*, Vol. 20, No. 4.
12. Romesh Thapar, (1985), "The Single- Leader Principle", *Economic and Political Weekly*, Vol. 20, No. 42.

15

India-ASEAN Evolving Security Cooperation in 21st Century

Challenges and Prospects

Abhishek Mohanty

Introduction

The Association of South East Asian Nations (ASEAN) is an intergovernmental organisation comprising countries of Southeast Asia, which was formed on 8th August 1967 when foreign ministers of Indonesia, Singapore, Thailand, Malaysia, and Philippines implemented the ASEAN Declaration in Bangkok. The setting up of ASEAN was initially stirred due to the failure of Southeast Asia Treaty Organisation (SEATO), mutual fear of communism, and yearning for economic prosperity. Currently, ASEAN has 10 member states: five founding member states, later on joined by Brunei in 1984, Vietnam in 1995, Laos and Myanmar jointly in 1997, and Cambodia in 1999. It has established numerous partnerships —like ASEAN Regional Forum, ASEAN+3 (China, Japan, and South Korea), Asia-

Pacific Economic Cooperation, and East Asia Summit to endure friendly affairs with the other states in and around the region (Chatterjee, 2017).

India had friendly bilateral partnerships with few Southeast Asian countries after independence, but relations with ASEAN were not cordial because of India was seem as siding with Soviet Union after the Treaty of Friendship in 1971. Regardless of that, the first official meeting between India and ASEAN was held in Kuala Lumpur in 1980 which reflected on strengthening partnership in the sectors of economic affairs and information technology. However, in a span of two months relations between India and ASEAN were depreciated after India pledged support to Vietnam in the Vietnamese-Cambodian War and recognized the HengSamrin regime. Prime Minister Rajiv Gandhi during his tenure tried coaxing ASEAN for mutual partnership, but ASEAN had developed uncertainty for regional partnership with India, as it was not sure of India's global point of view. However, after the fall of Soviet Union, ASEAN agreed to reinforce partnership with India.

PV Narasimha Rao, former Prime Minister of Indiaunveiled "The Look East Policy" in 1992 with the objective of strengthening political cooperation, raising the standards of economic prosperity and developing regional security cooperation with ASEAN. After that, India and ASEAN relations have been transformed from 'Sectoral Dialogue Partnership' in 1992 to a 'Comprehensive Dialogue Partnership' in December 1995. Membership in ASEAN Regional Forum in 1996 gave India the opportunity to share the dais with dominant global powers like the United States, China, and Russia, alongside ASEAN, on security concerns hovering the Indo-Pacific region. In 2002, the cordial partnership got a major boost when the 1st India-ASEAN Summit was held in Phnom Penh, Cambodia, and in 2012, the partnership touched new heights during the 10th Commemorative Summit held in New Delhi when the relations were transformed into a 'Comprehensive Strategic Partnership'.

Under the vision of present-day Prime Minister Narendra Modi, the Look East Policy has now been modernized into a more wide-ranging "Act East Policy" which symbolizes India's shifting priorities in the changing geopolitical scenario and fits impeccably into the notion of India's extended neighborhood foreign policy. The pioneering Act East Policy was affirmed at the 12th India-ASEAN Summit, which took place at Nay Pyi Taw, Myanmar, in November 2014. Subsequently, India and ASEAN have progressed their relations and now setting the path to prospective Asian century.

Spheres of Security Cooperation

Initially, India's major engagement with ASEAN was only centred towards trade and investment. But during the two successive ASEAN Summits in Bali and Vientiane in 2003 and 2004 respectively, there was a major shift in India's partnership with ASEAN. Both parties signed up the Treaty of Peace, Cooperation and Amity which marked the beginning of India-ASEAN security cooperation. In 2004, India and ASEAN signed the "India-ASEAN Partnership for Peace, Progress, and Shared Prosperity". It laid the roadmap and comprehensive spheres of cooperation between both sides up to 2020. In the sphere of security cooperation, both acknowledged to act together in several areas such as regional maritime security, counter-terrorism, illegal human and arms trafficking, non-usage of Weapons of Mass Destruction (WMDs), conflict resolution and peace building etc.

Throughout the commemorative summit of 20 years

cooperation between India and ASEAN held in New Delhi in December 2012, relations were transformed into a more comprehensive strategic partnership. The key highlights of the summit were joint cooperation in upholding regional harmony and prolonged existence, ASEAN's significance in the emerging regional framework, greater India-ASEAN collaboration in the sphere of maritime security, self-regulating navigation, and the peaceful resolution of regional conflicts in consensus with the UN designated international laws, especially the 1982 UNCLOS.

The central platform for India-ASEAN security dialogue is ASEAN Regional Forum (ARF). Since its approval of membership in 1996, India has uninterruptedly shown up at all the annual meetings of the forum and has enthusiastically partook in its numerous events. The ASEAN Defence Minister's Meeting (ADMM) is the most significant regional security dialogue in ASEAN. The ADMM+ is presided by the defence ministers of ASEAN members and regional partners like India, United States, Japan, Australia, Russia, Republic of Korea, New Zealand, and China on a biannual basis. Nirmala Sitharaman, the current Indian Defence Minister attended the 4th ADMM plus summit held in Pampanga, Philippines from 23-24 October 2017. Expanded ASEAN Maritime Forum (EAMF) is a stage for track 1.5 diplomacy which specifically focusses on mutual concerns in maritime security affairs. India participated in the 5th EAMF which was held in Jakarta, Indonesia on 7th December 2017.

In this paper, five main spheres of security cooperation have been discussed, i.e. Maritime Security, Counter Terrorism, Energy Security, Border Security and Cyber Security and also puts an attention on role of US in influencing India-ASEAN Security Cooperation.

Maritime Security

The starting point in any dialogue on maritime security cooperation in Asia is the centrality of Indian Ocean. With the beginning of 21st century, Indian Navy has led the role of chief protagonist in formulating cooperative maritime security relationships with several ASEAN states through joint naval exercises and holding the MILAN, a biennial multilateral naval exercise under the tutelage of Andaman and Nicobar Command at Port Blair. In its maiden edition in 1995, the exercise was attended by navies from Indonesia, Singapore and Thailand. In the successive editions, navies joined from Malaysia, Myanmar, Brunei, Cambodia, Philippines and Vietnam.

During 2004 when the Tsunami struck a disaster in the Indian Ocean region, the Indian Navy was swift enough to respond one-sidedly in providing relief and aid work in Southeast Asia. Following that, India also conducted several maritime patrols with ASEAN member navies in the Malacca Straits, because piracy through this maritime route was challenging the overall maritime security architecture of the region. In 2008, Indian Ocean Naval Symposium (IONS) was held in New Delhi and Goa, which was a brainchild of Indian Navy. Since then, the periodically held IONS has been developed into discussion forum amongst navies of ASEAN members on regional maritime cooperation.

The Indian Navy with other navies from ASEAN took part in the first ever Komodo multilateral joint exercise hosted by the Indonesian Navy from 28 March–3 April 2014 at Batam, Indonesia. It is a multilateral "Humanitarian Assistance and Disaster Relief (HADR)" exercise to bolster joint naval cooperation proficiencies in calamity assistance in the region, but also pays a huge attention to the hostile activities of the Chinese authorities in the disputed areas of South China Sea. The third edition of Exercise Komodo will be held on 4-9 May 2018 at Lombok, Indonesia.

In 2018, during the India-ASEAN Commemorative Summit in Delhi, which marked India's 25 years of partnership with ASEAN, the topmost priority of the discussions was strengthening the maritime security. ASEAN leaders have made their optimisms for India's vigorous and unblemished assistance in the region, particularly relating to the South China Sea. The ownership concerns, control, use and misuse of oil, gas, fisheries, and mineral resources in the South China Sea has occurred as the foremost argument between China and quite a few ASEAN countries like Vietnam, Malaysia, Philippines and Brunei. India is anxious because nearly 50 percent of its trade floats over the South China Sea (Sakhuja and Jha, 2016).

Moving beyond the parameters and scope of the multilateral maritime cooperation, India has started materialising bilateral maritime security partnerships with several Southeast Asian countries, including Vietnam, Indonesia, Malaysia, Singapore, and Thailand. A major sector of Indian assistance is in port developments, joint exercises, maritime training, and fruitful dialogues between national maritime establishments.

Counter Terrorism

Within a span of few months after Atal Bihari Vajpayee took over the charge of Prime Minister of India in 1998, he added a security facet to India's 'Look East Policy' with regard to India's new apprehensions about probable close links between *Jihadist* groups in South Asia and Southeast Asia. Contacts among the South Asian and Southeast Asian *Jihadist* groups can be traced back to the 1980s, when Moro Islamic Liberation Front, a Philippines-based terrorist organisation battled in cooperation with Mujahedeen (Tribal Militias) during Soviet invasion of Afghanistan. At present, there are two notableand strong *Jihadist* groups in Southeast Asia: a) Abu Sayyaf, informally branded as the Islamic State – Philippines Province, settled in and around Jolo and Basilan islands in Philippines, and b) Jemmah Islamiyah, a multinational Jihadist group with networks in Phillipines, Indonesia, Malaysia, and Singapore.

In 2001, while having a discussion with other foreign ministers of ASEAN in Brunei, Indian Foreign Minister Jaswant Singh stated, "We now face an unprecedented challenge in the great threat posed to regional and international peace and security by the dark forces of terrorism. As a major victim of terrorism herself, India fully supports ASEAN's efforts to develop bilateral and regional cooperation to combat terrorism. India is ready to work together both bilaterally with ASEAN countries and in the India-ASEAN framework, to develop practical programmes of cooperation (Sridharan, 2005).

During the 2003 India-ASEAN Summit in Bali, both parties adopted the "Joint Declaration for Cooperation in Combatting International Terrorism". This declaration is considered to be the most important aspect of bilateral counter-terrorism cooperation. In this, both sides acknowledged the global relevance of threats arising from terrorist activities and keeping that in view strived for a closer cooperation in several sectors, such as "exchange of information on terrorist financing, intelligence sharing, training, and education through seminars and conferences for counter-terrorism professionals; enhancement of relationships between respective law implementation agencies; and assistance on immigration and transportation challenges and conducting joint operations, as appropriate.

At the Commemorative Summit in January 2018, the Delhi Declaration approved to strengthen the counter-terrorism strategy developed by India and ASEAN. An important argument was the necessity to eradicate cross-border terrorism and pull terrorists out of their safe havens. The declaration also highlighted text calling for "compliance with the applicable United Nations Security Council resolutions vis-à-vis counter-terrorism" and strengthen the contemporary discourses of the "Comprehensive Convention on International Terrorism (CCIT) at the United Nations (UN)". In this purview, India in recent times has become ASEAN's trustworthy companion for countering terrorism.

Beyond ASEAN, Thailand had cooperated with India to toughen the battle against terrorism. Prime Minister of Thailand Prayut Chan-o-cha during his official visit to India in January 2016, acknowledged that India and Thailand need to strengthen their counter-terrorism approaches. Both leaders in a joint statement condemned all forms of terrorism and agreed to cooperate on developing a new framework for combatting global terrorism. Consequently, India's backing to countries on counter-terrorism has been recognised and respected. Its strategies to help in shaping the capabilities of the Southeast Asian countries came to eminence in the course of the Marawi siege in the Philippines. Above and beyond providing a generous amount of $500,000 to the Philippines, India also sent several of its cyber terrorism specialists to train the Filipino troops, who were anguishing from a severe deficiency of such experts.

Energy Security

Both India and ASEAN are facing huge demands for sustainable use of energy resources. Developing a new framework for regional energy security cooperation will have firm control on long term bilateral partnership. The initial signs towards this cooperation were developed in 2007 with the establishment of the India-ASEAN Green Fund, and in 2010 India-ASEAN Network for Climate Change was established. In 2012, India and ASEAN organised their first ministerial level summit on renewable energy in New Delhi, which aimed at bolstering commercial and institutional sector investment in the region. Dr. Farooq Abdullah, then the Minister of Renewable Energy hailed the "India-ASEAN Renewable Energy Family" and illustrated numerous stepping stones for cooperation: capacity building, human resource development, information sharing, and knowledge management. He stated that, "India's liberalised policy regime for FDI opens up prospects for business establishments from ASEAN countries to take benefit of India's prosperous clean energy sector" (ASEAN Official Statement, 2012).

In September 2014 during the 32nd ASEAN Ministers on Energy Meeting, a new theme for the "ASEAN Plan of Action for Energy Cooperation (APAEC)" was discussed. The ministerial meeting recommended to the integrate market economy and enhance energy connectivity in ASEAN in order to achieve comprehensive energy security, affordability, availability, and sustainability for all. Together with the establishment of Trans-ASEAN pipeline and ASEAN power grid, the APAEC 2016-2025 report explicitly mentioned new avenues for energy cooperation between India and ASEAN. It encompassed the establishment of ASEAN Centre for Energy to work on research and development in the domains of energy security, policy planning, resource management, and action-oriented programmes; running campaigns for clean and green energy with energy conservation technologies via institutional capacity-building; decrease the energy intensity by 20 per cent till 2020, and strive to strengthen the usage of renewable energy to 23 per cent in ASEAN by 2025.

The additional areas of cooperation comprise encouraging private sector commitment in the broadening and consumption of renewable and unconventional energy sources; and India's provision for the rural household electrification initiatives in ASEAN member states by means of bio-mass, bio-gas, solar energy, off-grid and micro-hydro electrification to reduce the barriers confronting the developmental process in the rural-urban context in the member states. The plan also aspires to develop new initiatives through ASEAN-India Green Fund, with all the required financial aid, technical support, and institutional capacity-building to ASEAN member states which would help them to strengthen environmental governance and tackle the menaces arising from climate change.

India is facilitating the infrastructure development for energy sources in the ASEAN region, mainly in the CLMV group (Cambodia-Laos-Myanmar-Vietnam). India is also investing in hydropower projects, power transmitters and stations, and gas/oil pipelines in the Southeast Asian countries. Tata Power, Hindustan Power, Hero Future Energies and other Indian companies have comprehensively invested in energy resources of Southeast Asian countries like natural gas, oil and coal.

Border Security

Myanmar is the lone ASEAN country with which India shares a territorial border and, for that reason it is India's entryway to Southeast Asia and a very important aspect of "Act East Policy". Border supervision concerning the two sides has been outlined around a variety of apprehensions, from the security hazards India diagnoses from insurgent groups in Northeast region to the directiveguidelines of local commercial activity in cooperation amongst people on bothsides of the international border, which weighs much significance from both countries to unravel the prospects of cross-border connectivity while handling the complications that it brings with it.

India and Myanmar have been signatories of various agreements vis-à-vis border security cooperation. In 2010, S. Singh, Joint Secretary of Indian Home Ministry and U. Nay Win, Army Commander for Chin state, signed "Mutual Legal Assistance Agreement". In 2012, during the state visit of former Indian Prime Minister Manmohan Singh to Myanmar, a MoU was signed on India-Myanmar Border Area Development and establishing Border Haats across the borders. In 2014, Ambassador of India to Myanmar, Gautam Mukhopadhyay, and Deputy Defence Minister of Myanmar, Major General Kyaw Nyunt, signed a MoU on Border Cooperation. This agreement provided a mechanism for a comprehensive partnership on a range of security issues, from intelligence exchange to joint border patrols. Some recent high level visits have raised the border security concerns. General Min Aung Hlaing, the Chief of Myanmar Army was in India in the end of July 2015 and met the Prime Minister, Defence Minister and Chief of Army Staff. India's National Security Advisor Ajit Doval was in Myanmar in June 2015 and had dialogues with the President, Foreign Minister and Chief of Army.

India and Myanmar have gradually progressed on unambiguous components of border security, be it the efforten route for the planning of new border points or alignment on visa procedures. India has also initiated some imperative measures along India-Myanmar borders to cope any imminent infiltration, together with deploying additional military personnel and technology and the contemplating of new approaches of guidelines. The Ministry of Home Affairs is making an allowance for the formation of a 29-battalion India-Myanmar Border Force, in which 25 from the corps of the Assam Rifles and 4 from Indo-Tibetan Border Force will safeguard India's 1, 643-km long rugged border with

Myanmar to inhibit drugs and arms trafficking and also crumple the anti-national activities of Manipuri and Naga rebels who take benefit of the permeable border.

Cyber Security

The cooperation in the sector of cyber security between India and ASEAN is still burgeoning, and both should contemplate each other and be a pivotal voice in setting norms and enlightening inter-regional cooperation for addressing cyber security-related challenges and prospects. While India is broadly acknowledged as a major IT power, cyber coercions still persist to be a big challenge to India's IT and security framework. Acknowledging India's accomplishments in this sphere, the ASEAN Secretariat in 2014 entreated India to organise an India-ASEAN Conference in an attempt to propagate the opportunities of mutual partnership in this decisive area. The decision was almost immediately accepted by Sushma Swaraj, Indian Minister of External Affairs, who assured to all Foreign Ministers of ASEAN throughout the ASEAN Foreign Ministers Meeting in August 2014 at Nay Pyi Taw, that India would be pleased to arrange the conference in near future. The promise was fulfilled and on January 9, 2015, the first India-ASEAN Cyber Security Conference was held in New Delhi. The conference fetched numerous cyber experts from India and ASEAN to exchange concepts and notions on the present state of play in the accessible technical information in cyber security and the prerequisite procedures to develop additional capabilities in this sphere (MEA Statement, 2015).

At the 15th India-ASEAN Summit held on 14 November, 2015 at Manila, both sides focussed on the ways to enhance India-ASEAN cooperation in cyber security as well as holding a new India-ASEAN Cyber Dialogue in 2016, which was anticipated to discuss the prospects for India's cooperation towards developing "ASEAN Cyber Centre and Networks of National Computer Emergency Response Teams" (CERTS) (Chairman statement, 2017). However due to some inevitable conditions the dialogue couldn't be commenced as scheduled.

During the 2018 India-ASEAN Commemorative Summit, both parties agreed to strengthen cooperation on cyber security capacity building and policy management, together with assisting the enactment of the "ARF Work Plan on Security of and in the Use of Information and Communication Technologies" (ICTs), the work of 'ARF Inter-Sessional Meeting on Security of and in the Use of ICTs', 'ASEAN Cyber Security Cooperation Strategy', improve the capacity-building of regional cyber security initiatives, and plan for the highly anticipated India-ASEAN Cyber Dialogue as soon as possible.

Role of the United States

Since the last decade, the United States has encouraged India to take the obligation of a larger role in maintaining balance of power in Southeast Asia, by developing security partnerships with mutual allies of Washington in the region. US is aggressively pitching the concept of "Indo-Pacific" as maritime security region, which clearly exhibits the important role of India in the region. Since the Trump administration transformed the strategy of "Pivot to Asia" to "free and open Indo-Pacific", without any doubt it is sure that the US will be playing a dominant role in this region in times to come.

The US is playing a worth mentioning role in the provision of security in the Indo-Pacific region, with Australia and Japan emerging as vital regional partners in this effort. In cooperation with India, the evolving partnership is known as Quad. Quad's objective is to preserve the maritime channels of the Indo-Pacific free and open for a comprehensive and flourishing Indo-Pacific region and have cordial partnership with ASEAN. Exercise Malabar delivers the prototype for maritime cooperation between the Quad with emphasis on anti- submarine warfare, antipiracy manoeuvres, sea interdiction, humanitarian and disaster assistance and collective patrolling in the Indo-Pacific region.

In the forthcoming years, US interests comprise of a greater security role in the South China Sea and the Malacca Strait, the two most important maritime points in the Indo-Pacific region. The United States has mounted huge expectations on India that it might become asignificant political comrade in Southeast Asia, which can back its geopolitical rivalry against Chinese strategic goals in the region. This was also exemplified by Indian Prime Minister Narendra Modi in his statement to the US Congress on June 8, 2016, "A strong India-US partnership can anchor peace, prosperity and stability from Asia to Africa and from the Indian Ocean to Pacific" (AP, 2016).

Challenges

Due to the rapid acceleration of security cooperation between India and ASEAN, China perceives India as a ballast in Southeast Asia and the most imminent contender for hegemony in Asia. It has been involved in asphyxiating India with indirect means like using Pakistan and Myanmar as a proxy for creating cross-border issues and its "string of pearls strategy" in the northern Indian Ocean region. Until recently, India hadn't developed any joint counter strategy to tackle China's aggressive supremacy in the region. However, this is now shifting slowly but surely as India has taken support of ASEAN for joint cooperation against China's strategic ambitions not only in Indian Ocean but South China Sea also. While countering China is the major challenge of all, India and ASEAN first need to strengthen their maritime security cooperation in order to accomplish their mission.

Drug trafficking is known to be the one of the numerous threats between India and ASEAN. According to several reports, Manipur's towns of Moreh, Somdal, and Behiang and Mizoram's Champai town which are near to the borders of Myanmar have been labelled as the entry points and safe havens for drug smugglers from Southeast Asia (Ranjan, 2003). Myanmar has a huge significance in India's Act East Policy, as it is the gateway to Southeast Asia and holds huge commercial prospects for India. Almost all major Indian connectivity projects with ASEAN including the upcoming Trilateral Highway pass to Myanmar, so India and ASEAN need to articulate and disseminate a durable policy on border security cooperation.

Another major challenge is the trafficking of small arms and light weapons. The grey and black markets for these weapons are especially on the India-Myanmar-China border and also on the border of Thailand. These have been the primary sources of arms supply to many insurgency movements in Southeast Asia and India. There have been several instances when Indian Army, Indian Navy, and Coast Guard have intercepted the movement of ammunitions passing through land and sea. The first step towards peace and stability in the region is to eliminate this threat. This also becomes one of the foremost challenges which needs to be addressed mutually by India and ASEAN.

Cyber-crime is the latest crime method which has emerged in the 21st century and is anticipated to raise at a mammoth frequency in the near future. Hacking of official government websites, online peddling of drugs, weapons, counterfeit notes and surreptitious broadcasting of virtual religious fundamentalism are the modern forms of challenges for which there is a dire need to address these issues. Here the technological savoir faire needs to be circulated through mutual cooperation. India and ASEAN must put efforts on boosting their joint cyber networks and develop robust cyber security policies.

At present, India and ASEAN are facing a big challenge from the Rohingya refugee crisis. The Rohingyas are designated as stateless people by UNHCR due to persecution in Myanmar and they are taking illegal refuge in India, Thailand, Malaysia, Indonesia and Philippines, which has resulted in demographic change in India to some extent. Indian and Myanmar authorities have also accused Rohingyas getting involved in terrorism, drug smuggling and human trafficking activities, which has now become a major security issue for India and ASEAN. All the above mentioned challenges have contemporary relevance and may pose a dangerous threat in future so both India and ASEAN should cooperate in developing policies and strategies to eliminate all the security threats pertaining to the region.

Future Prospects

The ASEAN Regional Forum (ARF) should be seen as a prototype for conflict management and resolution. India should use this forum to assert itself as the ballast and solidify its stake as a foremost contender for the regional balance of the 21st century. Multilateral channels of communication and collaboration are indispensable to boost expectations and diminish all kinds of pressure and turn into optimally stable. Cordial relations and mutual interests between India and ASEAN can without any doubt help to control Dragon's aggression in the region. India's dynamic involvement in the ARF's exercise of deterrent diplomacy will be significant in India-ASEAN Security Cooperation.

India and ASEAN have a huge scope in safeguarding maritime cooperation through numerous arrangements.

Both India and ASEAN are shoreline states with an elegant antiquity of maritime commerce. It is therefore very significant to resuscitate and give a boost to those ancient maritime linkages within a contemporary framework. India-ASEAN maritime security cooperation has the potential to become the main agent for anti-piracy strategies, freedom of navigation, unhindered lawful maritime trade, and a platform for vast opportunities intensifying the regional integration process. Improving maritime cooperation is henceforth a major requisite for the region's opulence, sustained growth, and constancy.

ASEAN, like India, is a victim of trans-border terror and unlawful activities. India's partnership with ASEAN in combating global terrorism and encouraging regional and bilateral defence and security synergies in the spirit of the "Treaty of Amity and Cooperation in Southeast Asia" will be influential in addressing mutual political challenges and stimulating much desired peace and security in the region. To counter terrorism, the most imperative characteristic is to share intelligence. Intelligence sharing would empower India and ASEAN to synchronise their manoeuvres and annihilate terrorism. The subsequent characteristic relates to training in counter terrorism institutions. India has numerous defence training institutes, which can train defence personnel of the ASEAN states on this serious theme.

The energy security sector offers a fresh area of cooperation against the over dependences on energy sources in the region. ASEAN members have always asked for establishment of India's service sector in their respective countries and India must pay heed to their requests, bearing in mind the long-term mutual benefits. India and Myanmar have also invigorated the dialogue on the gas pipeline construction sandwiched between the two countries via Bangladesh. In future, India will gain the opportunity from this initiative to access energy resources not only from Myanmar but also from the rest of the ASEAN members.

Conclusion

It is apparent from the paper that security cooperation between India and ASEAN is still evolving and has lots of challenges in its way. Overpowering these teething troubles will be a very strenuous mission. But due to mutual interests of India and ASEAN, this mission is not impossible to accomplish. The contemporary phase of India-ASEAN security cooperation is the resultant of the much influential Act East Policy and ASEAN's cooperative approaches for building security framework. Mutual traditional ethics, shared ancient connections, geographical contiguity, and regional security concerns are the aspects congealing the security cooperation between India and ASEAN.

For promoting regional security, ASEAN with no trouble can hinge on India, which is the most prevalent democracy in the world. According to Immanuel Kant's Democratic Peace Theory, democracies under no circumstances indulge in a full-fledged war and to a great extent assist in promoting peace and prosperity. ASEAN and India's relationship have been evolving confidently over time. India's role as an emerging global power delivers numerous prospects for cooperation with ASEAN in the security field. ASEAN and India have to utilise this opportunity to bolster their security cooperation and walk unruffled on the road to prospective Asian Century.

From Look East Policy to Act East Policy, India has splendidly developed its security cooperation with ASEAN. The security concerns hovering around India and ASEAN are intricately concomitant with each other. India and ASEAN share mutual security dilemmasin both traditional non-traditional spheres. Therefore, prospering of India-

ASEAN Security Cooperation is not only an obligation but also a mutual objective.

References

AIC-RIS, New Delhi. *ASEAN-India Development and Cooperation Report 2015*. Retrieved April 15, 2018, from http://www.ris.org.in/sites/default/files/ASEAN-India%20 Development%20 Cooperation-Report%202015.pdf

Brewster, D. (2013). "Open Research Library, ANU." *India's Defense Strategy and the India-ASEAN Relationship*. Retrieved April 15, 2018, from http://openresearch-repository. anu.edu. au/bitstream/1885/13062/1/Brewster, %20D.%20India's% 20 Defence%20Strategy%20and%20the%20India-ASEAN%20relationship%202013.pdf

C. Banaloi, R. (February, 20, 2013). Delivered at the Delhi Dialogue V, New Delhi, India. *Challenges in India-ASEAN Security Cooperation*. Retrieved March 16, 2018, from http://www.slideshare.net/RommelBanlaoi/challenges-in-india-asean-security-relations-banlaoi-speech

Desai, S. (November 18, 2017). *The Diplomat Magazine*. Revisiting ASEAN-India Relations. Retrieved April 14, 2018, from http://thediplomat.com/2017/11/revisiting-asean-india-relations/

Extraordinary & Plenipotentiary: *Diplomatist Magazine. ASEAN 2017*. Retrieved April 16, 2018, from http://www.diplomatist.com/specialreport/2017asean/index.html

Fadli. (June 15, 2017). *The Jakarta Post. Batam to host Komodo naval joint exercise*. Retrieved April 13, 2018, from http://www.thejakartapost.com/news/2013/06/15/batam-host-komodo-naval-joint-exercise.html

Ganguli, S. (September 20, 2016). Dr. Syama Prasad Mookerjee Research Foundation. *India-ASEAN Relations: a Green Push*. Retrieved April 15, 2018, from http://www.spmrf.org/india-asean-relations-green-push/

Gupta, S. (January 18, 2018). *Hindustan Times. Home ministry looks to form 29-battalion Indo-Myanmar border force*. Retrieved April 13, 2018, from http://www.hindustantimes.com/india-news/home-ministry-looks-to-form-29-battalion-indo-myanmar-border-force/story-iImWizVCRAtDYG Ionj2OML.html

Jacob, J. (January 26, 2018). *Hindustan Times. India, ASEAN to bolster maritime security ties with eye on China.* Retrieved April 15, 2018, from http://www.hindustantimes.com/india-news/eye-on-china-india-asean-to-bolster-maritime-security-ties/story-9ALN8C7prLqNotTFoc9pUO.html

Jyoti. (2013). "India's Look East Policy: In its Second Phase". *Global Journal of Pharmaceutical Sciences and Education,* Research India Publications, 2(1), 1-14. Retrieved, from https://www.ripublication.com/gjpse/gjpsv1n1_01.pdf

Kumar Das, A. (2013,). S. Rajaratnam School of International Studies (RSIS). *India-ASEAN Defence Relations.* Retrieved April 14, 2018, from http://www.rsis.edu.sg/wp-content/uploads/2014/07/Monograph2813.pdf

Ministry of External Affairs, Government of India. *ASEAN- India Relations.* Retrieved April 13, 2018, from http://mea.gov.in/aseanindia/20-years.htm

Moudgil, S. (April 05, 2018). National Maritime Foundation. *India-ASEAN Maritime Cooperation Prospects.* Retrieved April 15, 2018, from http://www.maritimeindia.org/View%20Profile/636585053657368314.pdf

Muni, S.D. & Chak Mun, S. (May 25, 2012). ISAS Special Reports, National University of Singapore. *Asean-India Relations: Future Directions.* Retrieved April 16, 2018, from http://www.rsis.edu.sg/wp-content/uploads/2014/07/Monograph2813.pdf

Overview: ASEAN-India Dialogue Relations, As of February 2017. Retrieved April 12, 2018, from http://asean.org/storage/2012/05/Overview-ASEAN-India-as-of-February-2017r4CL.pdf

Parameswaran, P. (January 06, 2018). The Diplomat Magazine. *What's With the New India-Myanmar Border Pact?.* Retrieved January 14, 2018, from http://thediplomat. com/2018/01/whats-with-the-new-india-myanmar-border-pact/

PMO (January 25, 2018). *Press Information Bureau. Delhi Declaration of the ASEAN-India Commemorative Summit to mark the 25th Anniversary of ASEAN-India Dialogue Relations.* Retrieved April 12, 2018, from http://pib.nic.in/newsite/PrintRelease.aspx?relid=175908

Rajendra Kumar, G. (July 09, 2017). *The Hans India. India – Myanmar Border Management.* Retrieved April 14, 2018, from http://www.thehansindia.com/posts/index/Young-Hans/2017-07-09/India—Myanmar-Border-Management-/311243

Roy Chaudhury, D. (July 13, 2017). *The Economic Times. India expands counter terror coop with Philippines in ongoing fight against*

ISIS. Retrieved April 15, 2018, from http://economictimes.indiatimes.com/news/defence/india-expands-counter-terror-coop-with-philippines-in-ongoing-fight-against isis/articleshow/59572847.cmss://www.aseantoday.com/2017/10/are-thailands-counter-terrorism-measures-effective/

Sajjanhar, A. (January 04, 2018). Institute of Defence Studies and Analyses. *The India-ASEAN Partnership at 25*. Retrieved April 14, 2018, from http://idsa.in/idsacomments/india-asean-partnership-at-25_asajjanhar_040118

Shodhganga. *CHAPTER – II INDIA AND SOUTHEAST ASIA: A HISTORICAL OVERVIEW UPTO 1991*. Retrieved April 12, 2018, from http://shodhganga.inflibnet.ac.in/bitstream/10603/135169/8/08_chapter%202.pdf

Shodhganga. *CHAPTER - VI CHALLENGES AND PROSPECTS*. Retrieved April 16, 2018, from http://shodhganga.inflibnet.ac.in/bitstream/10603/8005/14/14_chapter%206.pdf

Sinan SIyech, M. (2018, January 31). *The Diplomat Magazine. The Delhi Declaration: A New Indo-ASEAN Counterterrorism Partnership. The Diplomat Magazine*. Retrieved April 13, 2018, from http://thediplomat.com/2018/01/the-delhi-declaration-a-new-indo-asean-counterterrorism-partnership/

Singh, A., Pande, A., M. Smith, J., Saran, S., Joshi, S. & Lohman, W. (2018, January 19). Observer Research Foundation. *The new India-US partnership in the Indo-Pacific: Peace, prosperity and security*. Retrieved April 16, 2018, from http://www.orfonline.org/wp-content/uploads/2018/01/ORF-Heritage-Hudson.pdf

Ted, O. (June, 2013). *Enhancing India-ASEAN Connectivity, Centre for Strategic and International Studies*. Lanham: Rowman and Littlefield. Retrieved from https://csis-prod.s3.amazonaws.com/s3fs-public/legacy_files/files/publication/130621_Osius_EnhancingIndiaASEAN_WEB.pdf

Thi Ha, H., & Chalermpalanupap, T. (2018). ASEAN-India Commemorative Summit: Matching "Act East" with Actions. *ISEAS-YusofIshak Institute Perspective, 8*(2018). Retrieved, from https://www.iseas.edu.sg/images/pdf/ISEAS_Perspective_2018_8@50.pdf doi: ISSN 2335-6677

Veera, S. & Yeo, I. (October 07, 2017). *ASEAN Today. Are Thailand's counter-terrorism measures effective?*. Retrieved April 14, 2018, from http://www.aseantoday.com/2017/10/are-thailands-counter-terrorism-measures-effective/

16

The Dynamics of Growth Amid India-Mongolia Relations

Ritesh Kumar Rai

Introduction

In a rapidly changing global balance of power, new powers and fresh alliances are emerging in world politics. Successive Indian governments in the past few years have integrated the phrase extended neighborhood while formulating the foreign policies. This policy of India has become important given the specific seam in time when the strategic and economic interests of the country is becoming increasingly entwined with the greater Asian hemisphere, much beyond our immediate South Asia neighborhood.

Despite the fact that India and Mongolia are geographically far apart, there is no stoppage in continuation of their civilization links spanning over a period of more than 2, 500 years. Both share a long historical and cultural bond. According to Soni, "India and Mongolia are two ancient Asian civilisations whose spiritual and cultural bonds go back to antiquity" (Soni 2016: 51).[2] In 1978, former EAM Vajpayee Ji stated that:[3]

India and Mongolia are ancient lands of the ancient people of Asia. The historic and cultural collaboration between India and Mongolia is most fascinating and unique and is as old as the history of the spread of Indian culture and ideas into Central Asia and Siberia. We in India consider the Mongol veneration of Sanskrit, a matter of special privilege. We hold the people of Mongolia in high esteem for preserving in translation as well as in manuscripts, the vast collection of our precious Sanskrit text on our philosophy, poetry, logic and astronomy lost by us over centuries. In modern times, too many Mongols visited India–the land of Buddhism.

In the modern sense, India has excellent relations with Mongolia despite its political systems or leaning. The relationship between India and modern-day Mongolia was formalised by an Indo-Mongol communiqué issued on 24 December 1955. In the process, Nyamdavaa analyzes that, "India became the first country outside the Soviet bloc to establish relations with Mongoliathen afterword called the Mongolia's People Republic".[4]

India-Mongolia relations will form a key component in determining the evolution of the balance of power in South Asia politics. India and Mongolia share vibrant political relations. Their democratic aspirations and urge for socio-economic development and scientific progress have provided new impetus in their bilateral relations. Although South Asian as well as Central Asian regions remain strategically contested, geo-economic tendencies have gained momentum. Consequently, both countries are exploring new avenues for expanding their economic and development partnership. Indian Prime Minister Narendra Modi's visit to Mongolia is being considered as a step forward in bilateral and multilateral partnership. It has further strengthened their common approach to inclusive development. India pledged to provide line of credit of US$ one billion and help in developing railways and other infrastructure projects.

On the other hand, New Delhi may also benefit from natural resources of Mongolia. As one of the fastest growing economies of the world, India needs constant supply of energy at affordable prices. Mongolia has potential to contribute to enhancing energy security of India. In the broader regional framework, Mongolia is integral to "India's Look East Policy" and now "Act East policy". Here, it needs to be analysed. Over the years, both conduct joint military exercise called Nomadic Elephant. Because at present, terrorism has become a common issue for South Asian countries so, we take a look here what are the goals and benefits of the recent India-Mongolia military exercises.

India-Mongolia Relations: Some Decisive Aspects

On 17 May 2015, Indian Prime Minister Narendra Modi visited Mongolia and participated in the 60th anniversary of diplomatic relations between Mongolia and India and his visit also aimed to boost up the strategic relations. "It has been regarded the first ever visit by an Indian Prime Minister to still a distant country as known to the world, though today Mongolia is one of the fastest growing economies in the world with a double digit growth rate since 2011 due to recent mining boom in coal, copper, gold, and uranium".[5] Prime Minister's visit to Mongolia contributed to strengthening investment cooperation, economic engagement, people-to-people exchanges, cultural, civilizational and spiritual linkages which is in accordance with the key objectives of India's Act East Policy.

However, the bilateral relations between these two

countries have been developing since 2009. But in the context of this recent visit by Prime Minister Modi, it energized relations in advance direction of a comprehensive partnership which is, traditionally based on the deep historic cultural bonding, familiar democratic traditions and shared interest for regional and international stability and peace.

Further, this visit also aimed at consolidating the comprehensive India-Mongolia relations by concurring to elevate the level of all inclusive relations to a strategic framework that is good for the common interests of India as well as Mongolia. If one is to look at the future, developing a strategic relation would be a recurrent yet a new aim of their respective foreign policies.[6] Soni observes the key directions that guided the real motives behind this high profile visit that marked the dawn of a new era in India Mongolia relations:

- *Act East Policy:* With the initiation of "Act East" policy, the erstwhile "Look East" policy, Northeast Asia is becoming a major factor in India's strategic vision in the East Asian region. Since Mongolia belongs to Northeast Asia Modi's visit was important strategically.
- *The China Factor:* China has been spending so much political energy in cultivating India's neighbours, be it South Asia or East Asia. India too needed to cultivate its good relations in China's periphery, and Modi's visit has worked in that direction as well.
- *Buddhist Factor:* Since India Mongolia relations are based on Buddhist linkages which are more than 2500 years old, Modi's visit has been part of this shared religious heritage with neighbours at the centre of his regional engagement. To a great extent, Buddhism, today, remains at the very forefront of India's new Asian outreach, both culturally as well

as diplomatically.

- *India's elevation as a third neighbour in Mongolia's foreign policy:* In its revised foreign policy of 2011 India has, for the first time, figured as one of Mongolia's third neighbours. This importance given to India has been responded positively by Modi's visit (Soni 2015).[7]

Act East Policy (AEP)

The Act East Policy of India, the link with Mongolia plays an important part towards India's linkages with Northeast Asian countries. The idea of this policy was inaugurated at Mayanmar in November 2014, at the East Asia Summit. Sajjanhar argues that, "some analysts seek to dismiss the transformation from the Look East Policy (LEP), initiated by Prime Minister Narasimha Rao in 1992, to AEP arguing that it merely represents a change in nomenclature".[8] "A closer look would reveal that while there is continuity, there are several significant areas where AEP has gone far beyond what LEP achieved in 20-plus years".[9]

This is also due to the fact that today's India is not the same old India of 1992, when their future regarding international policy was uncertain with the disintegration of Soviet Union and after having its foreign exchange reserves crashed. According to Sajjanhar, "India then needed to promote economic growth, which was done admirably through LEP. Bilateral trade between India and ASEAN rose from $2 billion in the early "90s to $12 billion in 2001 and to $72 billion by 2012" (Ibid). However, since then, there has been deterioration in the bilateral economic relation, partly because of the continuing international economic and financial crisis and following Eurozone sovereign debt crisis and feeble international demand.

India specifically is not focusing on promoting connectivity with other ASEAN states through Mayanmar and Thailand. In a bid to promote connectivity at the India-ASEAN Summit in Kuala Lumpur last November (2015), Modi had allocated $1 billion and this has highlighted the importance of "culture, connectivity and commerce".[10] Realization has hit India that it has to bring about economic and security development in northeast India in order to achieve the success of AEP.

Similarly, association with ASEAN countries have transformed to become multi-dimensional to enclose strategic, security and political, counter terrorism and defense cooperation on top of economic links. Cooperation to stop or reduce terrorism, specifically with the rise in the number of influences of Islamic State has gained importance. There has been improvement in the defense alliance with many ASEAN states. In the meantime, AEP has aimed to especially enlarge its geographical radar transcending ASEAN alone, to incorporate other countries like Australia, Japan, Pacific Island nations, Mongolia and South Korea.

India Impediment to China's Influence in Mongolia

Post the collapse of the Soviet Union, China has been playing a dominant role in the South Asian power balance post-Cold War. There is historical depth of the Central Asian Regions (CARs) with regards to great powers influence. During the polarized Cold War, the two superpowers tried to conserve regional balance ("tightly") through both soft and hard balancing (Thomas 2004: 313).[11] In this strict bipolar environment, the game of power brawl over Central Asia theatre was just between two blocs led by the US and USSR. However, China later was "the third active competitor" (Jahangir 2013: 51).[12]

With an increase in issues of energy security which practically overshadows many emerging geopolitical trends in South Asia, Central Asia and Afghanistan hold and play an imperative role. Currently, many scholars are of the opinion that while there has been integration of Eastern Europe into the European Union, the area right up to China's Xinjiang from Iran and to Northern India from the steppes of Russia is seen to have great geostrategic importance. "The Central Asian Republics (CARs) in tandem with Afghanistan make up a heartland in this context" (Cotter 2008: 108).[13] The one who is able to take a hold in this energy-rich Central Asia shall control the era, as per Mackinder's old heartland theory (1904).

The USA has off late revamped its policy towards Central Asia, while Russia and China were already busy before trying to get their respective regional economic and geostrategic interests. Central Asia has also been of keen interest to India and Pakistan but as competitors, both have not left stones unturned to hinder each other's access. One disadvantage that India has is that it does not have direct access to the CARs. So it is looking for another option most probably via Iran, to bypass Pakistan. On the other hand, "China, Russia and USA, engage in fresh power control games in Central Asia. Apart from opposing each other's domination, they also challenge the participation of regional countries".[14]

According to Soni that, in recent years, "China has made an effort to enlarge engagement with India's neighbours in the subcontinent as well as in the Indian Ocean" (Soni 2016: 53).[15] In fact, the 1990s saw China revamping its foreign policy towards its neighbouring countries in the Asia Pacific through what it calls its "periphery policy" or "good-neighbourhood policy" (Ji and Qingguo 1998: 128).[16] The primary idea for formulating a policy like this was directed at exploring "the common ground with Asian countries in both economic and security arenas by conveying the image of a responsible power willing to contribute to stability and cooperation in the region"(Zhao 2004: 258).[17] Hence both the non-traditional security paradigm such as economic diplomacy as well as traditional security concerns formed the main guiding principles of China's periphery policy.[18]

Alike most neighbors, China and Mongolia have a complex and long links. This relationship for most of history has been disputable. In fact, Erdenebileg argues that, "until the transition to a market economy began in the early 1990s, Mongolia had been under heavy Soviet influence".[19] Distrust of its large and populous neighbor to the south was widespread. Off late China's escalating global economic impact has been hugely felt in Mongolia. Immeasurably, Mongolia's largest export market is China. "As of early November 2016, about 80 per cent of Mongolia's total exports went to China. By a smaller margin, China is also Mongolia's largest import market, making up about 30 per cent of total imports by early November 2016".[20] Russia was the second largest import market. Because of restructuring of the economy in the past few years, there has been a drop in the demand for Mongolian exports to China. This obviously has had an acute impact in Mongolia and from 2015 to 2016 the country's economy saw a setback.

Availability of Energy Resources and Growing Market Economy

The pace of development attained by Mongolia over the past few years and the increasing demand of its own natural resources are lending new dimensions to its international diplomatic relations. The soaring quantum of demand appears to have enabled Mongolia to diplomatically position itself for a state of equilibrium in terms of energy security. As far as mineral exploration and development projects are concerned an upswing in the flow of Foreign Direct Investment (FDI)[21] and growing competition for it is noticeable throughout the globe. According to World Bank, "though FDI is generally considered to be beneficial for energy sector in the developing countries, there is still no plausible rationale for this being true in all contexts" (World Bank 2004: 50).[22]

However, the Asian Development Bank (ADB) forecasts that "FDI will increase significantly in 2017 because of strengthening countrys mining capacities, before stabilising in 2018, when the country will have maximised its coal mining capacity".[23] Simultaneously, however, as threats of climate change loom large, there has been mounting pressure to meet the new national and international social and environmental standards of sustainability and efficiency.

The energy sector of Mongolia has not fully realised so far the humongous potential it has, to attract more capital that can be infused in its energy market. It has been observed during the course of this study, that viable policies and planning were formulated by Mongolian leadership following the approval of the national "Law on Energy" in 2001, which "evolved the legal framework for energy sector reform, including the scope to open it up to the foreign investors".[24]

On a theoretical plane, the avowed objective of Mongolian policies was to seek investment from major powers. In practical terms, however, it was basically intended to reorient such policies towards "third neighbor" countries.[25] At this backdrop, it was found that, foreign investments in the energy sector of Mongolia, with reference to the support extended by the donor countries, international agencies and trading partners, for the sustainable development of energy resources in Mongolia. Besides taking into account the investments from its two immediate and influential neighbours, it also highlights those coming from the US, Japan, Republic of Korea, Australia, Canada and India. As Dierkes notices, such an engagement with these "third neighbours" has had a tangible effect on the economic, political and social development of Mongolia.[26]

India's Search for New Energy Market in Mongolia

As Mongolia grows economically, its resilient economy will throw up opportunities and possibilities for processing the mineral resources. In order to decrease its dependence on Australian coking coal which is highly priced there have been plans of India to obtain a mine in Mongolia. "Plans are also underway to set up the first steel plant in the quality coal rich country".[27] The grand design is to obtain the mine and use the coal for the steel plant. The rest will be exported to India through Chinese ports (Mongolia is a land locked country). India prefers Mongolia because it has vast mines of very good quality of coking coal. Indian companies willfind opportunities to cooperate with Mongolian business and industrial entities. If the Mongolian government so allocates good coking coal mines to India, India will have a mutual plan to build a steel plant there.

Inspite of being an escalating economy with surplus coal mines, Mongolia lacks its steel plant till today. According to PTI report, "this will be the first attempt by India to break away from the excessive dependence of Australian coking coal, which has become too costly in recent years pushing up the cost of steel production to very high level in India. India is importing 35 Million tonns of coking coal every year, about 60 to 70 per cent from Australia which is close to India and therest from the US and New Zealand.[28]

Despite all this, logistic issues will certainly dominate export of Mongolian resources and there are not many economically viable options to import Mongolian mineral products and export Indian consumer goods. The issue of connectivity is being addressed and the Indian Government is hopeful that there will be direct air connections between Ulaanbaatar and Delhi either through one of the airports in Central Asia or through China. According to the Ambassador of India to Mongolia, "India also has slightly different model of economic cooperation and believes in grow together". This is a win-win situation for both".[29]

New Energy Policy between Mongolia and India in post-Modi Visit

Soni analyses that, "Indian PM's visit has essentially given a much needed boost to Mongolia, as for quite some time now, the Mongolians felt that Mongolia is not considered in India as an important country the way Mongolia considers India".[30] Further, on the economic front, it is optimistic and futuristic observation that Mongolia would be an economically advantageous place for Indian companies. And Mongolia's mining sector is also explored by Indian companies through joint investment and ventures. Soni estimated that, "the country has 170 billion tonnes of coal, 205 million tonnes of petroleum and 68 thousand tonnes of uranium reserves. Possibly the relations between India and Mongolia, in future, will be reinforced by economic cooperation led by the mining industry".[31]

During this first visit by the Indian PM, India and Mongolia signed a civilian nuclear deal for uranium supplies way back on 14 September 2009. However, India is yet to get its first supply of uranium from Mongolia. Moreover, Soni argues that, "Mongolian uranium supply won't materialise to the country. That is because the Mongolian internal processes are still to be completed and uranium supplies are bogged down".[32] At the same time, India's energy security is one of the prime drive forces of India's foreign policy, where Indian Prime Minister has been trying to import Uranium from Mongolia. Pragmatically and absolutely, it was a huge ticket plan for Modi's official talks with Mongolian interlocutors. Hence, one of the first few countries to strike a uranium deal with India was Mongolia.

Both the countries have benefitted from this visit and have helped them in taking their bilateral relationship to another level for reciprocal advantage. Although Mongolia historically has had a great civilization and is a big country but today it stands geo-politically squeezed between Russia and China. Moreover, Mongolian government aimed at invigorating ties with India and expanding its foreign policy and business through "third neighbour" policy. For this reason, Mongolia wanted to outreach beyond China and Russia and also connect with India. Hence, According to Sharma, "it is also evident to note that Mongolia is the world's second largest landlocked country after Kazakhstan. It is rich in mineral resources like copper, iron, coal and uranium, which are the influencing factors for India's policy analysts in the matter of foreign affairs".[33]

To conclude the discussion, it is worthwhile to retrospect on the path-breaking developments in the early 1990s. The period marked rapid democratisation of Mongolian society which is coupled with the promise of mineral resource now to lend a fresh look to Mongolia's foreign policy due to which it can claim far more attention on the global stage than ever in the past. The policy of "third neighbour" as one of the prime drivers of its diplomacy of external relations, Ulaanbaatar has succeeded in attracting a number of key partners, which may reduce the overarching influence of Russia and China in Mongolia to some extent. Concerning the impact of Mongolia's "third neighbour" approach on India-Mongolia bilateral relations, the emergence of a new dimension is noticeable. As such, bilateral ties seem to have been transformed into a comprehensive partnership suggesting ways in which both sides have redefined their geostrategic interests.

Notes

1. S. Singh, (2013). *Parameters of India's Foreign Policy and India-Mongolia Relations*, 3 September 2018, URL: https://eoi.gov.in/ulaanbaatar/?1030?000
2. Sharad K. Soni, (2016). "Emerging Dimensions of India-Mongolia Relations", *Indian Foreign Affairs Journal*, 11 (1): 51-62.
3. Government of India (2018). *Brief on India-Mongolia Bilateral Relations*, Ministry of External Affairs, New Delhi, [online: web] Accessed 2 May 2018, URL: https://www.mea.gov.in/Portal/Foreign Relation/25_January_2018.pdf
4. Oidov Nyamdavaa, (2004). *Mongolia-Indian Relations*, New Delhi: Bhavana Books Prints.
5. Sharad K. Soni, (2015). "Strategic Partnership: Key to Modi's Mongolia Visit", Association of ASIA Scholars, New Delhi, 28 July 2015.
6. Ibid.
7. Ibid.
8. A. Sajjanhar, (2016). "2 Years on, Has Modi'sAct East Policy Made a Difference for India?" *The Diplomat*, Tokyo (Japan), 3 June 2016, URL: https://thediplomat.com/2016/06/2-years-on-has-modis-act-east-policy-made-a-difference-for-india/
9. Ibid.
10. Ibid.
11. Raju G.C. Thomas, (2004). "The South Asian Security Balance in a Western Dominant World", in T.V. Paul, James, J. Wirtz and Michel, F. (eds.) *Balance of Power: Theory and Practice in the 21st Century*, California: Stanford University Press.
12. A. Jahangir, (2013). "Changing Dynamics of South Asian Balance-of-Power", *Journal of South Asian Studies*, 1 (1): 50-58.
13. M.W. Cotter, (2008). "The New Face of Central Asia", *Ethics & International Affairs*, 22 (1): 107-112.
14. K. Stoner, (2013). "Old Games, New Rules? Great Powers in the New Central Asia", *Asia Policy*, 16 (1): 171–4.
15. Sharad K. Soni, (2016). "Emerging Dimensions of India-Mongolia Relations", *Indian Foreign Affairs Journal*, 11 (1): 51-62.

16. You Ji and Qingguo Jia, (1998). "China's Re-emergence and Its Foreign Policy Strategy", Quoted in J. Y. S. Cheng, (ed.), China Review, Hong Kong: Chinese University Press.
17. S. Zhao, (2004). "The Making of China s Periphery Policy", Quoted in, S. Zhao (ed.) 2004, *Chinese Foreign Policy: Pragmatism and Strategic Behavior*, Armonk: M. E. Sharpe.
18. Economic diplomacy was clearly identified by Chinese scholars as a key element of Beijing's, periphery diplomacy ; see Yang F., Qin, Y. and Heng X., *Contemporary China and its Foreign Policy*, Beijing: World Affairs Press, 2002, p. 195.
19. Z. Erdenebileg, (2017). "China-Mongolia Relations: Challenges and Opportunities", *China Briefing*, China, 6 January 2017.
20. Ibid.
21. Foreign Direct Investment is investment of foreign companies or individuals in domestic projects and investing entities controls projects partially or fully.
22. *World Bank (2004). "Mongolia Mining Sector: Managing the Future", [Online: web] Accessed 25 November 2015 URL: http://www.forum.mn/res_mat/MiningReport_en.pdf
23. Santander Trade Portal (2016). "Mongolia: Foreign Investment", [online: web] Accessed 12 November 2017, URL: https://en.portal.santandertrade.com/establish-overseas/mongolia/investing-3
24. C. Batbayar and D. Purevbayar, (2010). "Small Wind Energy in Mongolia", Energy Authority of Mongolia, [Online: web] Accessed 8 April 2016, URL: https: //www.usea.org/sites/default/files/012013_Energy%20issues%20for%20 Mongolia_ccc215.pdf
25. This approach came into existence as a technique to balance the Mongolia's two proximate neighbours.
26. Julian Dierkes, (2014). "Mongolia in the Region: Time for Economic Foreign Policy", *East Asia Forum*, Canberra, 23 March 2014.
27. "India to Acquire Coking Coal Mine in Mongolia", *The Hindu*, 10 May 2012, [Online: web] Accessed 24 June 2015 URL:http://www.thehindu.com/business/Economy/india-to-acquire-coking-coal-mine-in-mongolia/article3404225.ece
28. Ibid.
29. S. Singh, (2013). *op. cit.*, 3 September 2018, URL: https://eoi.gov.in/ulaanbaatar/?1030?000
30. Sharad K. Soni, (2015). "Strategic Partnership: Key to Modi's Mongolia Visit", Association of ASIA Scholars, New Delhi, 28

July 2015.

31. Ibid.
32. Ibid.
33. Rajeev Sharma, (2015). "Forget Uranium: Real Reason behind PM Modi's Mongolia Visit is Chaina", *FIRSTPOST*, India, 9 May 2015.

Index